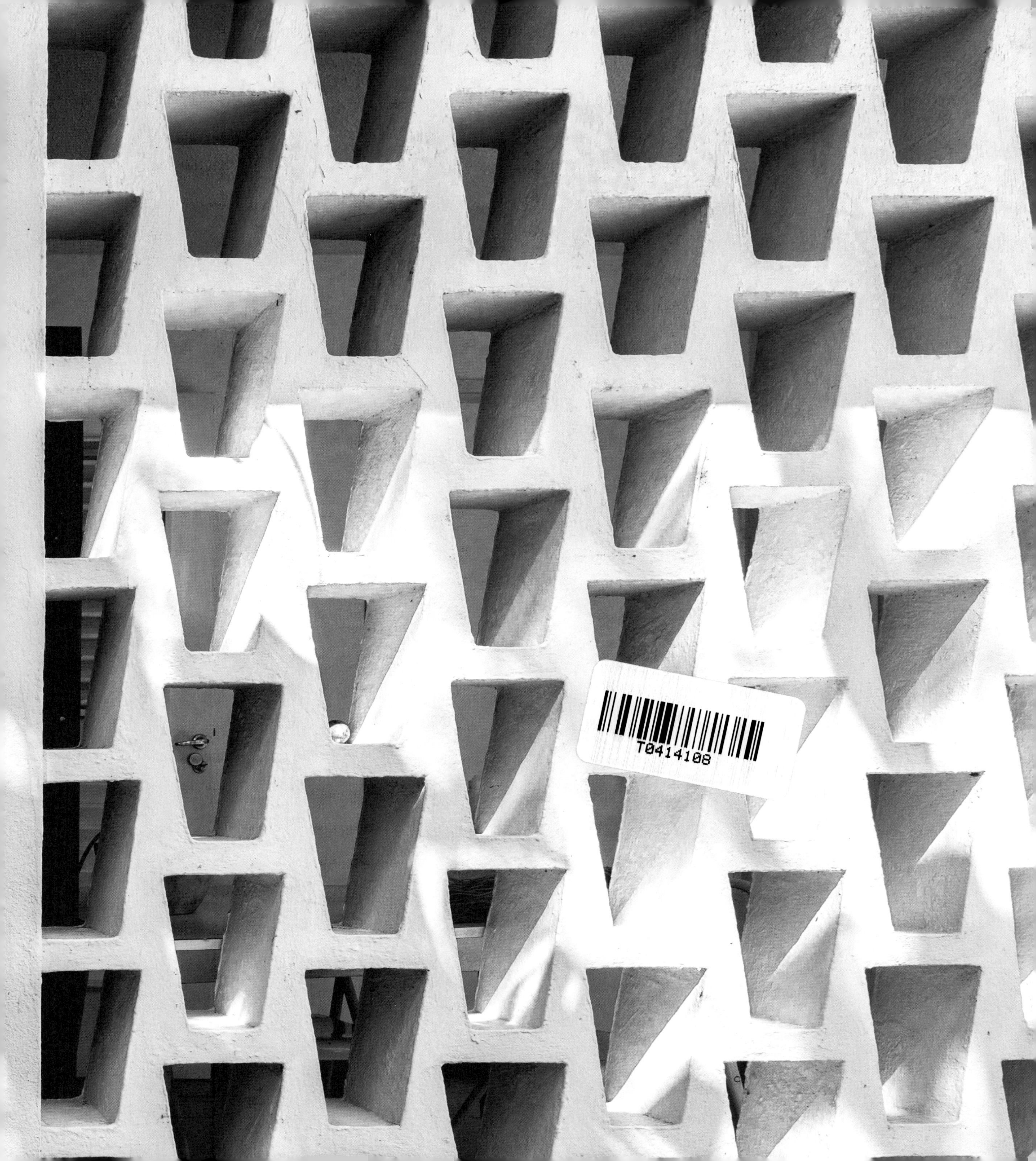

Foundation for the Documentation and
Conservation of the Modern Movement Curaçao

do.co,mo,mo_curaçao

MODERN ARCHITECTURE OF CURAÇAO_
1930 - 1960

Michael A. Newton

Photography **Ton Verkuijlen**

PREFACE_

do_co_mo_mo_curaçao

As the current DoCoMoMo Curaçao chairman, I am honored to present this book to our local and international community. The publication was preceded by a long period during which architects, art historians and other enthusiasts worked to protect and preserve good architecture on the island of Curaçao, especially the buildings in the distinctive style of the Modern Movement (1930-1960). The style is characterized by an emphasis on the interplay of building volumes, the rational use of often new materials, asymmetry and minimal ornamentation.

On March 2, 2009, the Foundation for Documentation and Conservation of the Modern Movement Curaçao was established. One of the first activities of the foundation, chaired by Sofia Saavedra Bruno, was organizing the First regional DoCoMoMo seminar, *"The Impact of Caribbean Modern Architecture"*, in collaboration with the University of the Netherlands Antilles (now the University of Curaçao). One of the speakers was Wessel de Jonge, co-founder of DoCoMoMo International, which now includes 79 national and regional working parties (chapters).

Ronald Gill, author of the book *"A century of architecture on Curaçao"*, compiled a list of buildings in the Modern Movement architectural style. A top ten list was created, featuring a diverse range of buildings, including office buildings, homes, a hospital and even water tanks, all thoroughly documented. This book contains all these beautiful buildings and more. Some have been well preserved, while others have unfortunately deteriorated over the years, making the original architecture barely recognizable.

With this book, we aim to showcase what architects have created during a specific period and how their buildings with international allure were adapted to the local tropical climate. We hope to increase community awareness of this architecture. The better examples from the past can also inspire the new generation of architects. Appreciation for good architecture is not always self-evident, sometimes due to unfamiliarity with the more modern architectural styles. There is already extensive literature about the older monuments on our island, but not enough about the more modern architecture. We hope that this book will serve as a catalyst for expanding this knowledge.

Special thanks to architect Michael A. Newton and photographer Ton Verkuijlen, who documented this legacy, and to all sponsors who made the publication of this book possible.

Ronny Lobo
Chairman DoCoMoMo Curaçao

CONTENTS_

do_co,mo,mo_curaçao

•	PREFACE	2
•	INTRODUCTION	6
1.	CHAPEL CAPRILES CLINIC	13
2.	POLICE STATION	23
3.	CUSTOMS OFFICE	27
4.	KNSM BUILDING	35
5.	CINELANDIA CINEMA	47
6.	PUBLIC READING ROOM & LIBRARY	53
7.	CURAÇAO TRADING COMPANY	65
8.	BEN SMIT RESIDENCE	69
9.	ST. THOMAS COLLEGE	81
10.	WATER RESERVOIRS LWV	85
11.	CURAÇAOSCHE COURANT	93
12.	ALEX BUILDING	97
13.	WATER FACTORY	101
14	BENESH RESIDENCE	111
15.	MGR. VERRIET INSTITUTE	117
16.	CPIM LABORATORY	129
17.	LA CONFIANZA	139
18.	SPRITZER RESIDENCE	143
19.	PALAIS ROYAL	155
20.	ST. ELISABETH HOSPITAL SOUTH-EASTWING	161
21.	PETER STUYVESANT COLLEGE / KOLEGIO ALEJANDRO PAULA	173
22.	CASA SIMON BOLIVAR	185
23.	ALVERNA CHAPEL & MONASTERY	195
24.	ROZENDAELS	211
25.	PLTS TECHNICAL SCHOOL	223
•	MAP OF CURAÇAO	234
•	BIBLIOGRAPHY	236
•	INDEX	238
•	COLOPHON	240

INTRO-
DUCTION_

do_co_mo_mo_curaçao

This book focuses on 25 buildings on the island of Curaçao, constructed between the 1930s and the 1960s, whose designs were influenced by the international architectural styles, called the Modern Movement and Art Deco.

In December 1997, the inner city of Willemstad, the capital of Curaçao, was designated as a UNESCO World Heritage site, which increased the local awareness of its historical architecture. However, out of almost 800 listed and protected buildings on Curaçao, fewer than 10 represent modern architecture.
Creating awareness of modern architecture and its cultural value is crucial for preserving the fine buildings of this period. This documentation aims primarily to achieve that goal.

Modern Architecture
In previous centuries, architectural styles applied in Curaçao were largely influenced by corresponding movements in Europe. This also applies to the Modern Movement and Art Deco architecture, which were introduced by Dutch architects working on the island. The Modern Movement and Art Deco are two distinct yet interrelated international styles that emerged in the early 20th century. Modern Movement architecture, which dominated the Western world between the 1930s and the 1960s, is also known as the International Style, Functionalism, Modernist architecture, and in Dutch 'Nieuwe Bouwen', and 'Nieuwe Zakelijkheid'.

The Modern Movement embraces new construction materials and technologies, such as reinforced concrete, steel, and large glass panels (curtain walls). This exploration of new materials and technologies led to a dramatic shift in the building design, moving away from traditional forms and construction techniques. The design focuses on simplicity, minimalism, and the absence of ornamentation. "Form follows function" is a core principle, meaning the design of a building should be based upon its intended use. Buildings often have a rectilinear, grid-like appearance and incorporate large windows connecting the interior with the exterior and bringing in air and light. "….not the wall but the opening in the wall has become the most important….the full enjoyment of light and air has been added…. " stated architect Ben Smit. (Möhlman,1955, p.71)

In Europe, the Bauhaus had a profound impact on the development of Modern architecture. This groundbreaking school of art, design and architecture operated in Germany from 1919 to 1933. Although the Bauhaus school existed for only 14 years, it laid the foundations for many aspects of modernist design. Among its most famous representatives are former teachers like Ludwig Mies van der Rohe, Marcel Breuer, and Walter Gropius, founder of the Bauhaus. Cornerstones of Bauhaus design principles include: "Form follows function" and "Less is more".

In addition to the Bauhaus, other influential architects who significantly contributed to the international development and spread of Modernism include Swiss-French architect Le Corbusier and Brazilian architect Oscar Niemeyer. Both architects also inspired several designers in Curaçao.

Le Corbusier's research into the use of the 'brise-soleil', shading slats as sun protection in his projects in tropical environments in the early 1930s, was significant for the Modern Architecture in the Tropics. In Curaçao, the rotating 'brise-soleil', as developed by Le Corbusier, was used by architects like Ben Smit in his own **residence [8]**, the **Spritzer residence [18]**, the **St. Elisabeth Hospital South-East wing [20]**, and **Alverna Chapel [23]**, and by Henk Nolte in the **PLTS [25]**.

Art Deco
Art Deco played a significant role in shaping the development of the Modern Movement and both styles were applied at almost the same time. Art Deco's ornamental yet streamlined approach served as a bridge to the more austere, minimalist tendencies of the Modern Movement architecture.

Art Deco, short for the French 'Arts Décoratifs', is a style of visual arts, architecture, and product design that first appeared in Paris in the 1910s during World War I and spread throughout Europe and the United States from the 1920s to 1950s. Art Deco designers often combined various architectural styles, using different elements at their discretion.

Curaçao's Art Deco is not directly derived from the European movement, but has its origins in the United States, specifically in Miami, where Art Deco flourished from 1925 to the 1950's. In Miami's South Beach, buildings were typically constructed according to three basic rules for a geometric façade: the center element being the strongest or most dramatic, flanked by two usually - but not always - similar elements or structures, resulting in symmetry. Besides these basic rules, the Art Deco architecture incorporated elements such as curves, long horizontal lines, and sometimes nautical motifs. In Miami, this style is now also known as "Tropical Deco".

Art Deco was the prevailing style at the time, and South Beach now has the world's largest remaining collection of this architectural style.

CURAÇAO MODERN ARCHITECTURE

Pre-World War II Modern Architecture
The first building in Curaçao constructed in the spirit of the Modern Movement was completed in 1929, quite early for the Caribbean region. Located on Brionplein along the waterfront in Otrobanda, it was commissioned by the Dutch firm 'Nederlandsche Indische Gasmaatschappij' (later O.G.E.M.) and designed by the Dutch architect Johan Heinrich Werner Jr., also known as Henk or Hans Werner. During his time in the Netherlands, Werner had worked for the renowned architects' firm Staal and Kropholler, where he likely encountered Modern Architecture, influenced by the Amsterdam School style.

In 1928, Werner moved to Curaçao, where he worked for the government for only a year and a half before establishing himself as a private architect. In written studies on Curaçao architecture, Werner's role and influence during the pre-WW-II period is often underestimated.

The O.G.E.M. building, which was destroyed by fire on May 30, 1969 during social riots, featured an asymmetrical design characterized by both horizontal and vertical lines. It incorporated various glass elements in the façade, such as strips with glass squares that emphasized the vertical tower on the right and a clock positioned atop the left tower. These elements were reminiscent of those used by Modern Movement architects in the Netherlands during that era, including architect W.M.Dudok.

On the ground floor, a heavy arched gallery covered the sidewalk, creating a shady area. We also find Werner's influence in other buildings, such as the **Chapel of the Capriles Clinic [1]** and the **Police Station [2]**, where he incorporated decorative Art Deco elements into the façades. Although these buildings retained traditional architectural features like steep tiled roofs, Werner's additions mark a transition to a new architectural era. Werner's most renowned building on the island is the Customs office [3] at the end of the Handelskade, which he designed for the government in 1937; its description follows in the subsequent pages.

Modern Architecture 1940 – 1965
The construction of the O.G.E.M. building in 1929 set a trend for the next few decades, during which local branches of major Dutch companies undertook significant construction projects, such as the **KNSM Building [4]**. Another prominent example was SHELL, which also left a distinct mark on the island's architecture in the first half of the 20th century. The principles of modernism were not solely introduced to the island by architects in the private sector, but also by their colleagues who worked for Curaçao's governmental Building Department. Architects like Anton de Vries, Cornelis (Kees) Bakker, Ben Smit, and Henk Nolte, all of Dutch origin, lived and worked on the island for varying

periods. They were responsible for designing many governmental offices, public buildings and schools.

Examples are the **Peter Stuyvesant College [21]** by de Vries and the **Public Reading Room & Library [6]** and **St. Thomas College [8]** by Bakker.

Most of the abovementioned architects, Kees Bakker, Ben Smit, and Henk Nolte, established their own architectural firm on the island after leaving the Building Department, and they were highly productive in the private sector during the 1940s, 1950s, and 1960s.

Examples described in this publication include the **Curaçao Trading Company [7]**, **Curaçaosche Courant [11]** and **Alex Building [12]** by Kees Bakker; the **Ben Smit Residence [8]**, **Benesh Residence [14]**, **Spritzer Residence [18]**, **St. Elisabeth Hospital South Eastwing [20]**, **Casa Simon Bolivar [22]** and **Alverna Chapel & Monastery [23]** by Ben Smit; and the **PLTS Technical School [25]** by Henk Nolte.

Despite their Dutch background, these architects demonstrated their ability to adapt Modern Architecture to the tropical climate of Curaçao. They also experimented with the use of local materials, which contributed to giving their designs a distinctive character.

Gerrit Rietveld – Invited to Curaçao
A unique local example of the Modern Movement is the **Mgr. Verriet Institute [15]** home for disabled children, designed by the renowned Dutch architect Gerrit Rietveld. He was invited to visit the island in 1949 and, within a few weeks, designed this exceptional building. Its characteristically open construction makes it perfectly suited for the tropical context of Curaçao.

Modern Architecture & Art Deco combined
Another influential figure responsible for various major constructions during the 1930s, 1940s, and 1950s was Pieter van Stuivenberg, a Dutchman who served as head of the Technical Department at the Governmental Department for Water Supply. He designed buildings for water production and distribution in Curaçao and Aruba, such as the **Water Reservoir LWV [10]** and the large **Water Factory in the Mundo Nobo district [13]**. Van Stuivenberg's designs clearly reflect influences from both the Modern Movement and Miami Art Deco.

While working for the water company, Van Stuivenberg also undertook private commissions. Almost simultaneously, he designed two cinemas in the inner-city: **Cinelandia Cinema [5]** in 1940 and West End Cinema in 1941.

The West-End Cinema, situated prominently at Plaza Brion in the district of Otrobanda, was the largest Art Deco building on the island. It featured distinctive elements such as a tower near the entrance, a rounded corner with a restaurant, and a symmetrical façade facing the waterfront. It opened in 1941 but was unfortunately demolished in August 2000 due to neglect, despite efforts by heritage professionals to have it listed as a protected monument.

Despite Pieter van Stuivenberg's design of several buildings with strong Art Deco influences, this architectural style has been rarely replicated on the island.

During the 1960's, Modern Architecture lost its vitality, and unique buildings in this style ceased to be designed. Instead, there was a proliferation of uninspired structures with flat roofs, hastily drawn up in a matter of days. Considerations such as balanced proportions and designs suited to the tropical environment became increasingly rare.

ir. Michael A. Newton
August 2024

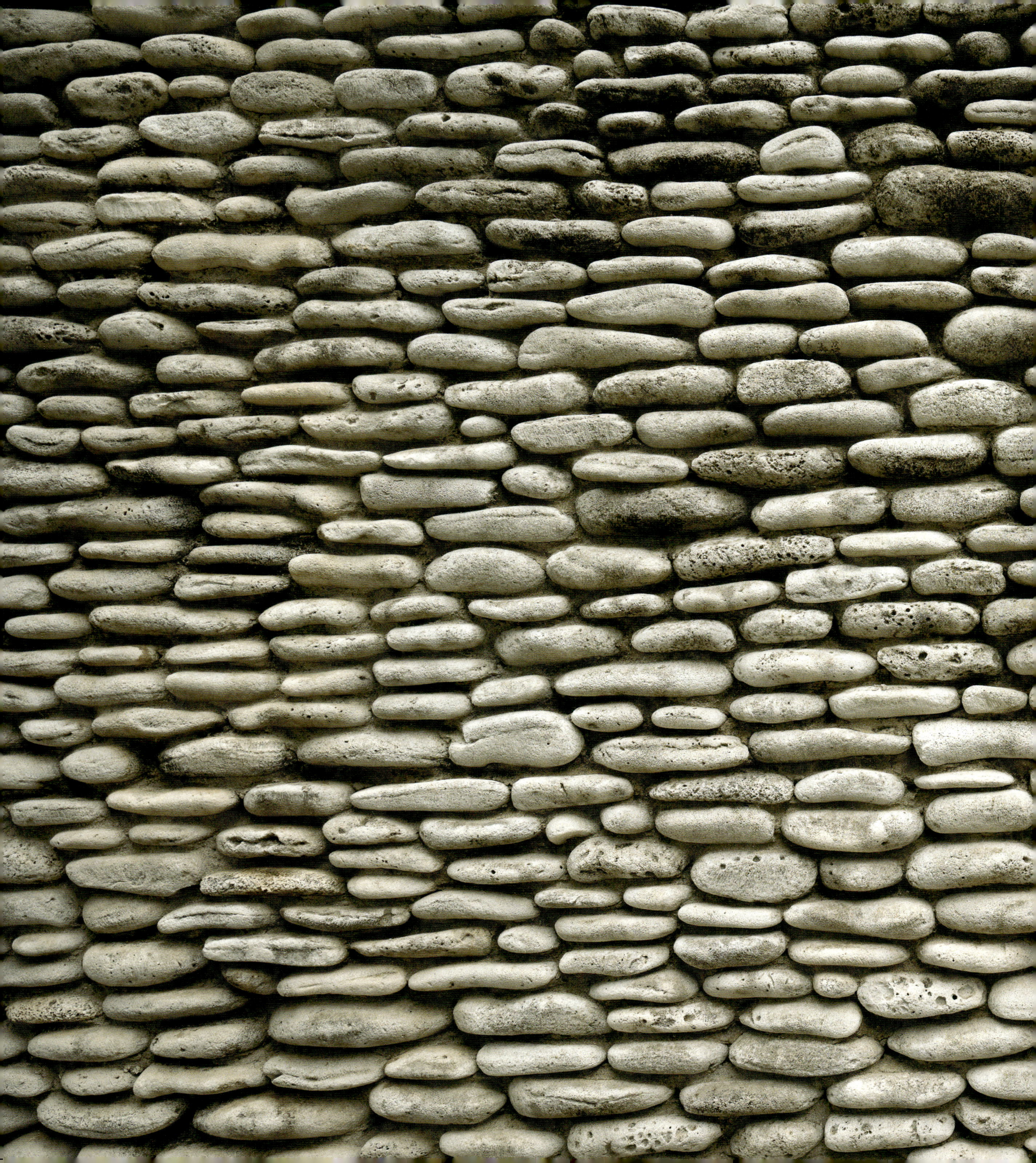

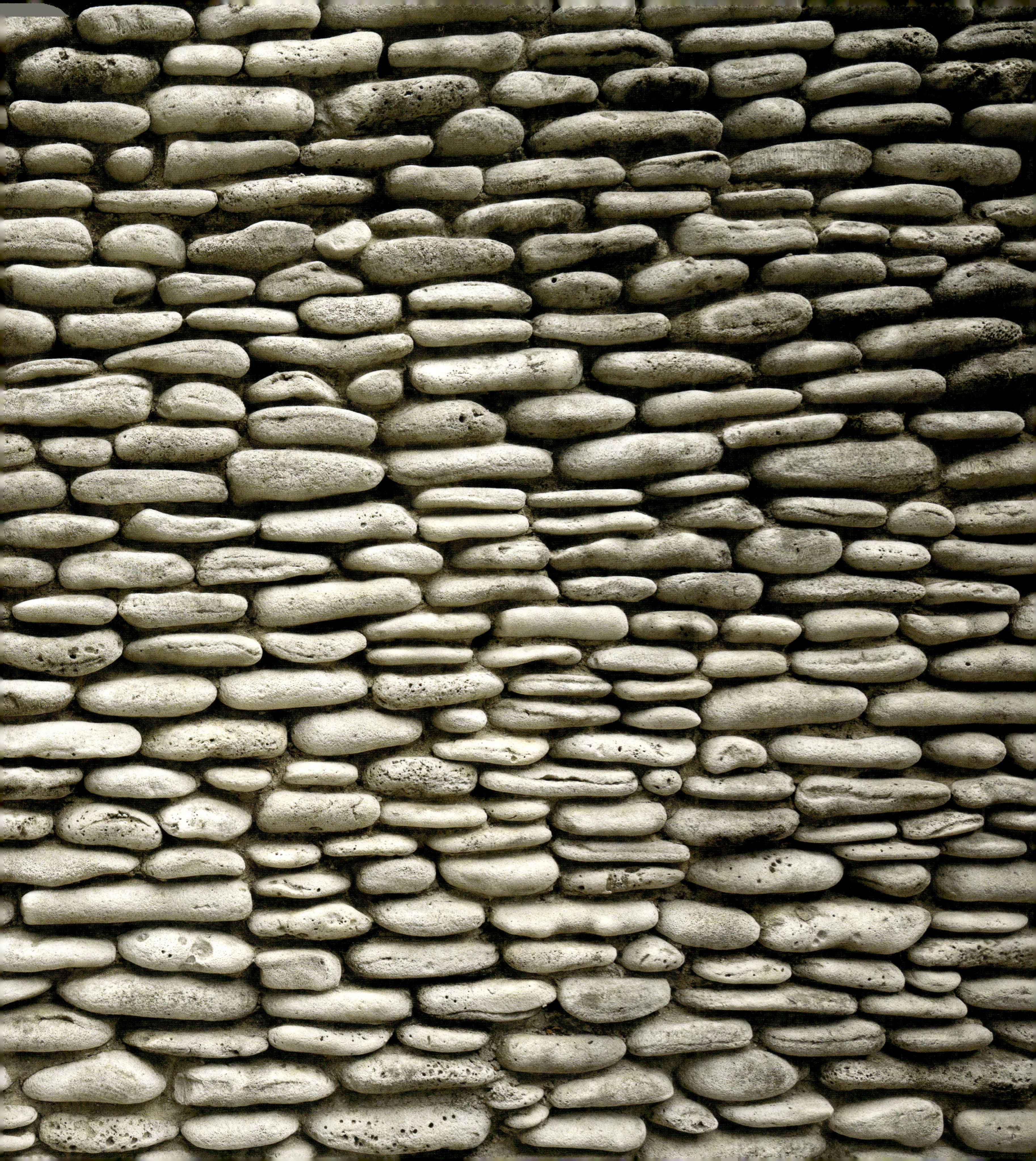

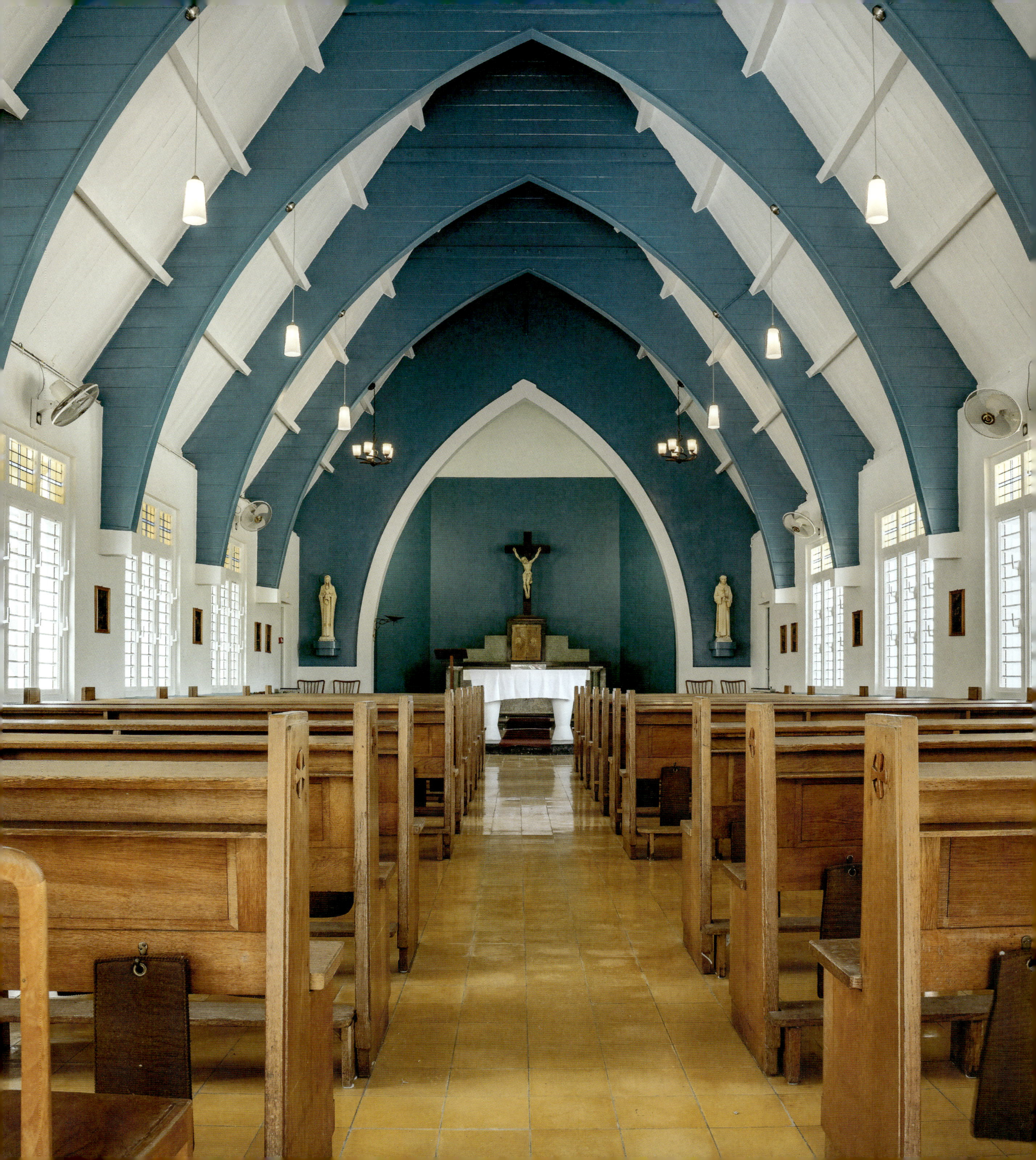

National grid reference: **12°08'31.1"N 68°54'26.2"W**

01.
CHAPEL CAPRILES CLINIC_

MOHIKANENWEG 8

Historic Background_

Mental health care in Curaçao was significantly improved with the inauguration of a new modernized institution in the Groot Kwartier suburb on April 11, 1936, named "Rustoord Groot Kwartier". (Amigoe 15-04-1936).

This development was driven by psychiatrist Dr. van Lienden, who arrived on the island in 1934. Commissioned by the governor, Dr. van Lienden undertook the task of upgrading the island's outdated 19th-century mental health care system. Almost half a century later, the institution was renamed the "Dr. David Ricardo Capriles Clinic", in honor of Dr. David Ricardo Capriles, who had served as a physician at the Monte Cristo asylum during the last decades of the 19th century.
The new complex featured spacious, symmetrically arranged pavilions with sufficient space around the buildings to ensure optimal cross ventilation.

Centrally located behind the main front building stands the Catholic chapel, notable for its pointed slim turret atop ventilation grilles.

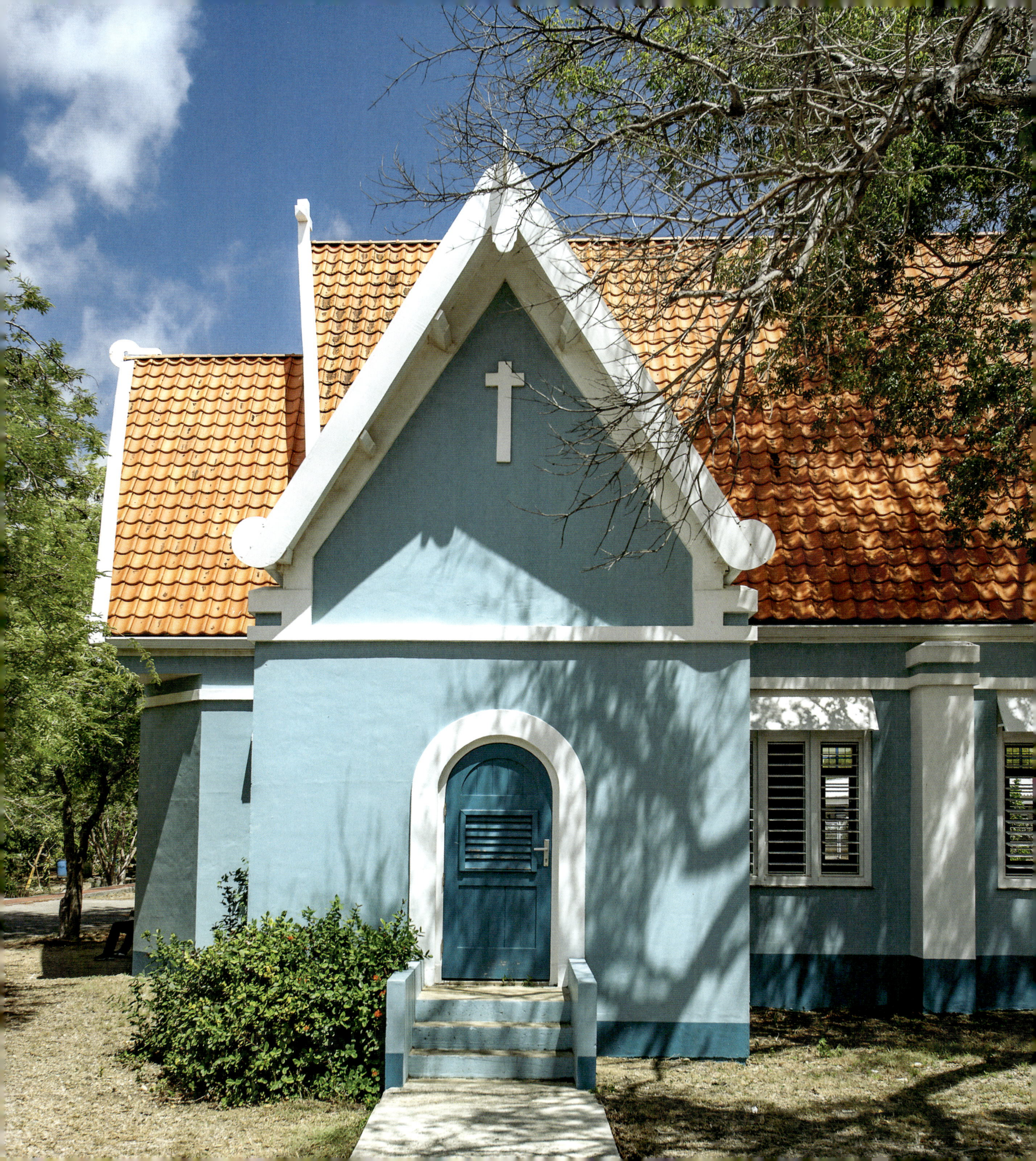

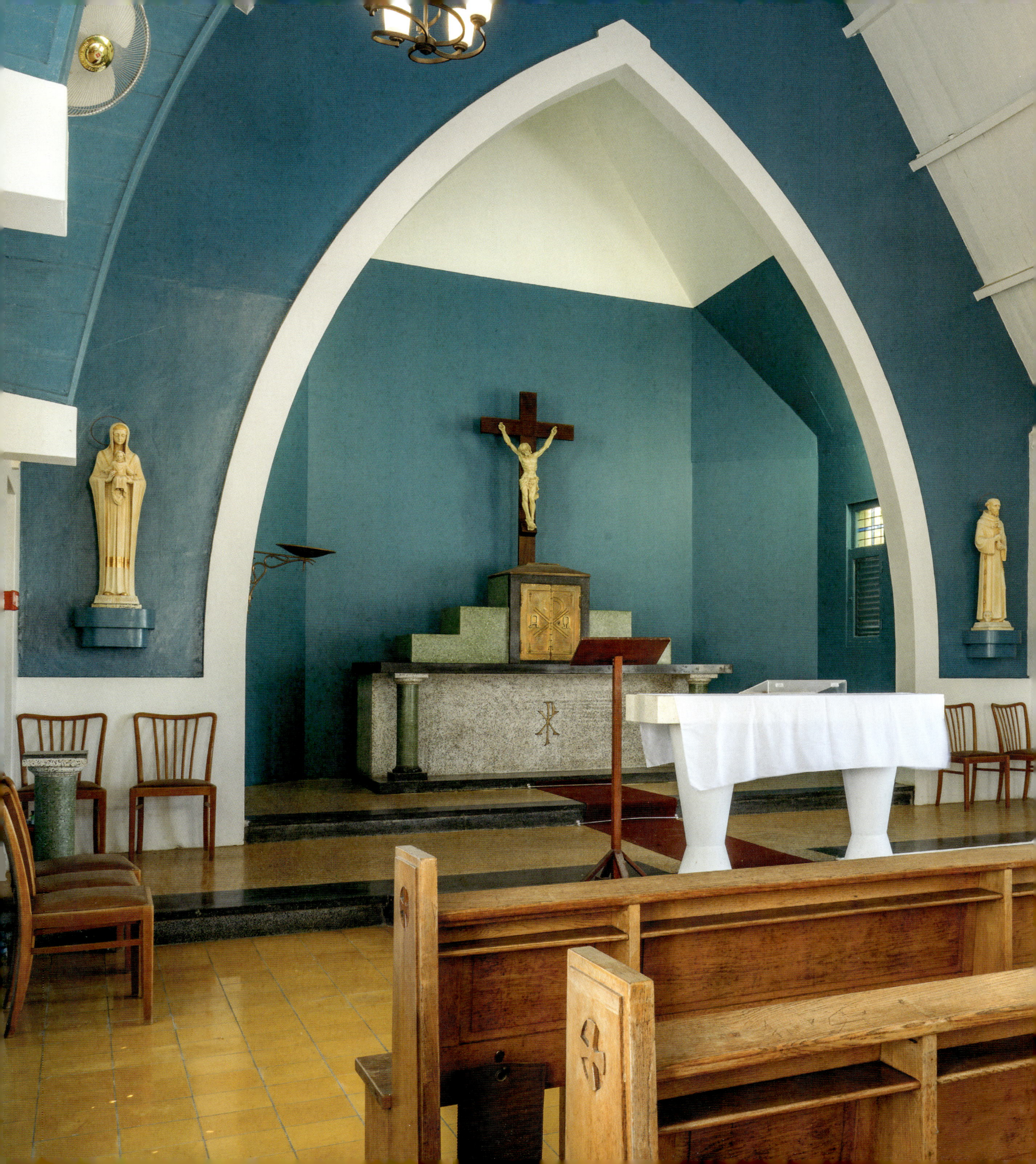

It represents an early transition from the local neo-styles of the late 19th and early 20th centuries to the Modern Movement architecture.

Architectural Design_

According to a 1936 newspaper report, (Amigoe, April 8,1936) the plan for the asylum was created by the medical director, Dr. Van Lienden. His plan was based on a design for an unbuilt insane asylum in the Dutch East Indies. The Public Works Department assisted in further developing and drafting Dr. van Lienden's plan, and the construction was carried out by the Nederhorst company.

The chapel of the Capriles clinic cannot be classified as an example of Modern Movement architecture. However, it represents an early transition from the local neo-styles of the late 19th and early 20th centuries to the Modern Movement. The leaning ridges of the roof reflect an East Indies influence, while the grooved ends of the exterior buttresses illustrate the shift toward Art Deco. These modern elements may well have been introduced by the Dutch architect J.H. Werner, who significantly influenced the implementation of modern architecture on Curaçao. Werner briefly worked for the Department of Public Works around 1928, but continued to create designs for the department after he left and started his own office.

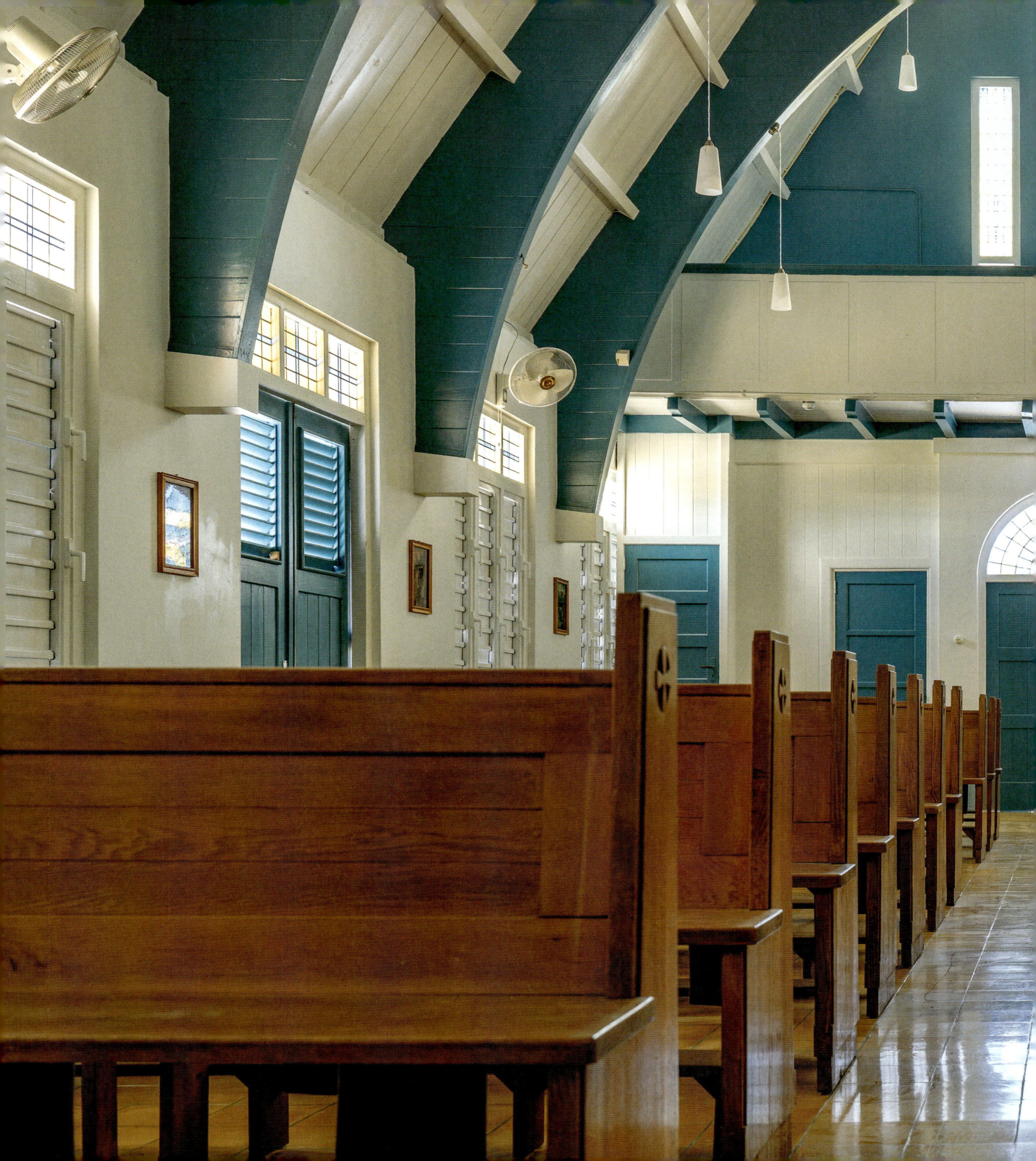

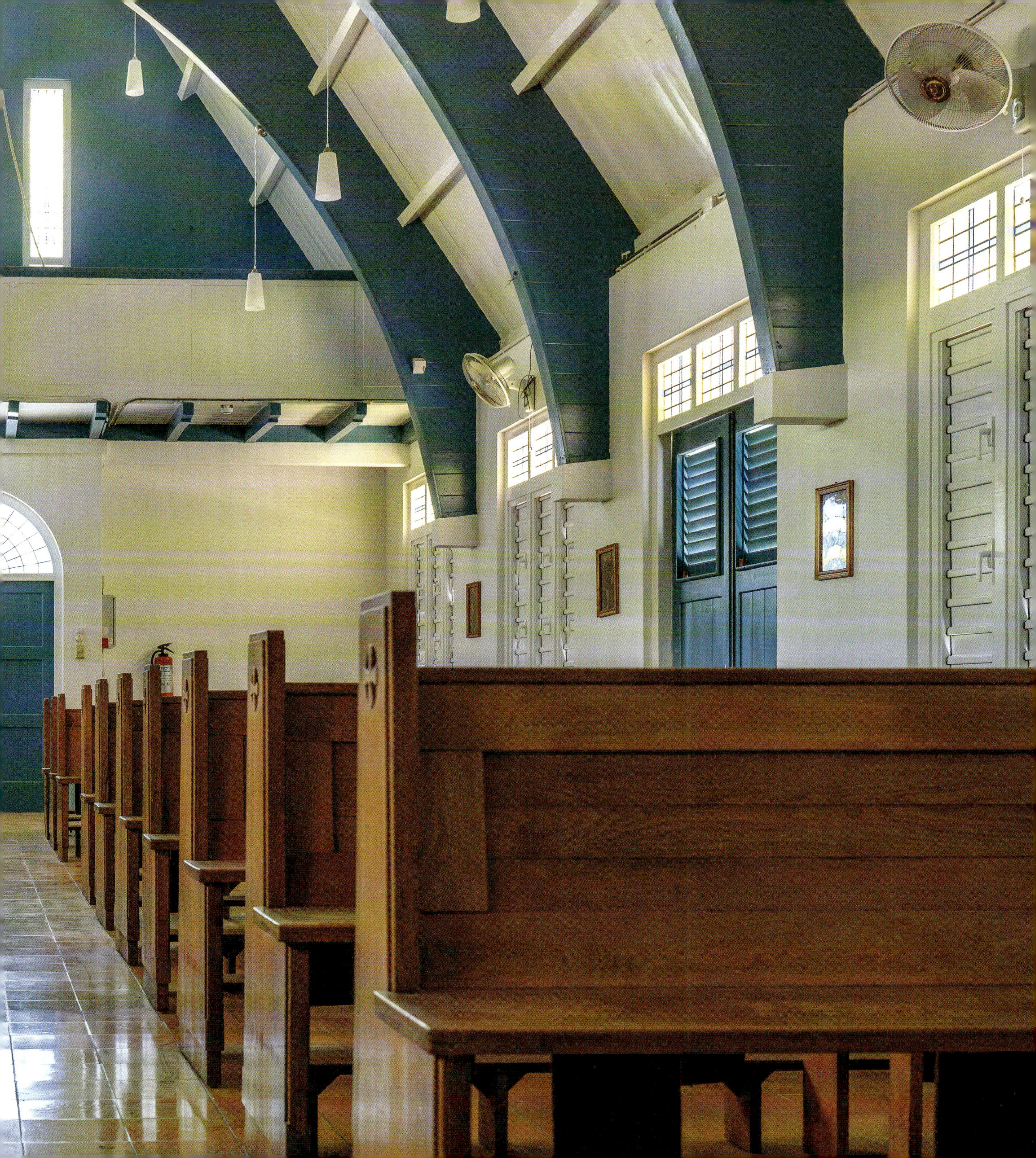

Description_

The rectangular chapel, with small side rooms on both sides of the altar, is covered by a steep tiled roof supported by relatively large trusses in the shape of neo-Gotic pointed arches. Remarkably, these trusses are composed of wooden planks.

The chapel, with approximately 200 seats, was renovated by the Capriles Clinic in 2019. Following the renovation, the pews were donated by the Sint Rochuskerk in Rijkevoort, Netherlands.

References:

- Gill, Ronald G. (2008) Een eeuw architectuur op Curaçao. Curaçao: Ronald G. Gill, (Original work published 1999)
- Maduro-Molhuijsen, Helma (2013) Johan Heinrich Werner, de 'doodgezwegen' architect;   De Archiefvriend, maart 2013

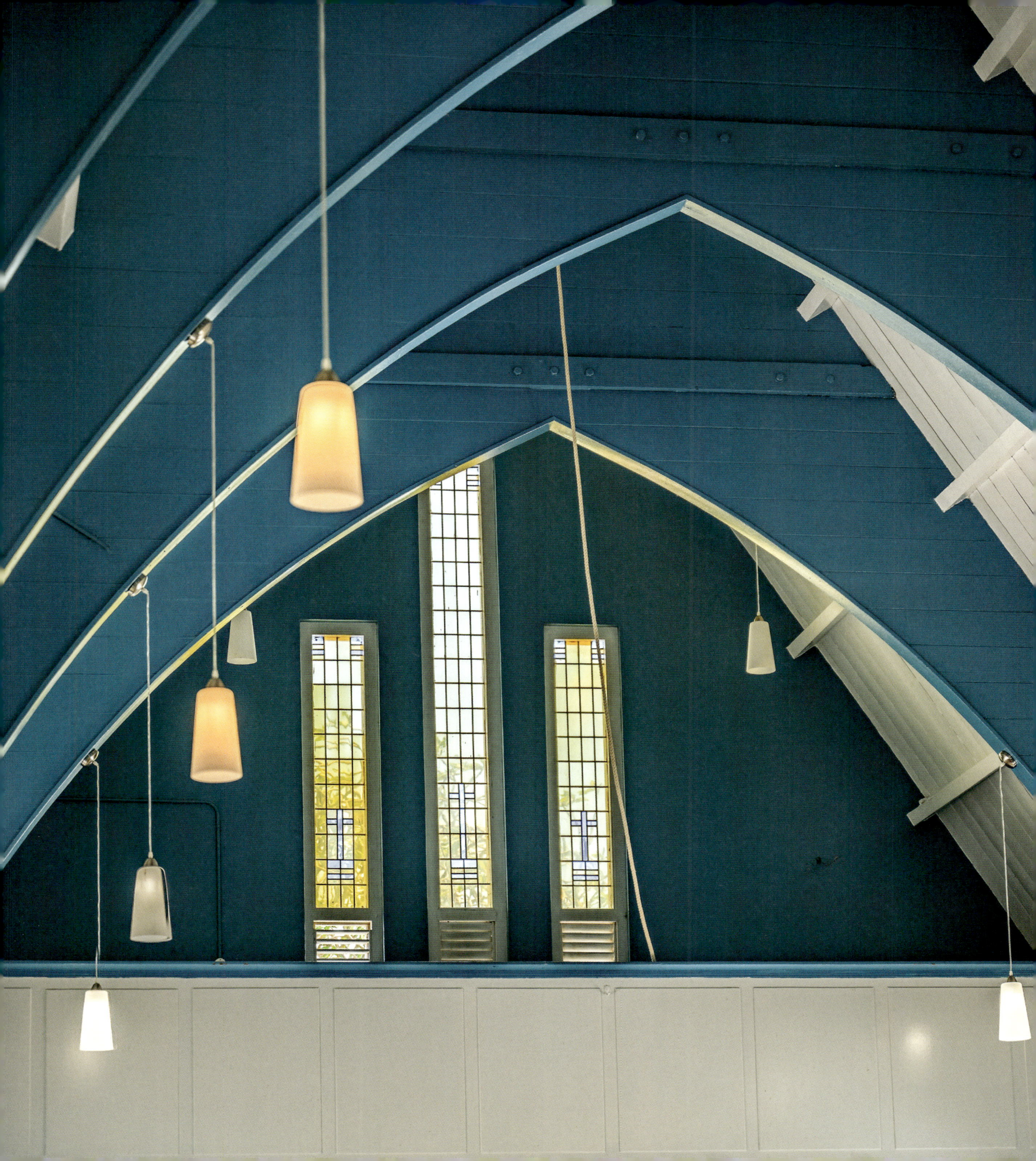

POLITIE

National grid reference: **12°06'15.1"N 68°56'03.1"W**

02.
POLICE STATION_

WILHELMINAPLEIN 2A

National Archive Curaçao / Coll. Fisher

Historic Background_

In the 1930's, the police force of the Dutch Caribbean was thoroughly reorganized. The police accommodations also required improvement, as the main police station in Curaçao was housed in a small office near Fort Amsterdam on Breedestraat. A new location was chosen just outside Fort Amsterdam, the government center, and adjacent to the court and the then prison beneath the parliament building. All police departments were moved to the new building.

The distinctive, tall, vertical Art Deco-style elements on either side of the entrance are likely his creation and are one of the first influences of Art Deco on the island.

Architectural Design_

On June 18th 1936, Governor Van Slobbe officially opened the police station on the Wilhelminaplein. To this day the building serves the same purpose.

According to a newspaper report of the opening the drawings were made by Mr. Jacobus Beiderwellen, who worked for the Department of Public Works, but the architect Mr. J.H. Werner "collaborated in the artistic part". (Amigoe, 20 June 1936). Werner had worked for Public Works from 1928-1930, after which he established himself as an independent architect. This architect – although little known – was one of the most influential designers during this transitional period to modern architecture. The distinctive, tall, vertical Art Deco-style elements on either side of the entrance are likely his creation and are one of the first influences of Art Deco on the island. The police station was built by the then well-known contractor of Italian origin, Giovanni Pizziolo.

Description_

The two-storey building is very simple at first glance, with its rectangular floor plan and steep saddle roof between two funnel-shaped gables. These reflect the traditional local architecture. Characteristic are the above mentioned Art Deco style vertical, slightly jutting posts against the front. The plasterwork is also notable, featuring prominent horizontal and vertical grooves, a technique commonly used to mimic large stone blocks. The windows on the ground and first floor are separated by two horizontal bands. The thin white moldings above the first floor windows are also typical for the building period.

References:

- Gehlen, Gerda & Ditzhuijzen, Jeannette van, (2017) Warda di Polis – Police Station; MONUMENTO HABRI '17 – Punda, Curaçao: Fundashon Pro Monumento, pp. 22 – 25
- Gill, Ronald G. (2008) Een eeuw architectuur op Curaçao. Curaçao: Ronald G. Gill, (Original work published 1999)
- Newton, Michael A. (1990) Fo'l porta, The Wilhelminapark and its surroundings. Building up the future from the past. Zutphen: De Walburg Pers, p. 39
- Paul, P. (1959) Gedenkboek Tien jaar Korps Politie Nederlandse Antillen: 1949 – 1 oktober – 1959. Curaçao, p.61

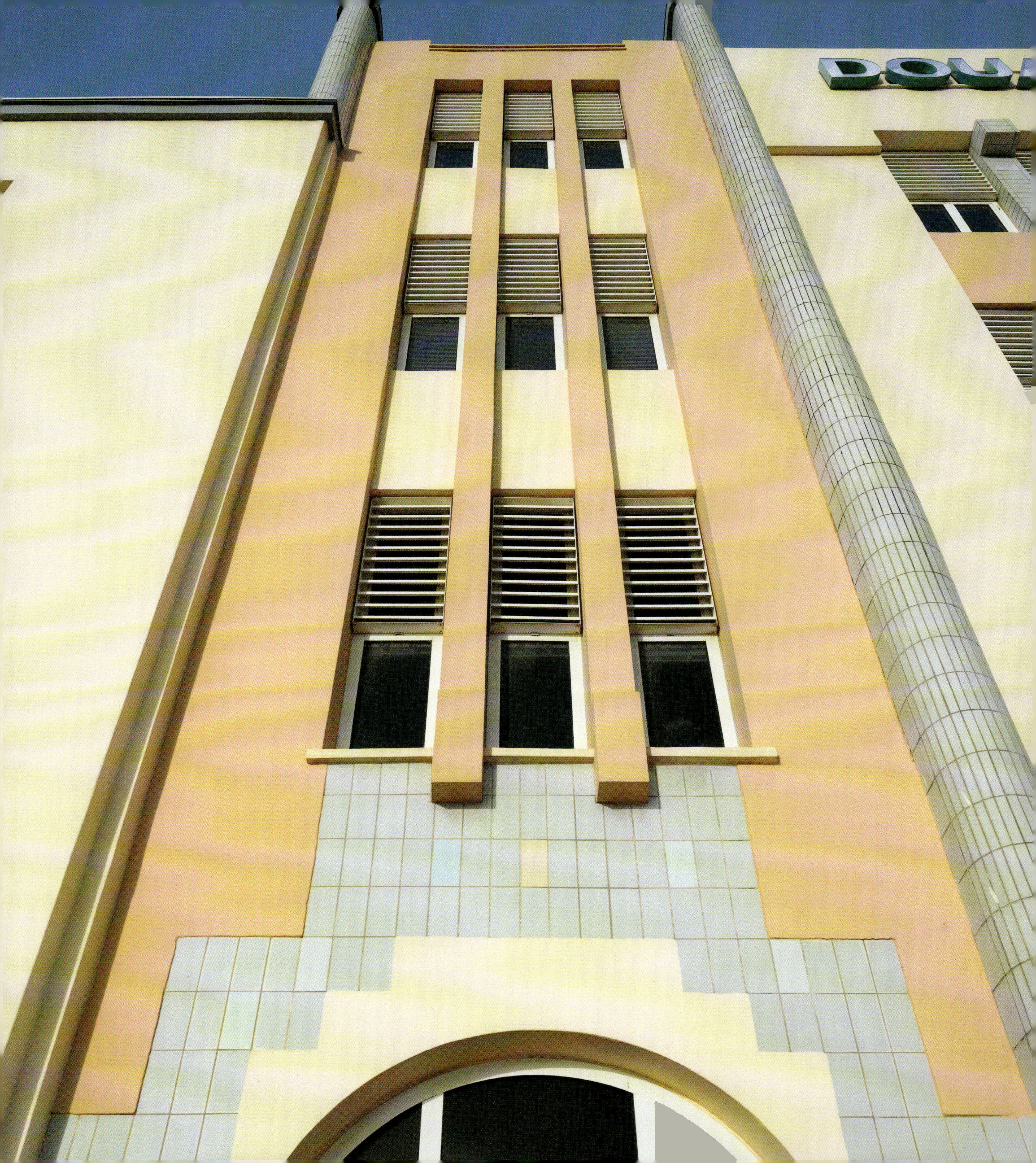
DOU

National grid reference: **12°06'24.3"N 68°56'00.1"W**

03.
CUSTOMS OFFICE_

SHA AND LIO CAPRILESKADE Z/N

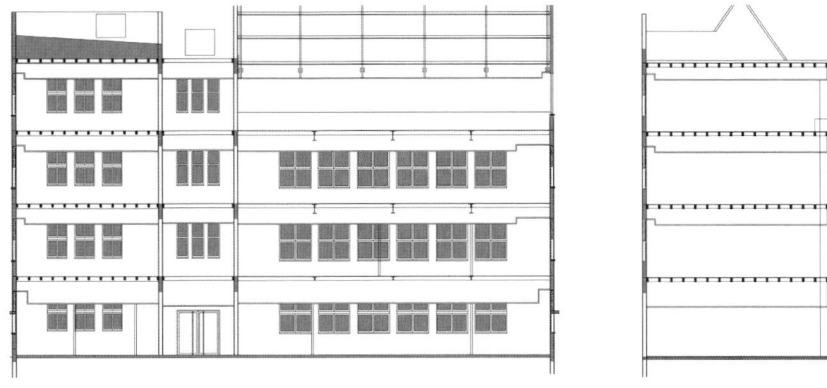

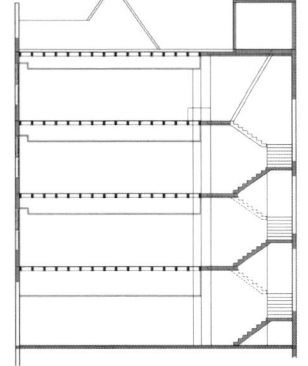

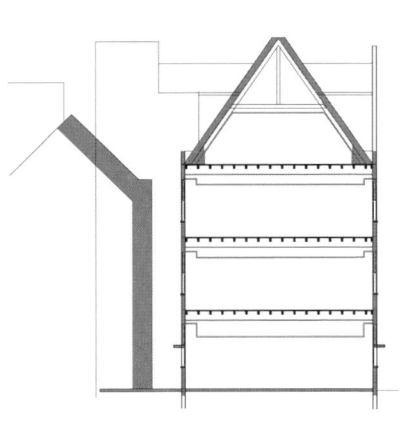

Customs Office. Drawing: Atelier Lobo & Raymann / Rosberg Engineering, 2016

Historic Background_

The oil industry in Curaçao was established in 1915. Crude oil from Venezuela was shipped to the island, first for transshipment but in 1918 the Royal SHELL opened an oil refinery on the northern borders of the Schottegat, the natural inner harbour. This was the beginning of a large-scale industrialization of the island. The population and economy increased considerably in the course of the subsequent decades. The increased income enabled the government to fund new public investments and allowed for the construction of government offices.

The customs office was built next to the St. Annabay, the harbour entrance in the center of Willemstad, where most of the ships were loaded and unloaded. A new port was only built in the early 1950s, further inland in the Schottegat. An old building was demolished to make way for the new Douanekantoor.

The call for tenders for the construction of the new customs office was held on the November 19, 1936. The principal was the Curaçao Department of Public Works. The official opening was on October 4, 1937. It is the oldest building still in existence that was built according to the ideas of the Modern Movement and the first civic building in this style. The building still fulfills the same function.

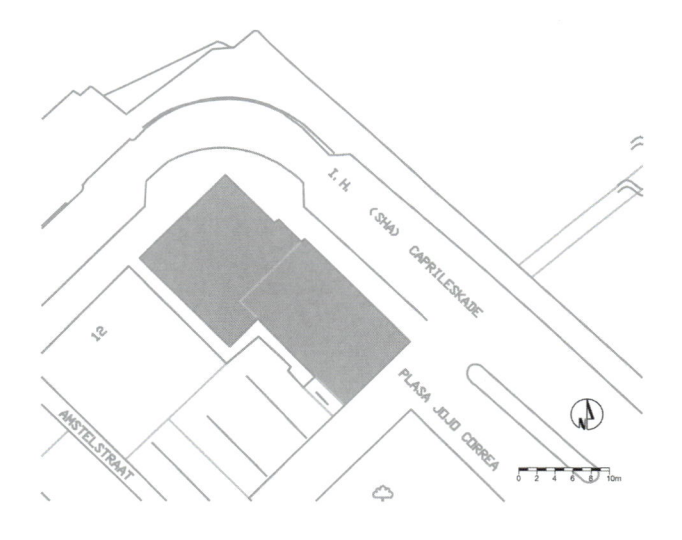

Customs Office. Drawing: Atelier Lobo & Raymann / Rosberg Engineering, 2016

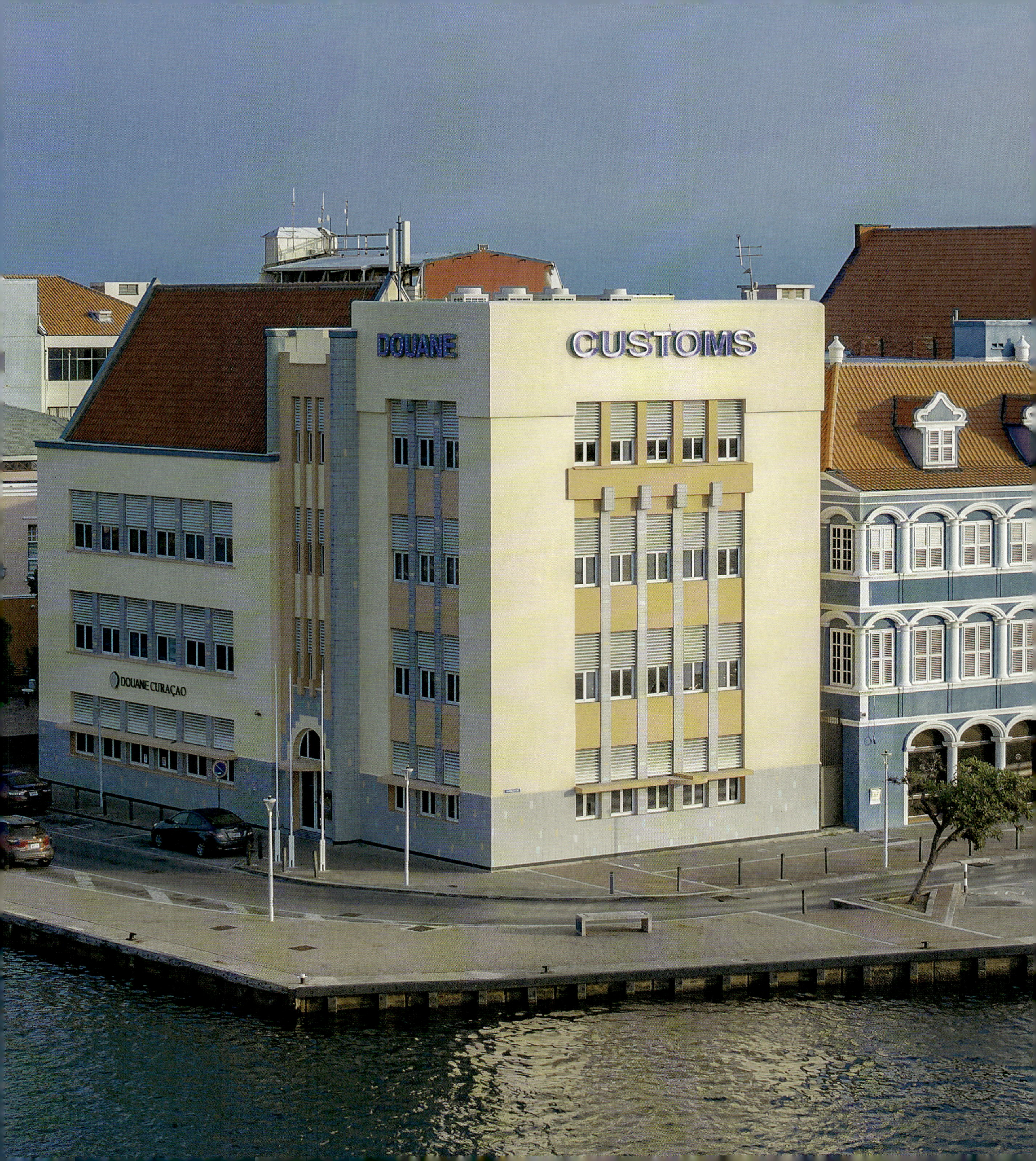
DOUANE
CUSTOMS
DOUANE CURAÇAO

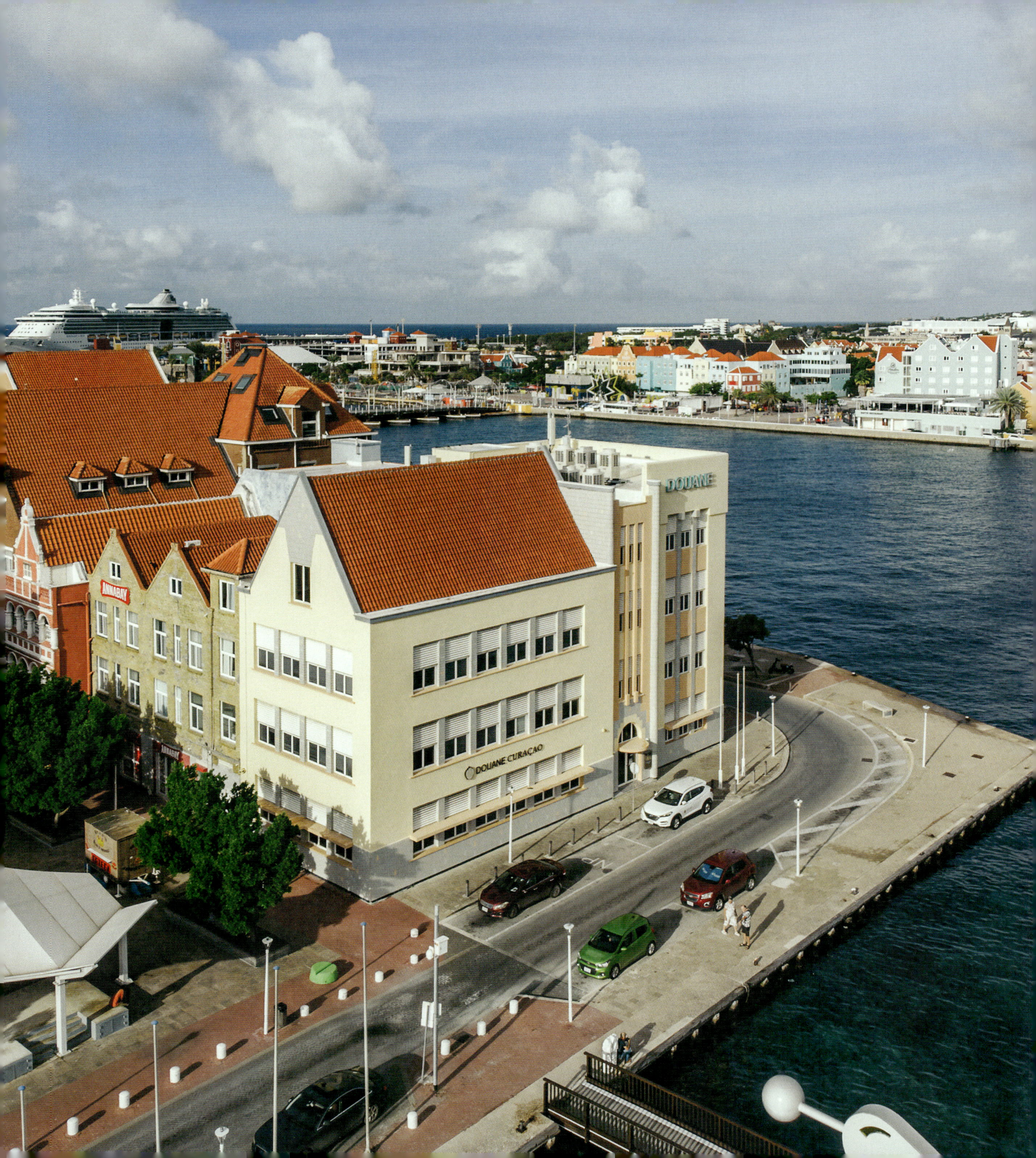
DOUANE
ANNABAY
DOUANE CURAÇAO

Although little known, he is one of the most influential designers associated with the transitional period from traditional to modern architecture.

Architectural Design_

The building was designed by Johan Heinrich Werner Jr., also known as Henk Werner or Hans Werner, a Dutch architect who started working in the Netherlands as an independent architect in 1908. He came to Curaçao in the 1920's and worked for the Department of Public Works from 1928 until 1930. In 1930 he re-established himself as an independent architect on the island. Werner designed various buildings and was the first to design in the spirit of the Modern Movement architecture, most probably influenced by his experiences in the Netherlands. Although little known, he is one of the most influential designers associated with the transitional period from traditional to modern architecture. For decades, the block-shaped building with its flat roof at the end of the Handelskade, at the harbour entrance, was regarded by the general public as an unsuitable presence in the historic district.

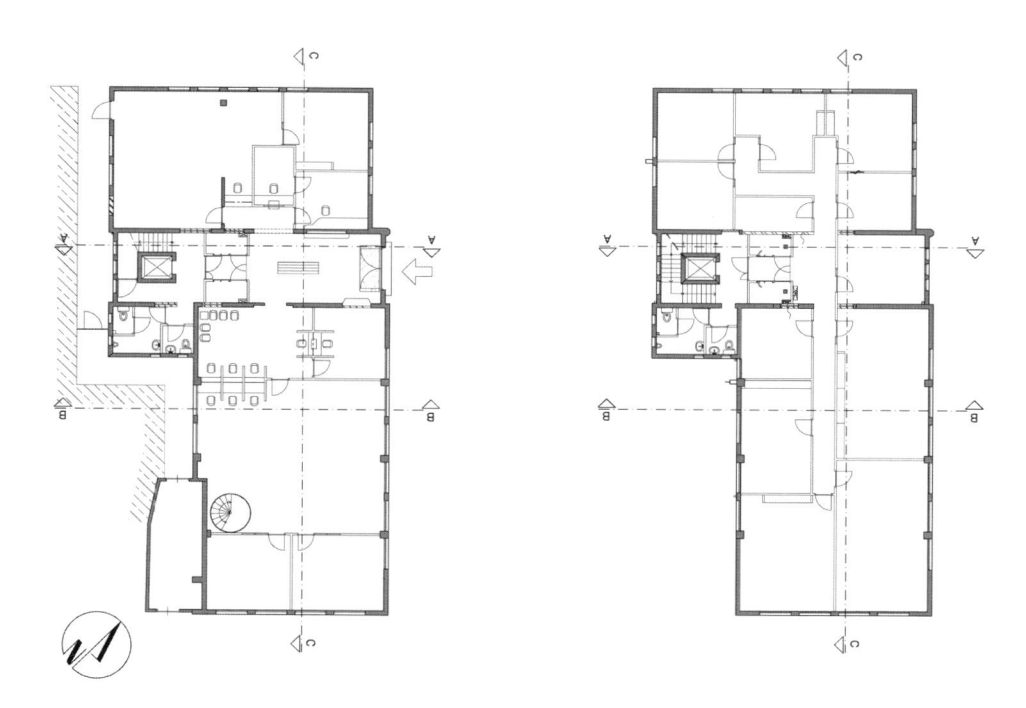

Customs Office. Drawing: Atelier Lobo & Raymann / Rosberg Engineering, 2016

References:

- Gill, Ronald G. (2008) Een eeuw architectuur op Curaçao. Curaçao: Ronald G. Gill, (Original work published 1999)
- Maduro-Molhuijsen, Helma (2013) Johan Heinrich Werner, de 'doodgezwegen' architect; *De Archiefvriend, maart 2013*
- Newton, Michael (2009) OGEM & Customs office – The first modern movement in Curaçao; *The impact of Caribbean Modern Architecture, First regional DOCOMOMO seminar, hosted by the University of the Netherlands Antilles, Curaçao, pp. 46-47*

Description_

The Customs office is situated on a corner at the end of a row of traditionally designed buildings on the famous Handelskade. The four-story block of the Customs office, with its flat roof, is dominated by verticality, achieved by using vertical columns between the windows. Although the whole building was constructed at the same time, its two-facedness is remarkable. The north-eastern side of the building is much more traditional with its tilled saddle roof and being dominated by horizontal elements. The building is mainly constructed of plastered concrete blocks. Except for the ground floor, all of the floors are constructed of wooden floorboards on wooden beams supported by steel beams.

Werner did not adapt his "European" Modern Movement architecture much to the tropical climate, unlike various other architects of the 1940s and 1950s who were commissioned by the Department of Public Works.

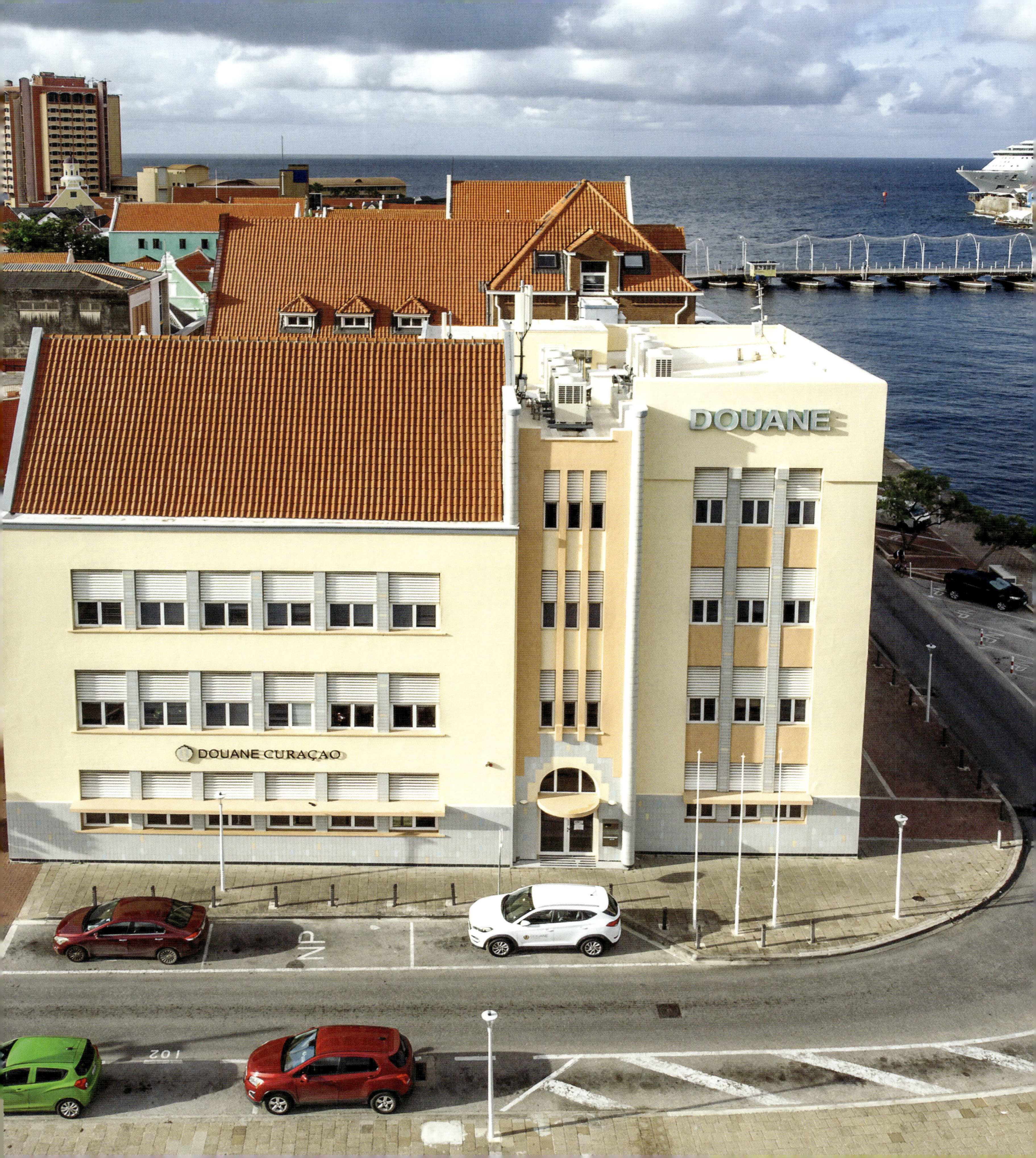
DOUANE
DOUANE CURAÇAO
NP

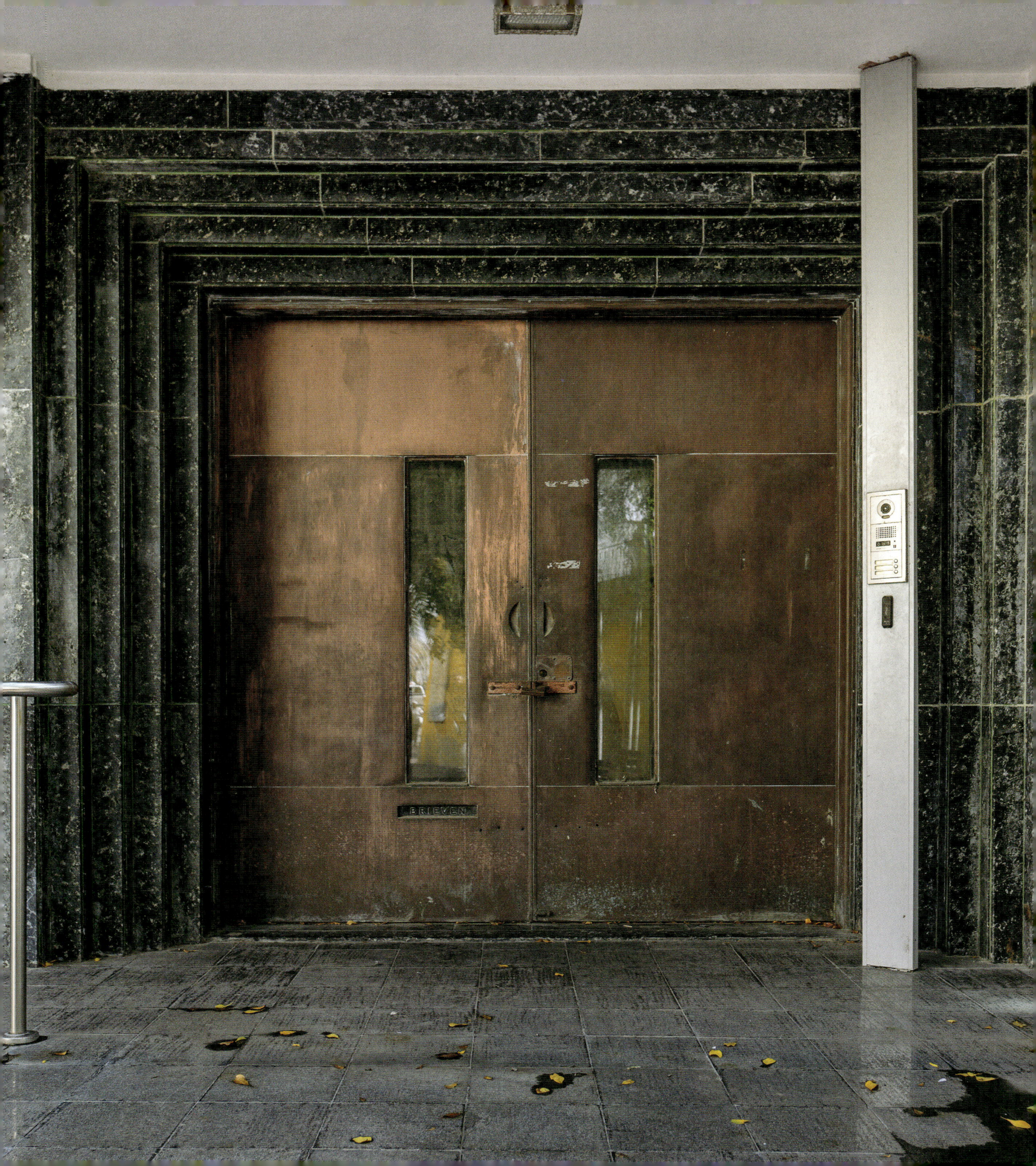
BRIEVEN

National grid reference: **12°06'19.2"N 68°56'03.6"W**

04.
KNSM BUILDING_

BREEDESTRAAT 39 - PUNDA

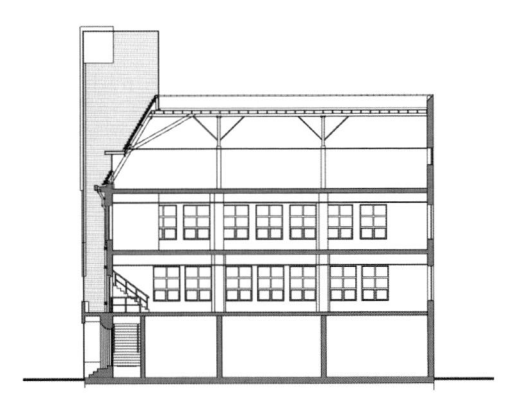

35

KNSM building, Drawing: Project Planners & Designers, 2004-2005 / Rosberg Engineering, 2016

Historic Background_

The Koninklijke Nederlandsche Stoomboot-Maatschappij n.v. (Royal Dutch Steamboat Company Ltd.), known as the KNSM, was a shipping company established in Amsterdam in 1856. Operating regular sailings between the Americas, the Caribbean and Europe, the company boasted a large fleet catering not only to freight but also to passenger accommodations. In Curaçao, with its century-long maritime heritage, KNSM was a major player in the freight industry and of significant economic importance for the island.

In 1938, KNSM acquired a lot from the Curaçao government to construct their office in the heart of historic Willemstad, adjacent to St. Annabay, the harbor entrance. The existing building on the site was demolished, and construction of the office commenced between 1939 and 1941. On March 1, 1942, the KNSM building was inaugurated, marking its distinction as the company's largest office in the Americas.

In 1981, KNSM merged with Nedlloyd, which later amalgamated with P&O to form P&O Nedlloyd, now a subsidiary of Maersk. Three years after, in 1984, the building was sold to the Curaçao government. For years, the government development bank KORPODEKO had its office on the second floor. In 2004, it was sold to a private entrepreneur.

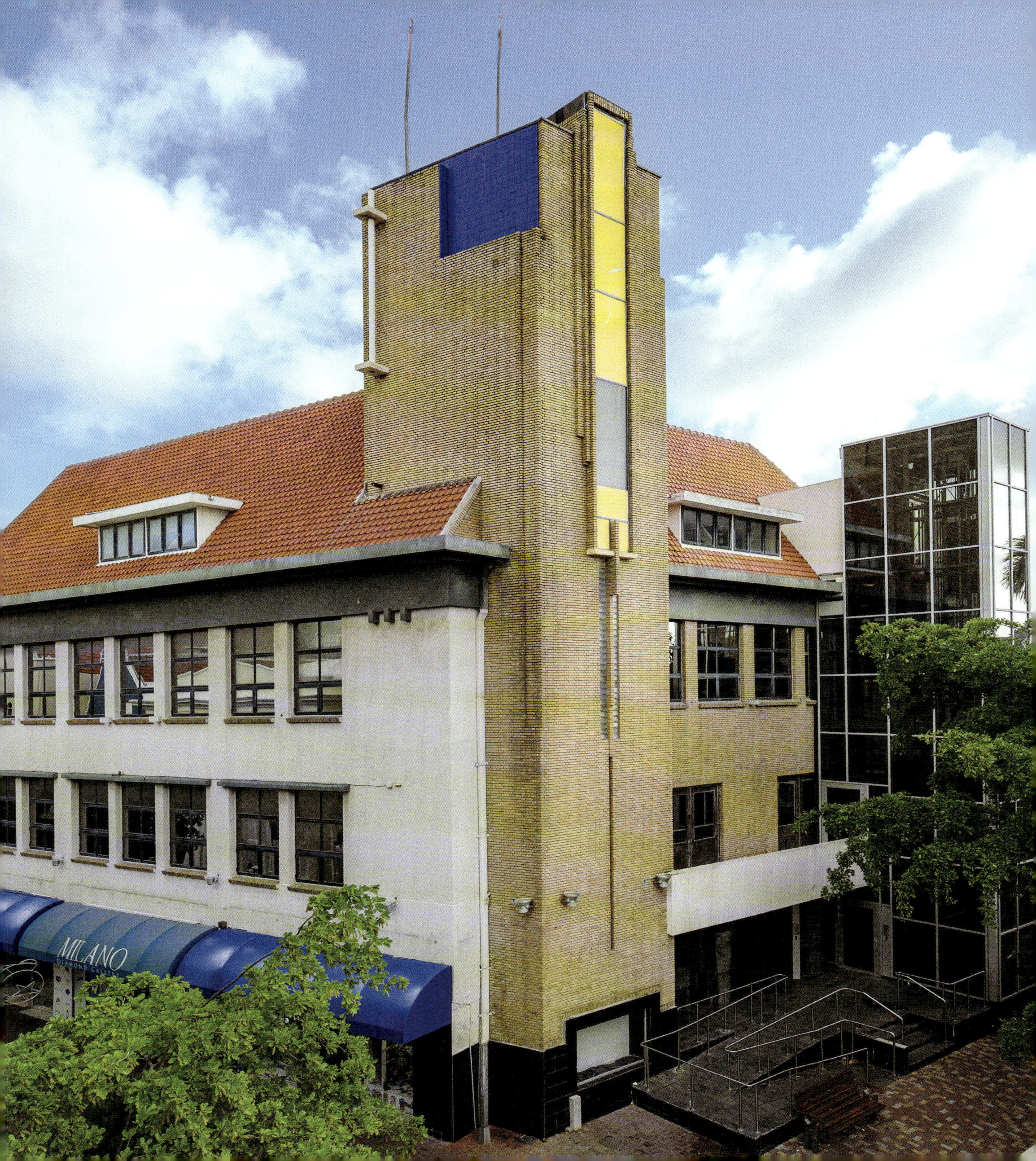
MILANO

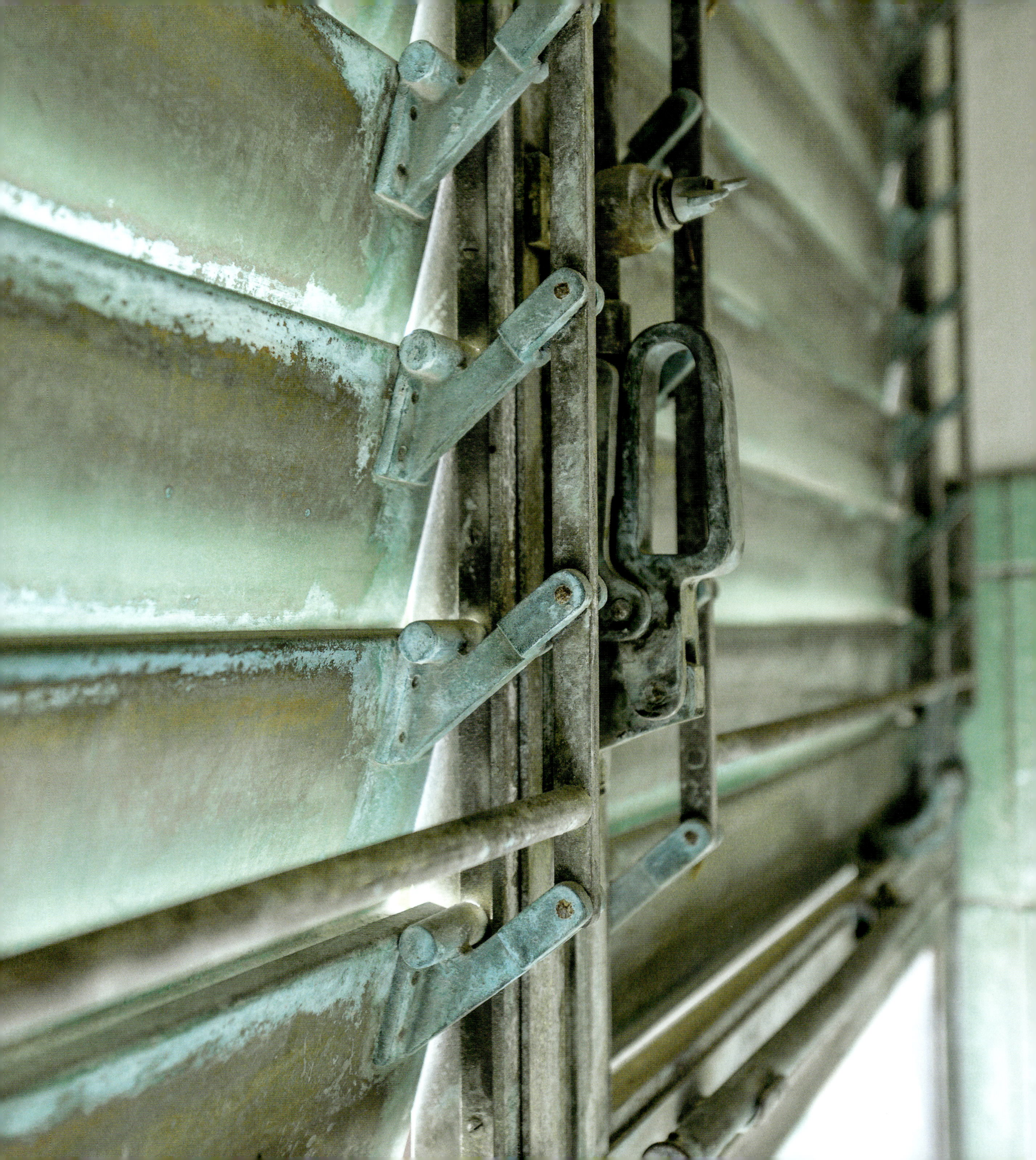

Though the architect remains unknown, it is presumed that the KNSM Building was designed by the Construction Bureau of KNSM in Amsterdam.

Architectural Design_

Though the architect remains unknown, it is presumed that the KNSM Building was designed by the Construction Bureau of KNSM in Amsterdam. On the other hand, the work is also attributed to Pieter van Stuivenberg, a Dutch engineer who was the manager of the Technical Department of the local Governmental Department for Water Supply, and also worked as an architect for the private sector. Given the clear architectural influence of the famous Dutch architect Dudok, it is likely that the design was made in the Netherlands, with Stuivenberg probably serving as the executive architect.

The design reflects Dutch architectural styles of the era. The tall, slimline tower at the corner of the building, the ochre-coloured bricks, and the striking brick pattern are reminiscent of the renowned Dutch architect W.M. Dudok (1884-1974). The blue tiles in the ridge of the yellow stair tower are also an unmistakable clue to this influence. Notably, the main façade on the St. Annabay side remains unplastered, unlike the prevalent practice of plastering walls in Curaçao since the 17th century. The building's unique features, including its unplastered façade, add to its architectural significance. However, in the same period the KNSM Building was built, a few more unplastered brick buildings were constructed.

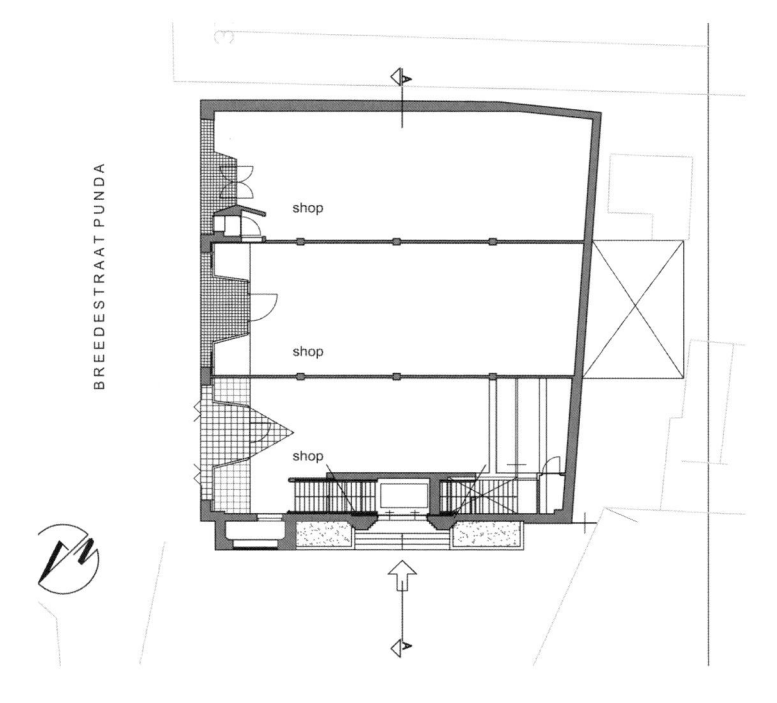

KNSM building, Drawing: Project Planners & Designers, 2004-2005 / Rosberg Engineering, 2016

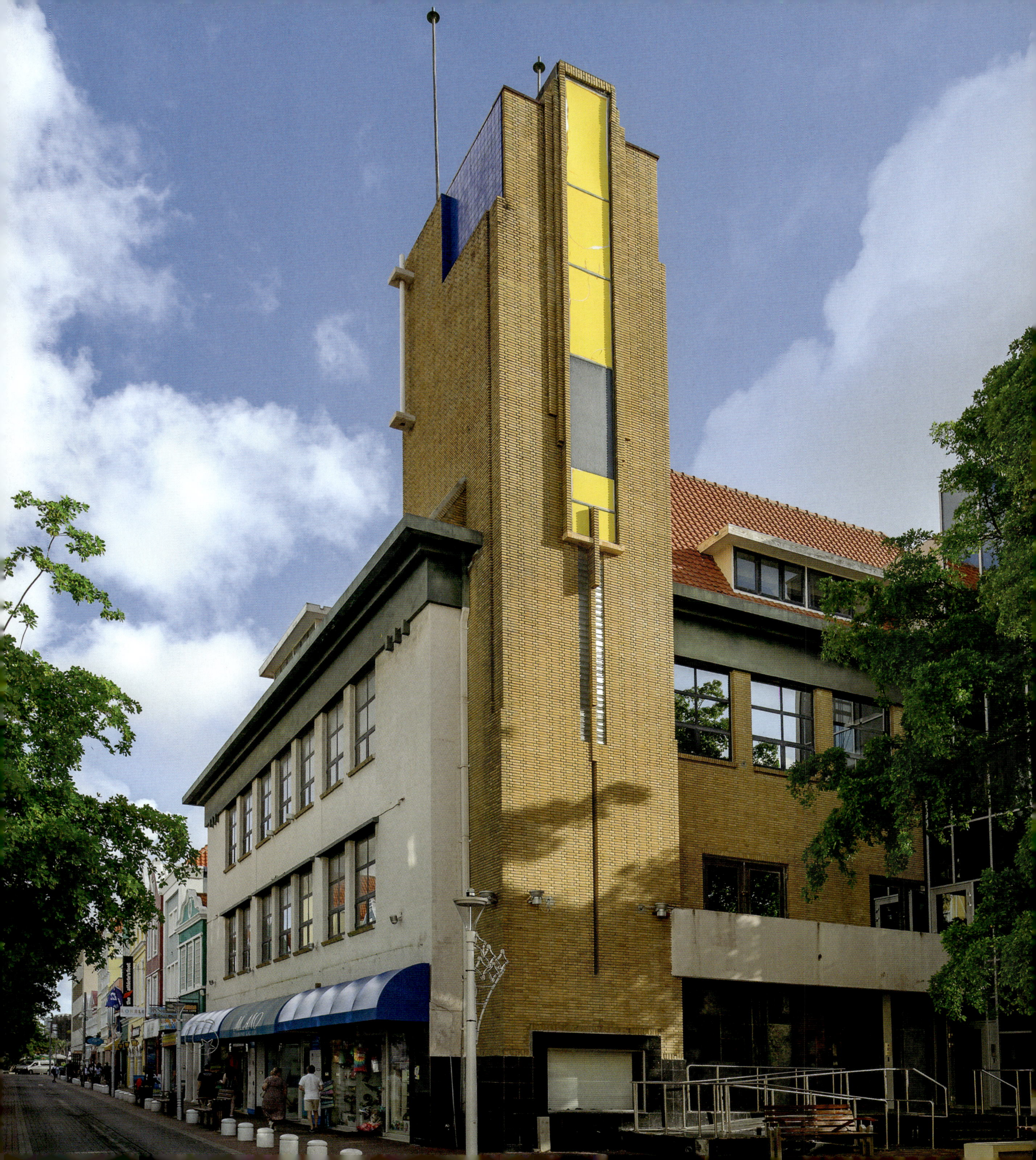

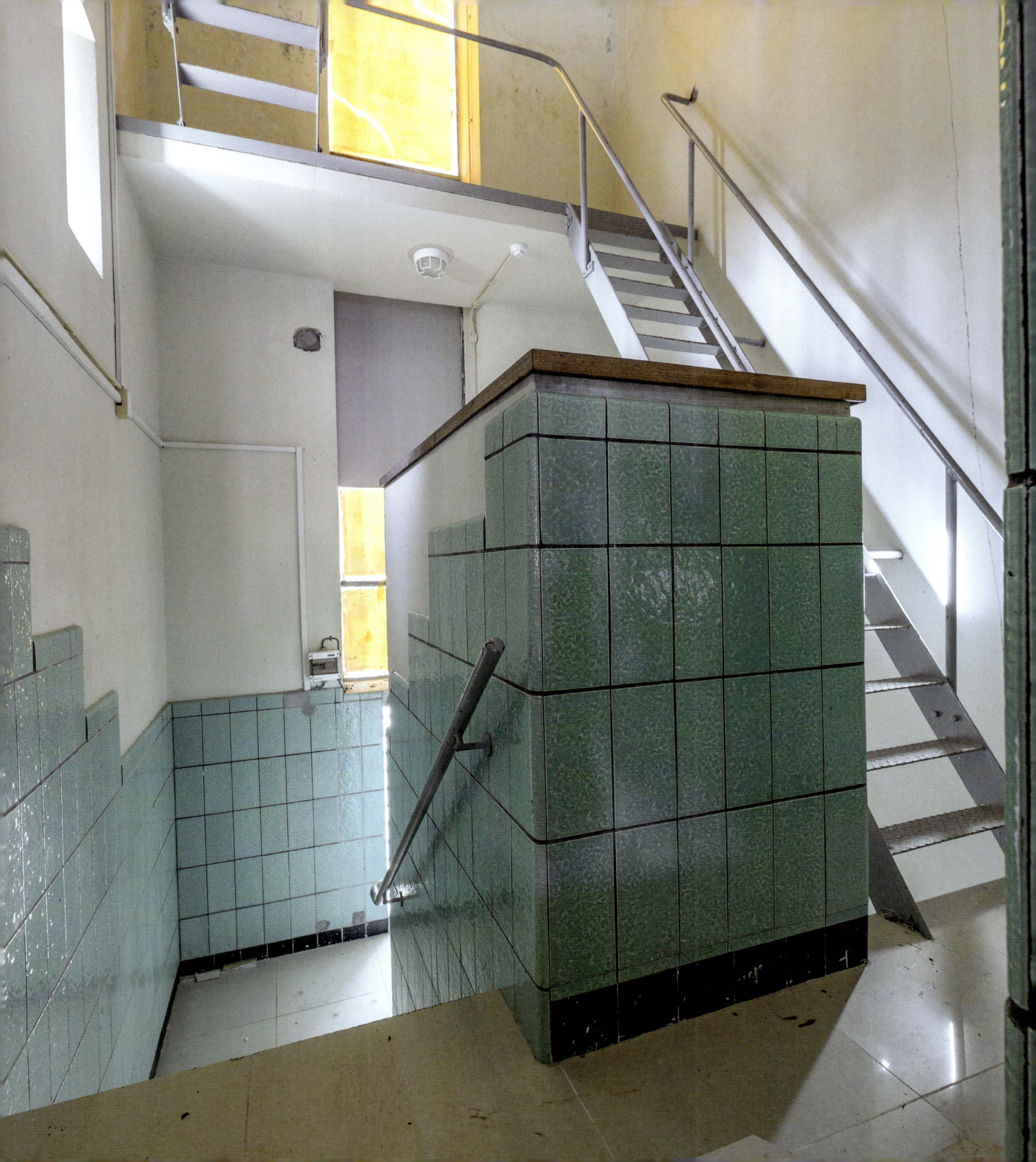

Description_

The former KNSM Building comprises a substantial block-shaped structure with a tower at the north-western corner. Its inner walls are a combination of reinforced concrete and concrete blocks. Allthough originally planned, the elevator in the tower was never constructed. The building features three stories with a steep, truncated tiled roof. The ground floor houses three shop outlets, traditionally leased to third parties.

Upon entry, two staircases lead directly to the second floor. The first floor previously housed public spaces, including ticket sales and freight handling counters, along with the 'public relations' department. The second floor accommodated bookkeeping and insurance claims departments, while the large attic served as storage space.

During World War II it was impossible to ship building materials from Europe. The building was designed with bronze exterior doors and windows, ready for shipping from Amsterdam when WW II broke out. The building had to be finished with the traditional wooden louvered windows. Remarkably, the original bronze windows and doors were recovered post-war and eventually installed. Part of these bronze windows were removed in 2004 and changed to aluminum.

In 2013, an outside elevator shaft was added at the front, along with a ramp to facilitate wheelchair access, partly affecting the character of the building. However, the structure is still a prominent landmark in Willemstad and remains a clear example of Dutch pre-WW II modern architecture.

References:

- Gehlen, Gerda (2009) The KNSM Building, unplastered brick, strikingly modern; *The impact of Caribbean Modern Architecture, First regional DOCOMOMO seminar, hosted by the University of the Netherlands Antilles, Curaçao, pp. 48-49*
- Gehlen, Gerda (2017) Het gebouw van de K.N.S.M.; *Monumento Habri '17 – Punda, Curacao, Fundashon Pro Monumento, pp 126-129*
- Gill, Ronald G. (2008) *Een eeuw architectuur op Curaçao.* Curaçao: Ronald G. Gill, (Original work published 1999)
- Knap, Ger. H., (1956) *Gekroonde Koopvaart, Reisresultaat van honderd jaar zeevaart door de Koninklijke Nederlandsche Stoomboot-maatschappij N.V. 1856 – 1956.* Amsterdam: J.H. de Bussy,
- Monsanto, Christel (2022) Pieter Antonie van Stuivenberg, architect. *De Archiefvriend, september 2022*
- Reichardt, Joke en Veendendaal, Peter (2024) *Inspired by Dudok.* Dudok.org / Dudok Architectuur centrum, pp 150-151

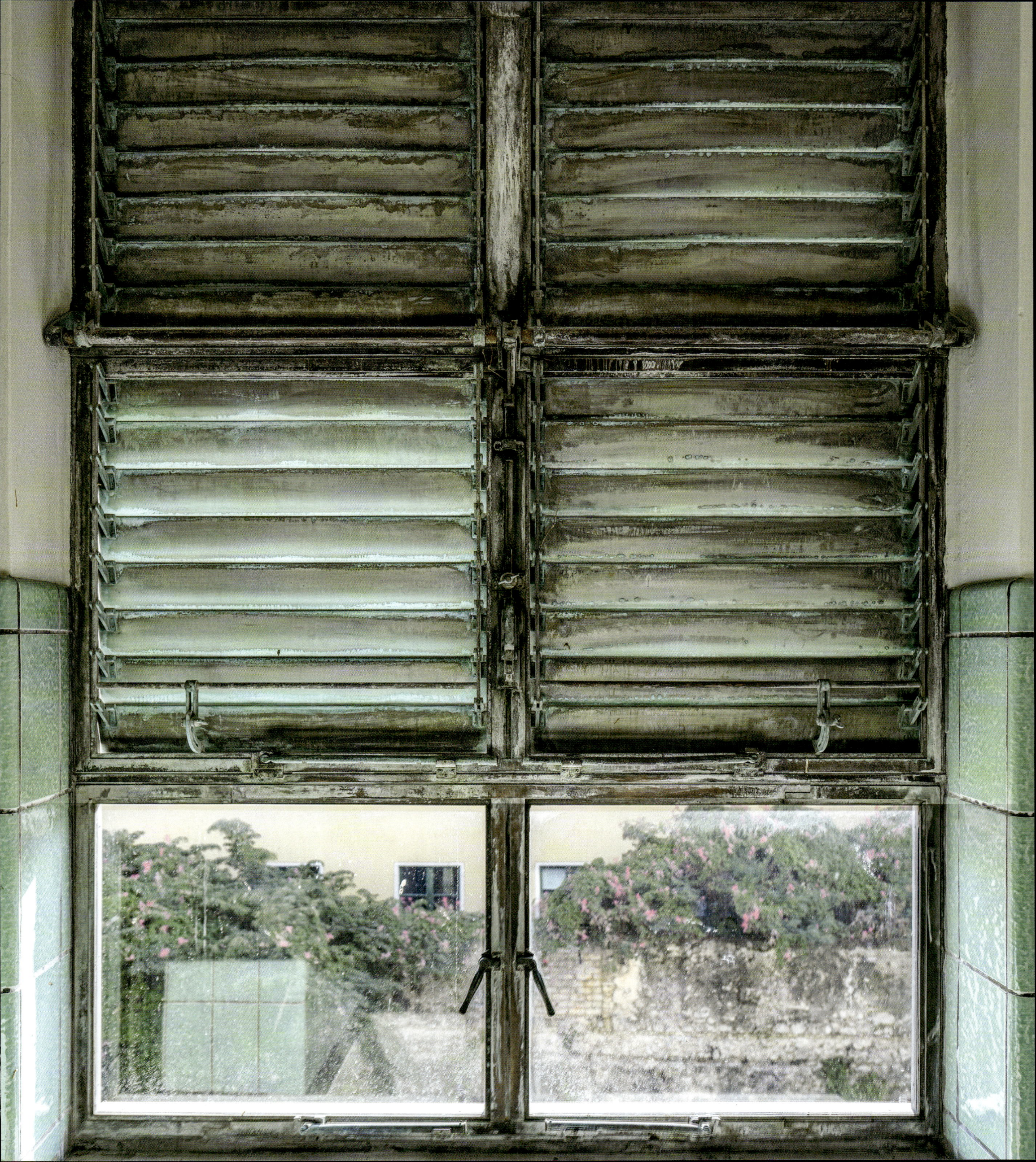

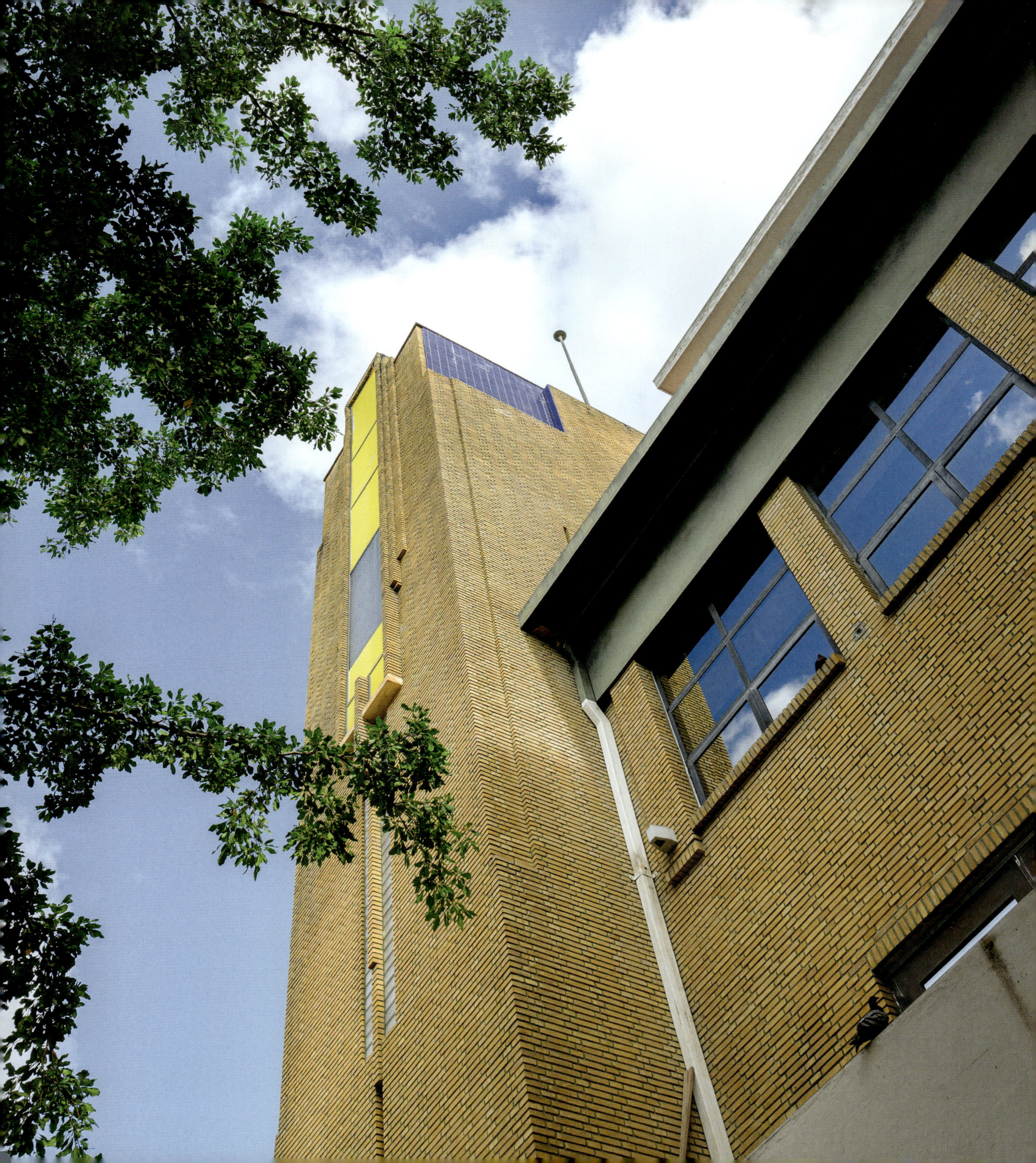

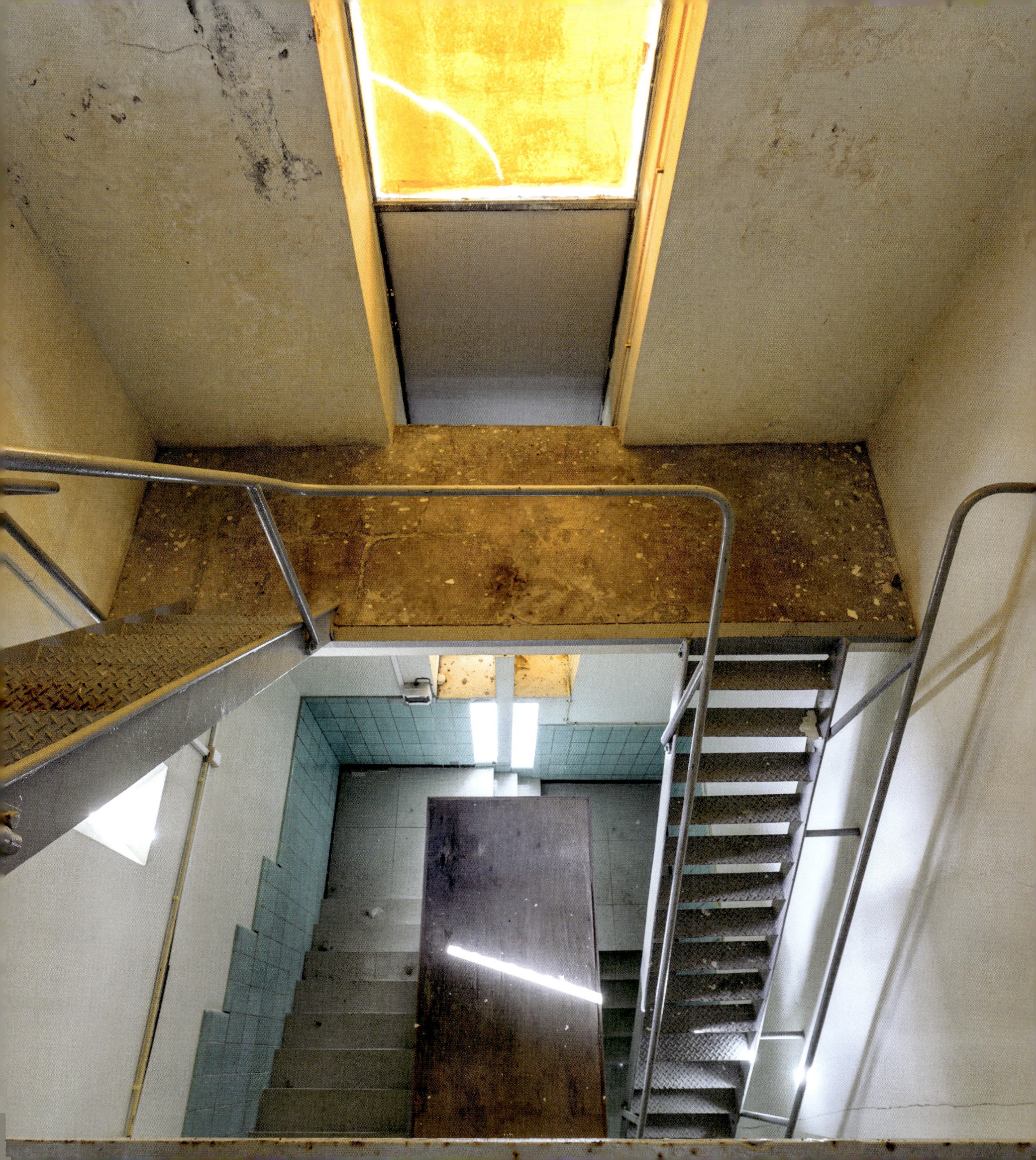

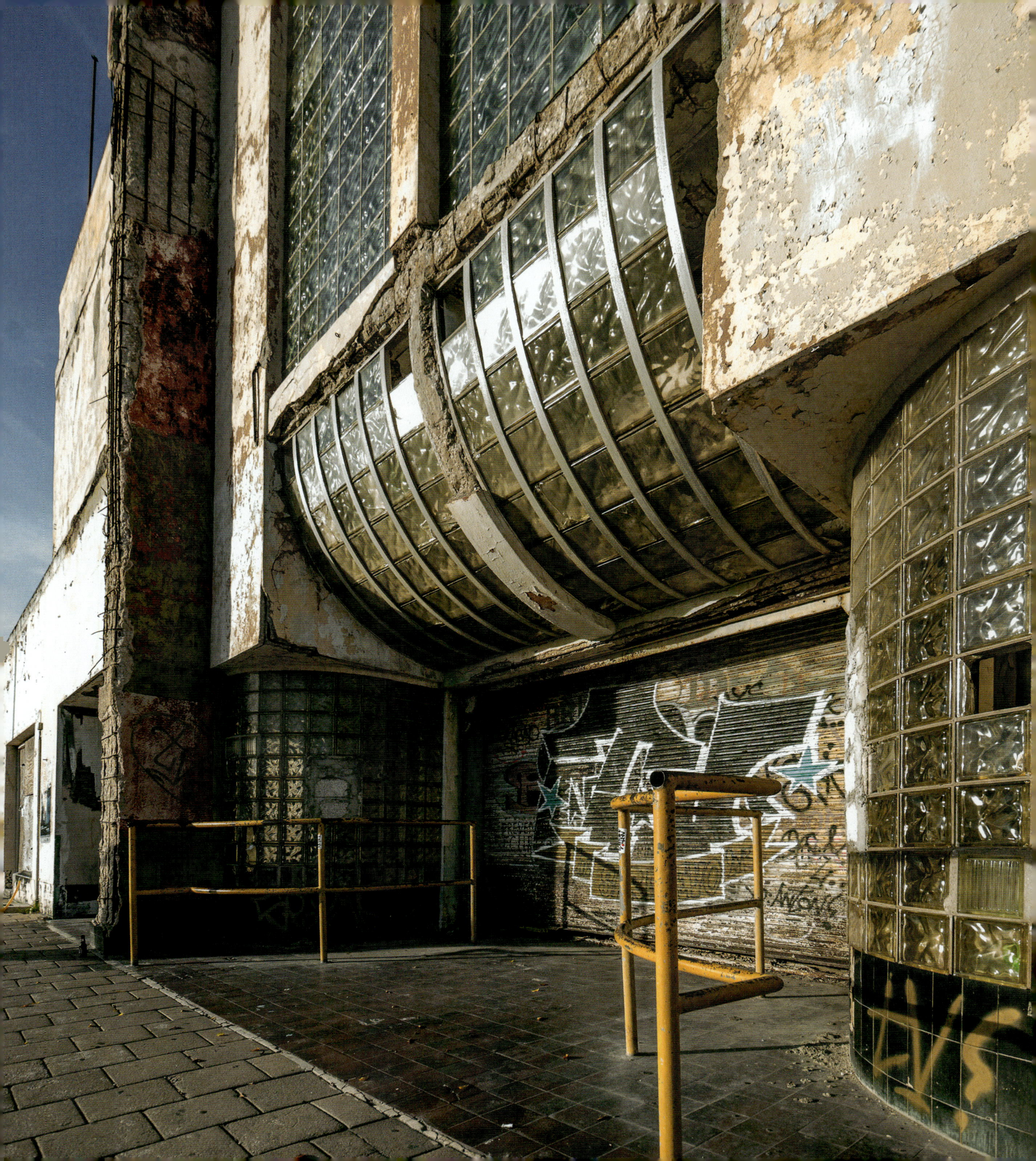

National grid reference: **12°06'14.7"N 68°55'56.7"W**

05.
CINELANDIA CINEMA_

HENDRIKPLEIN Z/N

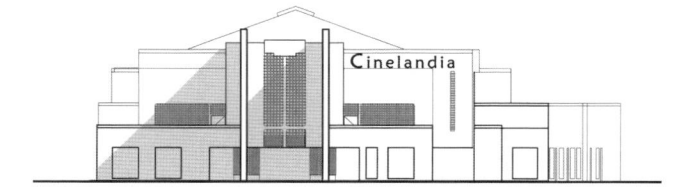

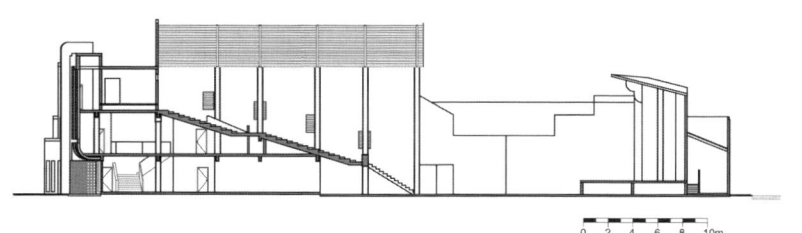

Cinelandia Building. Drawing Janko Lopez / Rosberg Engineering, 2016

National Archive Curaçao / Coll. Fisher

Historic Background_

Until the middle of the 19th century, the area where the Cinelandia building is located was an empty space just outside the city walls of Willemstad. After the demolition of the wall between 1860-1866, the lots were sold, but this one parcel remained vacant for several decades. In 1916, Alfredo Pellicer Hernandez, a Venezuelan who had presented film-shows on the island before, opened the first movie house in Curaçao on this plot. It was called Salón Habana. In 1932, it was destroyed by a fire but was subsequently reconstructed and rebranded as Cinelandia. Unfortunately, In 1939, this wooden building burned down once more. Two years later, the present open-air cinema opened. The owner at that time was Mr. Alfredo (Fetchi) Moron. It opened its doors to the public on January 16, 1941 (Amigoe di Curaçao, 15 January 1941).

Cinelandia, situated in the center of Willemstad, was the largest cinema in the region with a capacity of 2.200 seats. Among these, 600 seats were located on the balcony, while 1600 seats on the ground floor. It was operational for more than forty years. However, partly due to the emergence of films on video, the number of movie-goers decreased. Cinelandia closed its doors in mid-1983 and the building remained vacant ever since. The façade, along with the construction a few meters behind it, is listed as a protected monument.

Cinelandia is the principal example of the Miami Art Deco style on the island.

Architectural Design_

The building was designed by Pieter A. van Stuivenberg, a Dutch engineer who was the manager of the Technical Department of the "Landswatervoorzieningsdienst" – LWV, (the Governmental Department for Water Supply), established on January 1, 1928. In 1948, he would become the director of this Department. Besides designing structures for the LWV, he also worked for private clients. The West-End cinema in the Willemstad district of Otrobanda was also designed by Van Stuivenberg. It opened in 1941, but was, unfortunately, demolished in August 2000.

Most of Van Stuivenberg's designs were inspired by Art Deco architecture, in particular the so-called Miami Beach Art Deco style of the 1930's. Cinelandia is the principal example of the Miami Art Deco style on the island.

The building is characterized by a central entry block and asymmetrical façade elements on either side, with the name of the building displayed at the right top front. The center element, being the most impactful and dramatic, is formed by two large vertical concrete posts, slightly jutting forward and holding a wall of glass blocks. The wall of glass blocks is prolonged inside the building, curving into the cinema's entrance. The cashiers' offices on both sides of the entrance also feature curved walls of glass blocks. Such walls formed by numerous glass blocks were often used in Van Stuivenberg's designs.

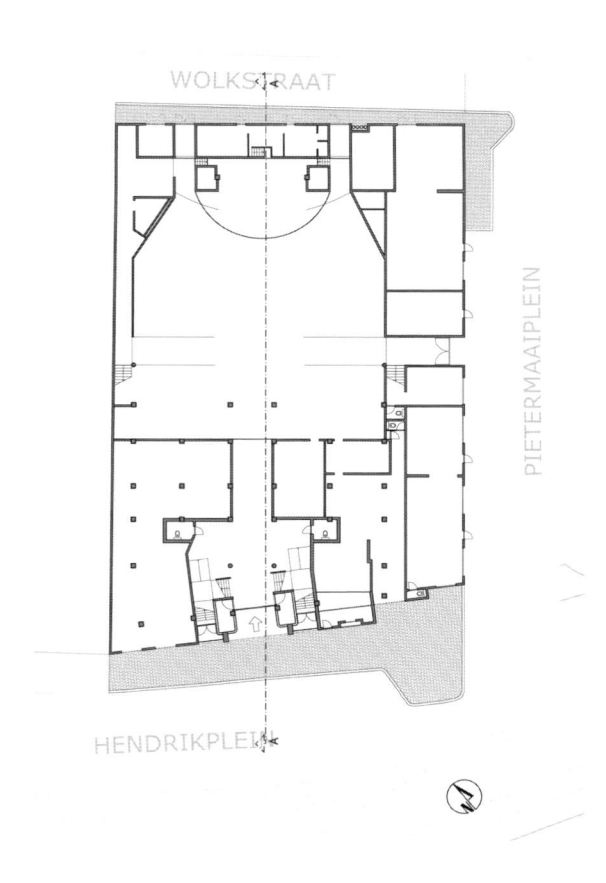

Cinelandia Building. Drawing Janko Lopez / Rosberg Engineering, 2016

do.co.mo.mo_curaçao

Description_

The main roofed part at the front of the building is only about ten meters deep and consists mainly of stairways and balconies. The back of building is occupied by the stage and the cinema screen. There is no roof over the central part of the building, making the cinema open to the air.

The building is constructed of reinforced concrete. Although this was not yet a very common construction method in the 1940s, the architect Van Stuivenberg often used it for projects of the Governmental Department for Water Supply.

Due to lack of maintenance over the past forty years, the degradation of the concrete is presently the main danger for the future of this significant example of Art Deco architecture on the island.

References:

- Gill, Ronald G. (2008) *Een eeuw architectuur op Curaçao*. Curaçao: Ronald G. Gill, (Original work published 1999)
- Monsanto, Christel (2022) Pieter Antonie van Stuivenberg, architect. *De Archiefvriend, september 2022*
- Newton, Michael A. (1990) Fo'i porta, The Wilhelminapark and its surroundings. *Building up the future from the past*. Zutphen: De Walburg Pers.
- Saavedra Bruno, Sofia (2009) The Cultural importance of saving Cinelandia; *The impact of Caribbean Modern Architecture, First regional DOCOMOMO seminar, hosted by the University of the Netherlands Antilles*, Curaçao, pp. 50-51

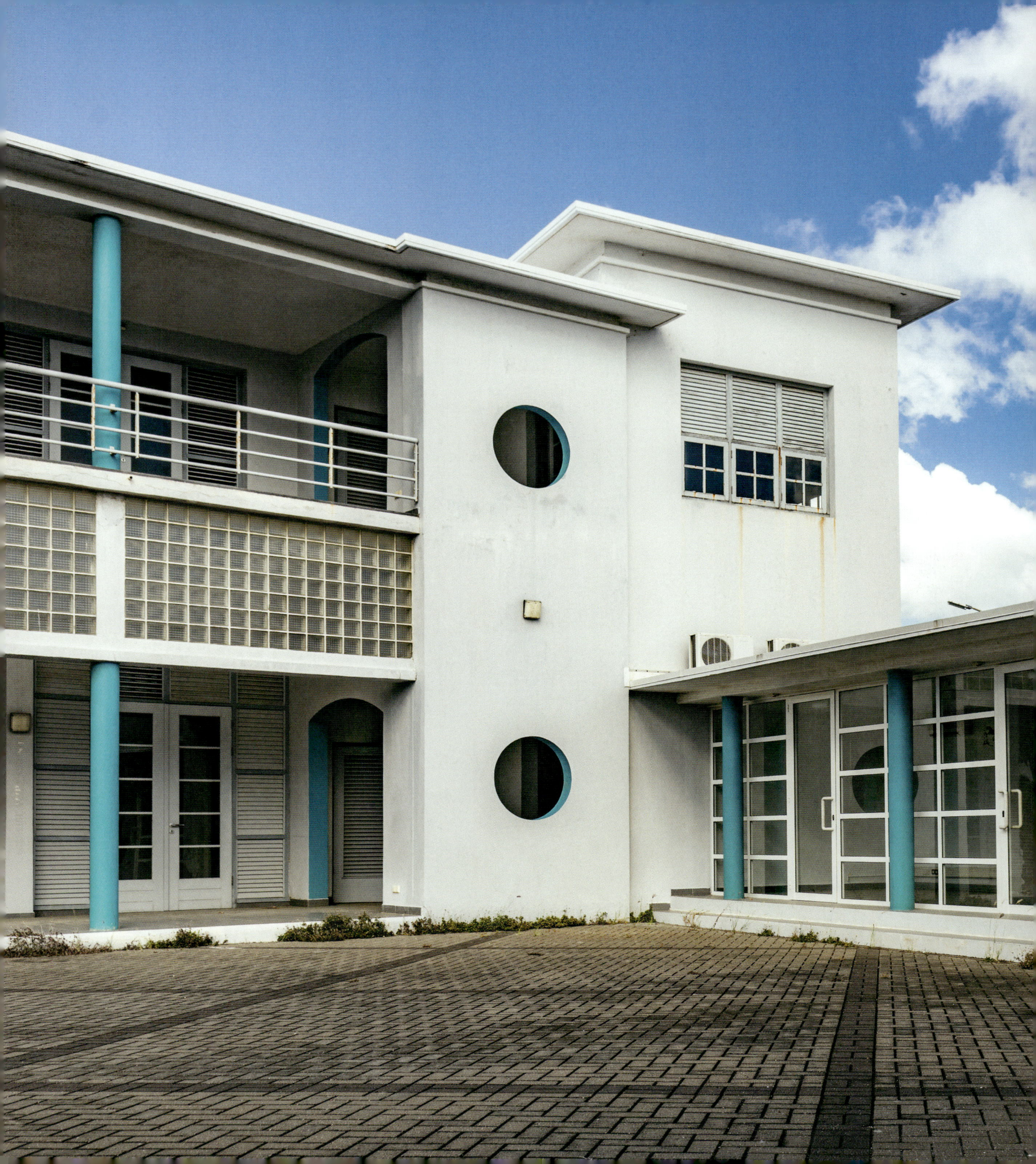

National grid reference: **12°06'09.3"N 68°55'35.5"W**

06.
PUBLIC READING ROOM & LIBRARY_

JOHAN VAN WALBEECKPLEIN 6-13

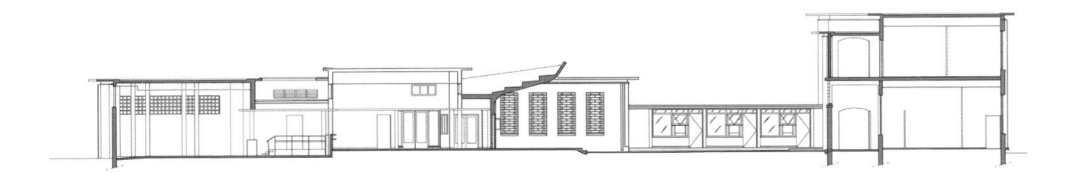

NAAM building. Drawing: IMD Design / Rosberg Engineering, 1998 / 2016

National Archive Curaçao / Coll. Fisher

Historic Background_

In the 1940s, the Curaçao Government decided to construct a joint building for the Public Reading Room and Library, along with the Education Inspectorate. The Damplein, as the Johan van Walbeeckplein in the Pietermaai district was called back then, was selected for its construction. Despite public discussion regarding the choice of the location, which was often used for festivals, fairs or circuses, the plans moved forward. A newspaper article about the official opening of the building in 1945 mentioned that it was situated in an "impractical" location (Amigoe di Curaçao, February 19, 1945).

Initially, the compound served as a food warehouse during the latter years of World War II. In 1945, the building was adapted for its original purpose, with the necessary modifications overseen by the architect Ben Smit. The Reading Room and Library accommodated in the eastern part of the building, while the western part housed the office of the Education Inspectorate. It officially opened on February 21, 1945.

When the Netherlands Antilles was formed in 1954, something peculiar happened. The property of the building was split in two. The eastern part, housing the public library, became property of the Island Territory of Curaçao. The western part came under the ownership of the Netherlands Antilles.

In 1988, the library moved to a new building in the Scharloo district, and the island government repurposed the library building as storage space. The western part was utilized to accommodate the Archaeological Antropological Institute Netherlands Antilles (AAINA) until 1998. In that year, the National Archaeological Antropological Museum (NAAM) was established, taking over the collection of AAINA. In 1998/1999, the NAAM foundation obtained ownership of both parts of the compound.

In October 1999, it became the first Modern Movement building to be listed as a protected monument by the Government.

In 2005, the property was transferred to the General Pension Fund of the Netherlands Antilles (APNA). The pension fund commissioned architects Jacqueline Woei a Sioe and Dennis Klaus to draw up a restoration plan, which was carried out from 2005 to 2007.

As of June 1, 2007 NAAM, whose name was changed to National Archaeological Antropological Memory Management, rents the eastern part of the compound from the pension fund.

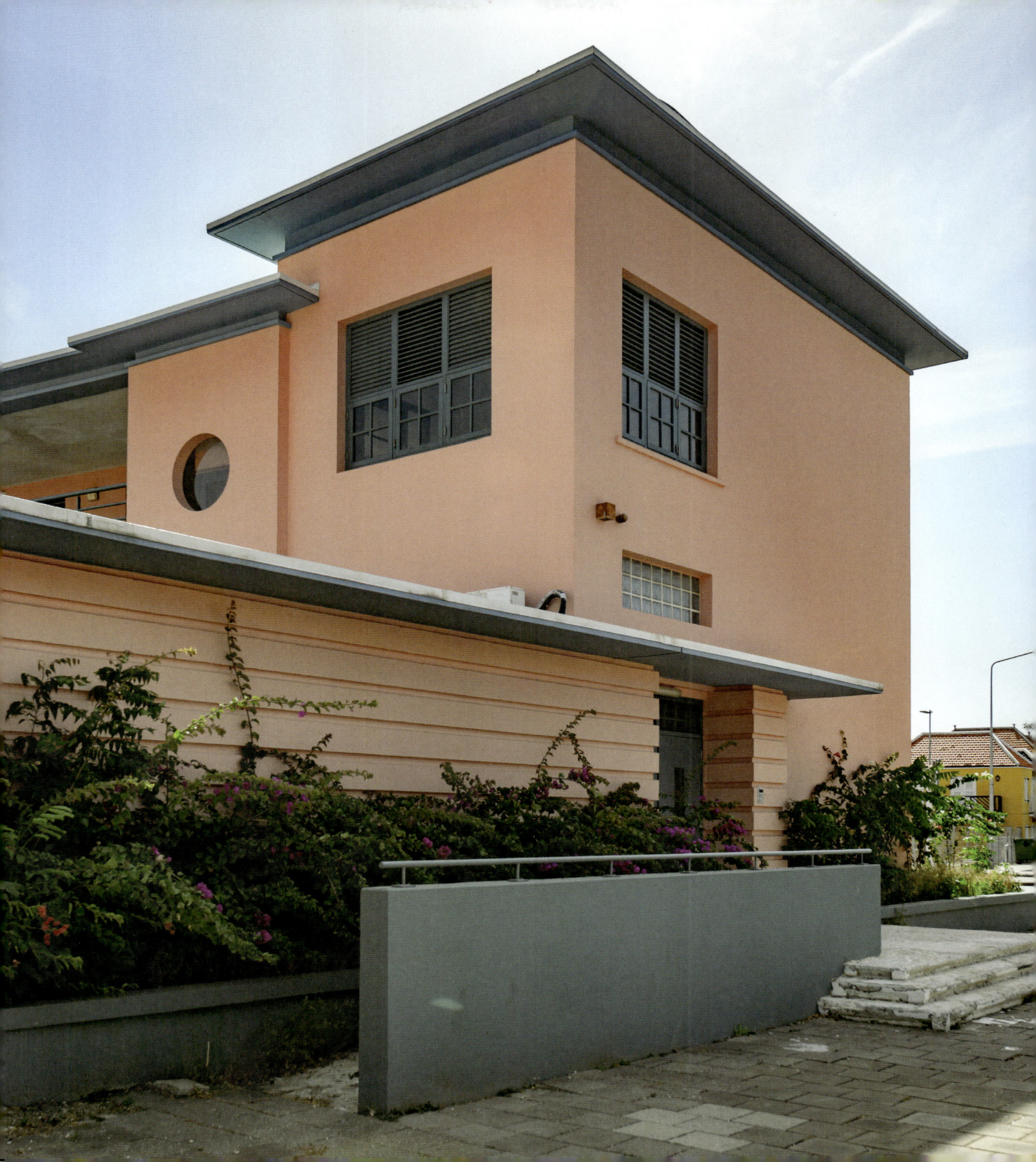

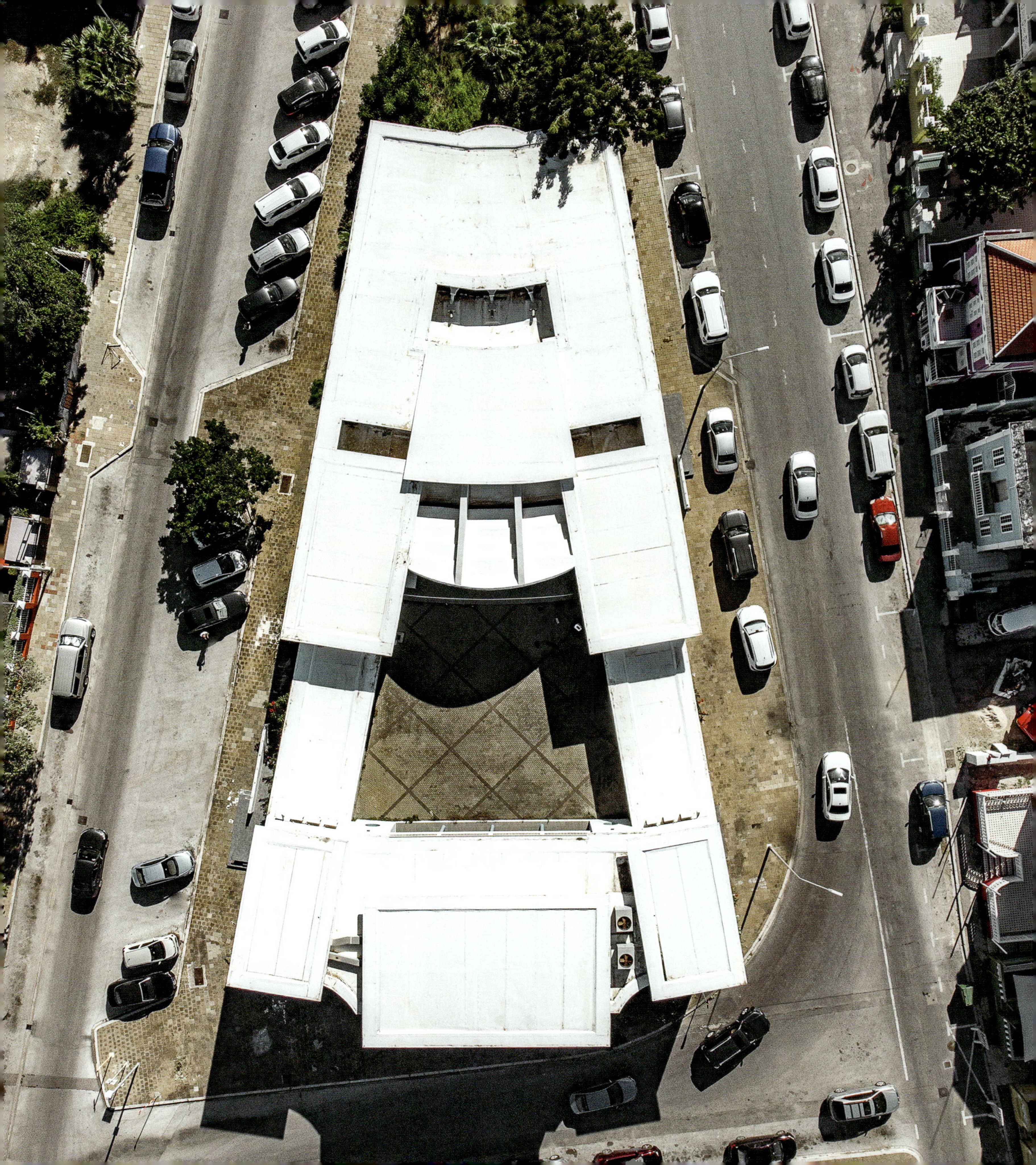

A significant example of the Dutch "Nieuwe Bouwen", part of the Modern Movement in the Netherlands, adapted to tropical climates.

Architectural Design_

The building was designed in 1943 by the Dutch architect Cornelis Marinus (Kees) Bakker M.Sc. He came to Curaçao in 1940 to work for the Curaçao Department of Public Works. In 1944 he left the Department to join the oil refinery. After 1948, he operated as an independent architect before immigrating to Canada in 1952.

The original building plot, situated at the former Damplein, had a triangular shape, serving as inspiration for Bakker's design. He chose to anchor the elongated compound on the short west side of the plaza, tapering it towards the east. The design principle aimed at symmetry on both sides of a longitudinal axis.

Given the building's intended multifunctionality, Bakker opted for two structures connected by a large internal patio in between. This patio was used as an open-air hall for lectures and movie showings. To enhance acoustics, a sturdy, slightly curved concrete canopy was erected across the podium on the east side of the patio. Characteristic of Bakker's architectural style are the horizontal grooves adorning sections of the façades and all entrances.

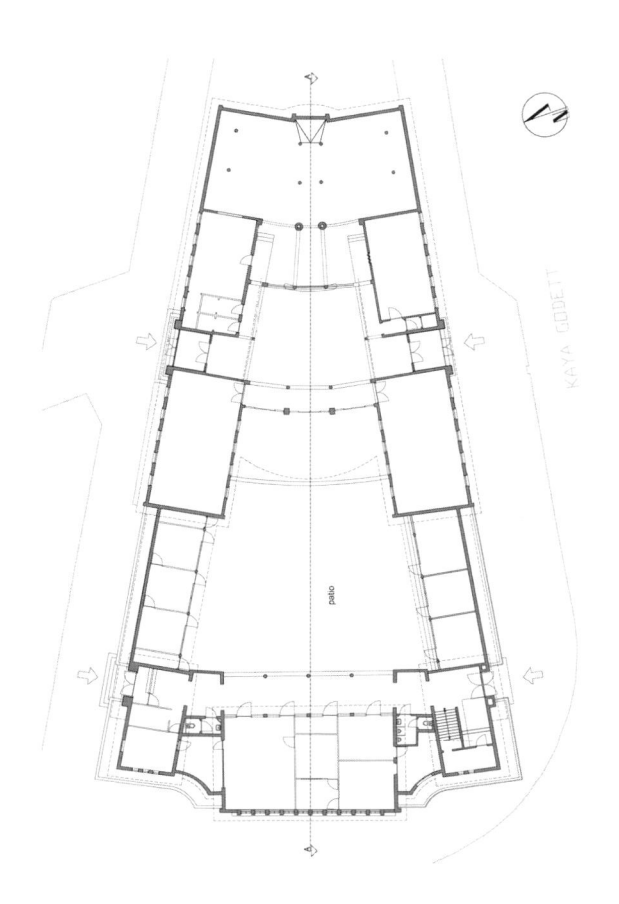

NAAM building. Drawing: IMD Design / Rosberg Engineering, 1998 / 2016

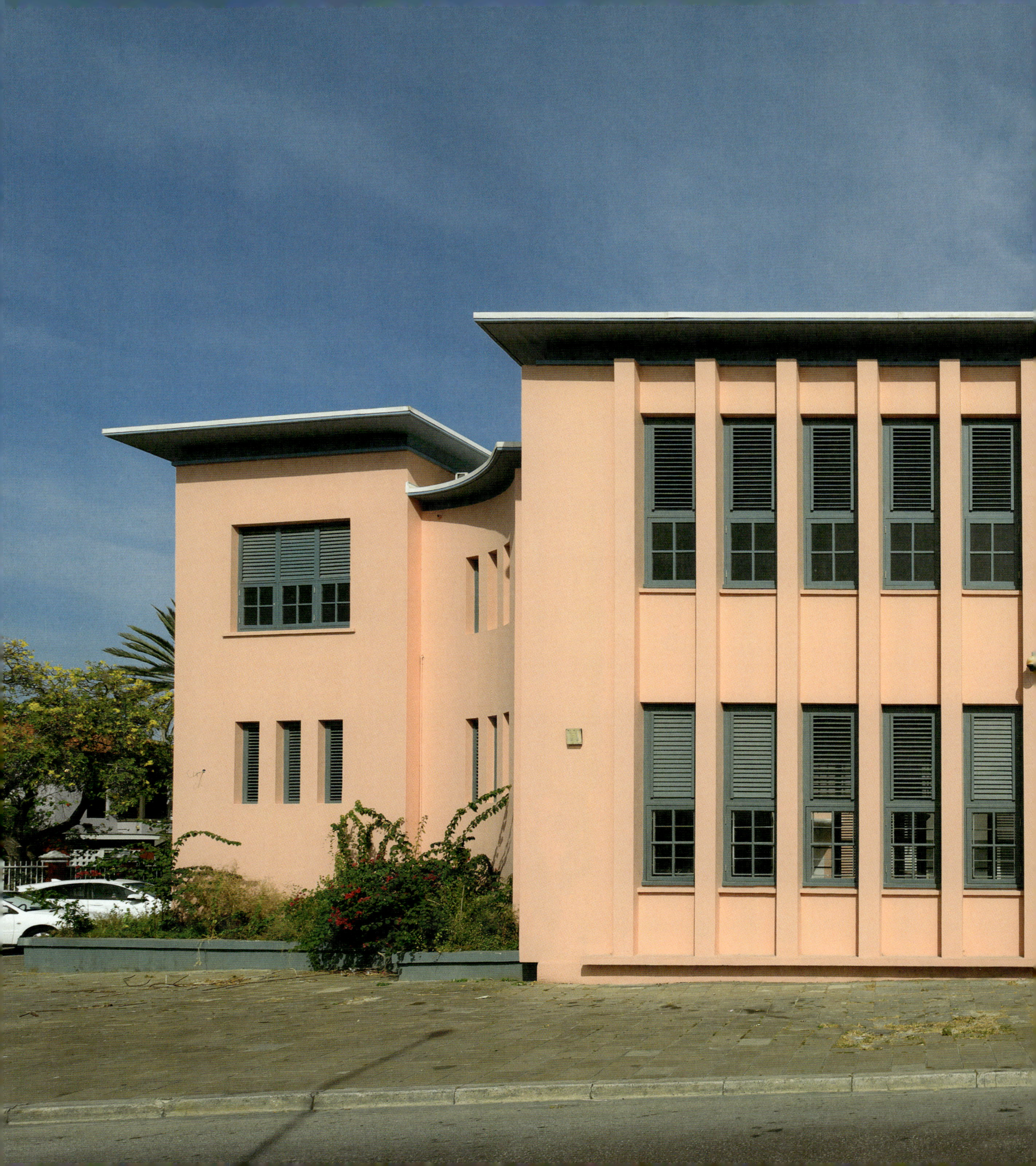

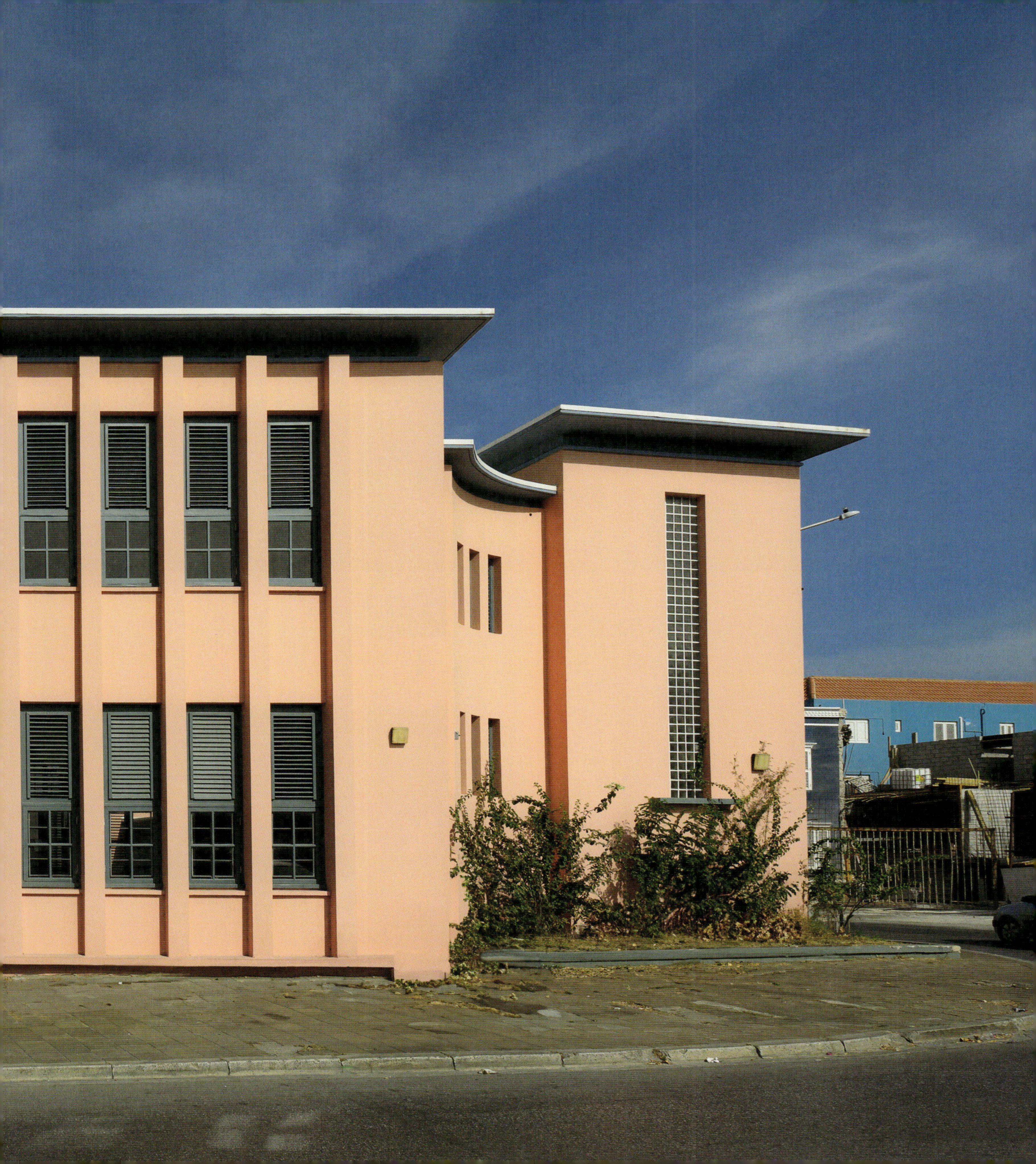

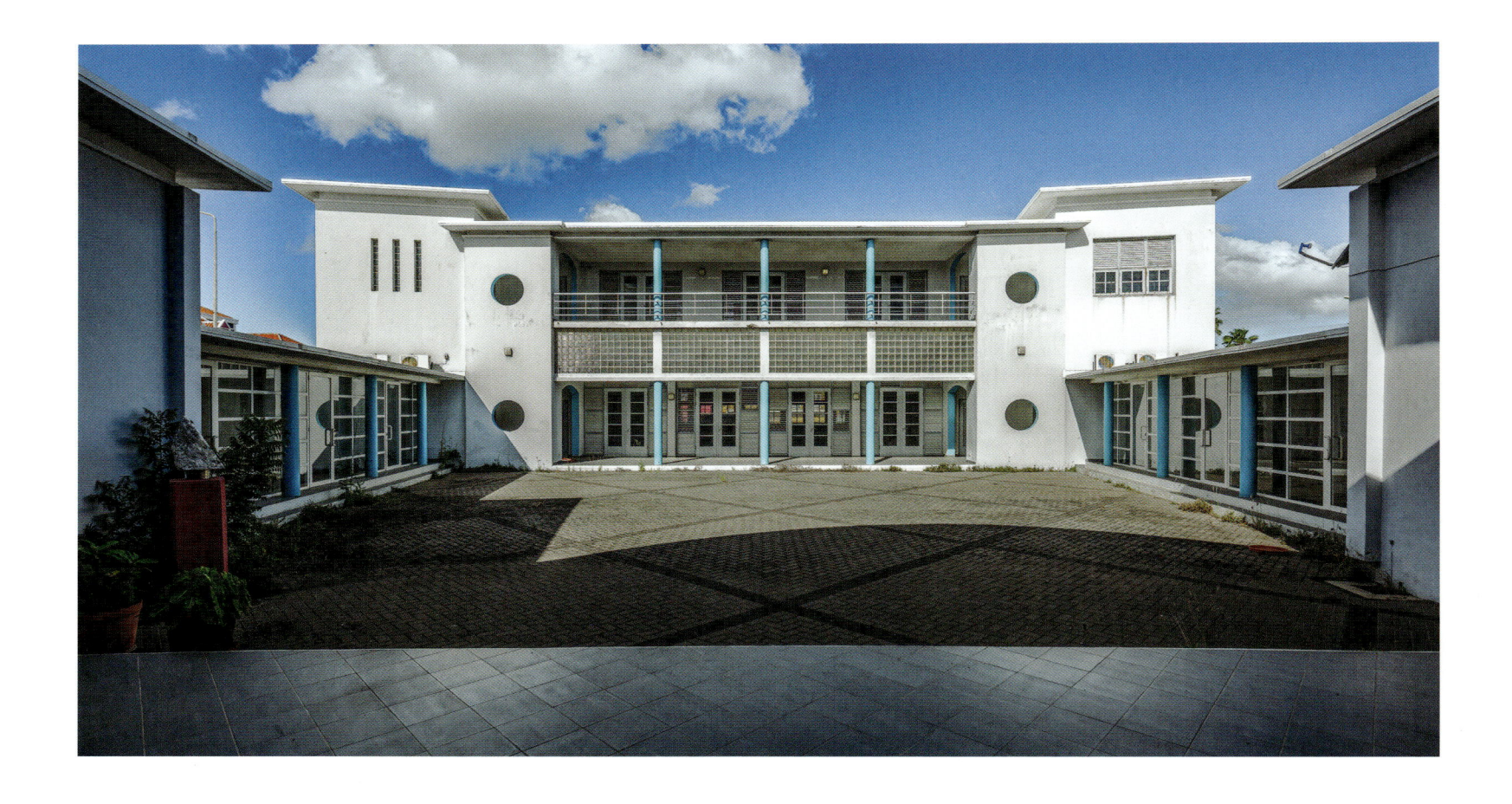

Description_

The building is mainly constructed of concrete blocks and reinforced concrete slabs, all of which were plastered. It is a significant example of the Dutch "Nieuwe Bouwen", part of the Modern Movement in the Netherlands, adapted to tropical climates. This adaptation is evident not only in the central patio, but also in the consideration of the prevailing eastern trade wind. The wind can flow freely across the lower east construction, reaching the west two story building unhindered. Another tropical adaptation is the design of narrow, high window openings with wooden louvers on top and glass at the bottom, which was important in the pre-air conditioning era.

Typical features include rows of small square ventilation openings under the edge of the roof and the use of square glass building blocks in the facades.

Buildings of the Modern Movement are usually light in color. This also applied to the NAAM building, which has always been almost white to light grey. In the middle of 2023, the walls of this complex were painted in a terracotta color, and the windows and doors were painted dark green. These colors do not match the original character of this Modern Movement building.

References:

- Bosch-Kruimel, Fosca (2007) Johan van Walbeeckplein 6/13; *Monumento Habri '07 – Pietermaai Smal, Curaçao: Fundashon Pro Monumento*, pp 44-47
- Bosh-Kruimel, Fosca (2009) Johan van Walbeeckplein 6 / 13; *The impact of Caribbean Modern Architecture, First regional DOCOMOMO seminar, hosted by the University of the Netherlands Antilles*, Curaçao, pp. 52-55
- Gill, Ronald G. (2008) *Een eeuw architectuur op Curaçao*. Curaçao: Ronald G. Gill, (Original work published 1999)
- Monsanto, Christel (2022) Ir. Cornelis Marinus (Kees) Bakker, architect (1903 Hilversum – 1989 Toronto). *De Archiefvriend, december 2022*

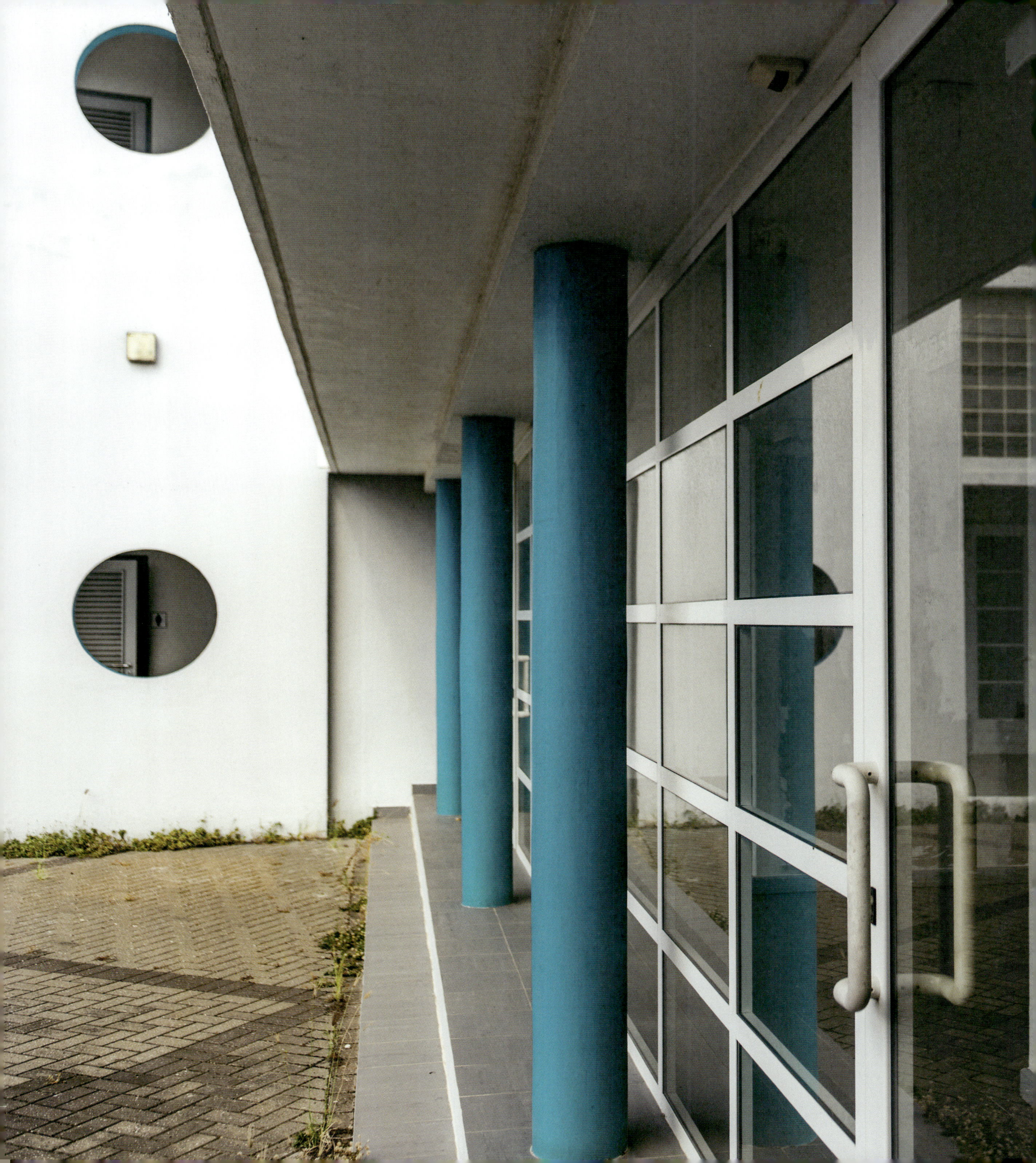

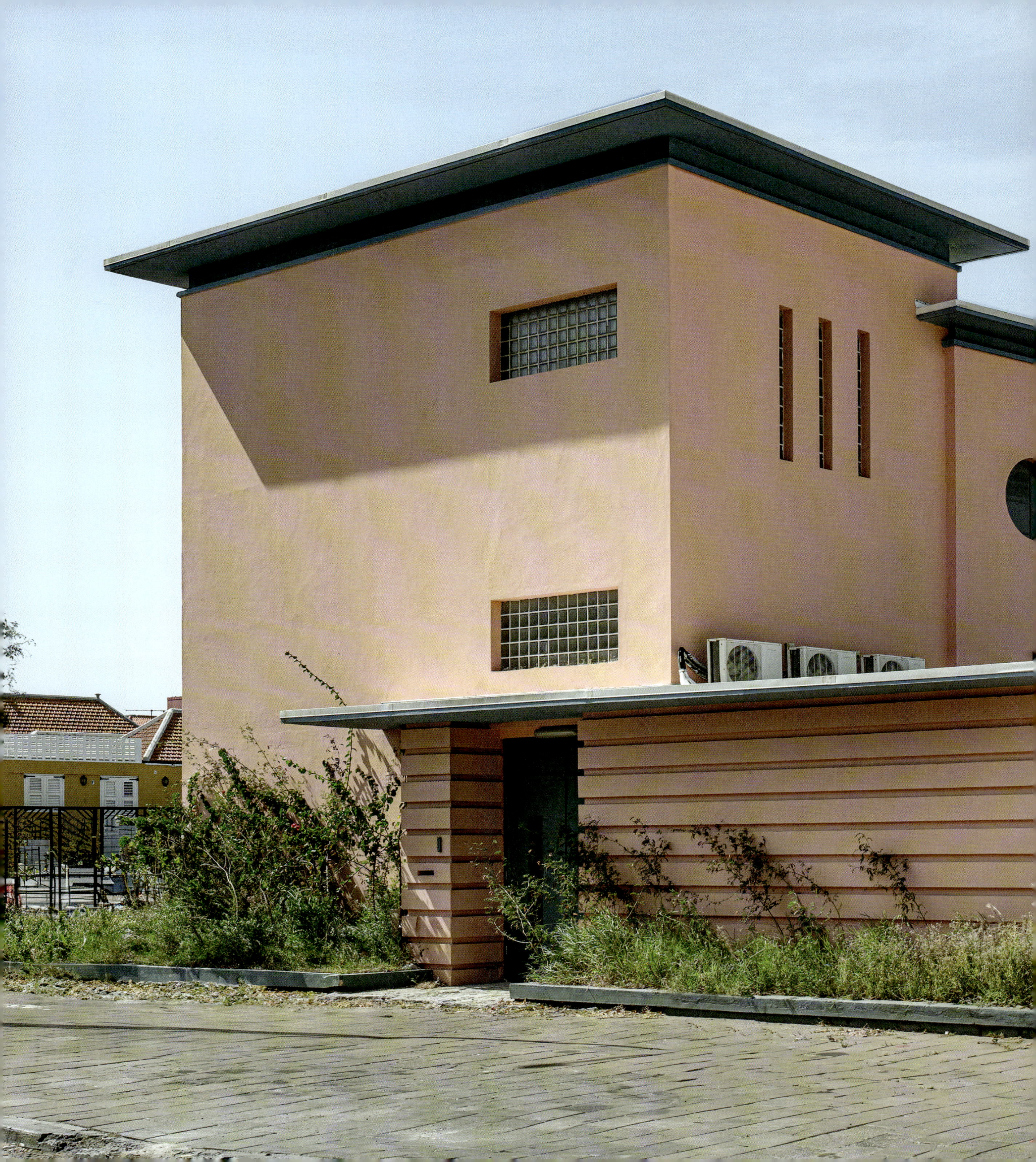

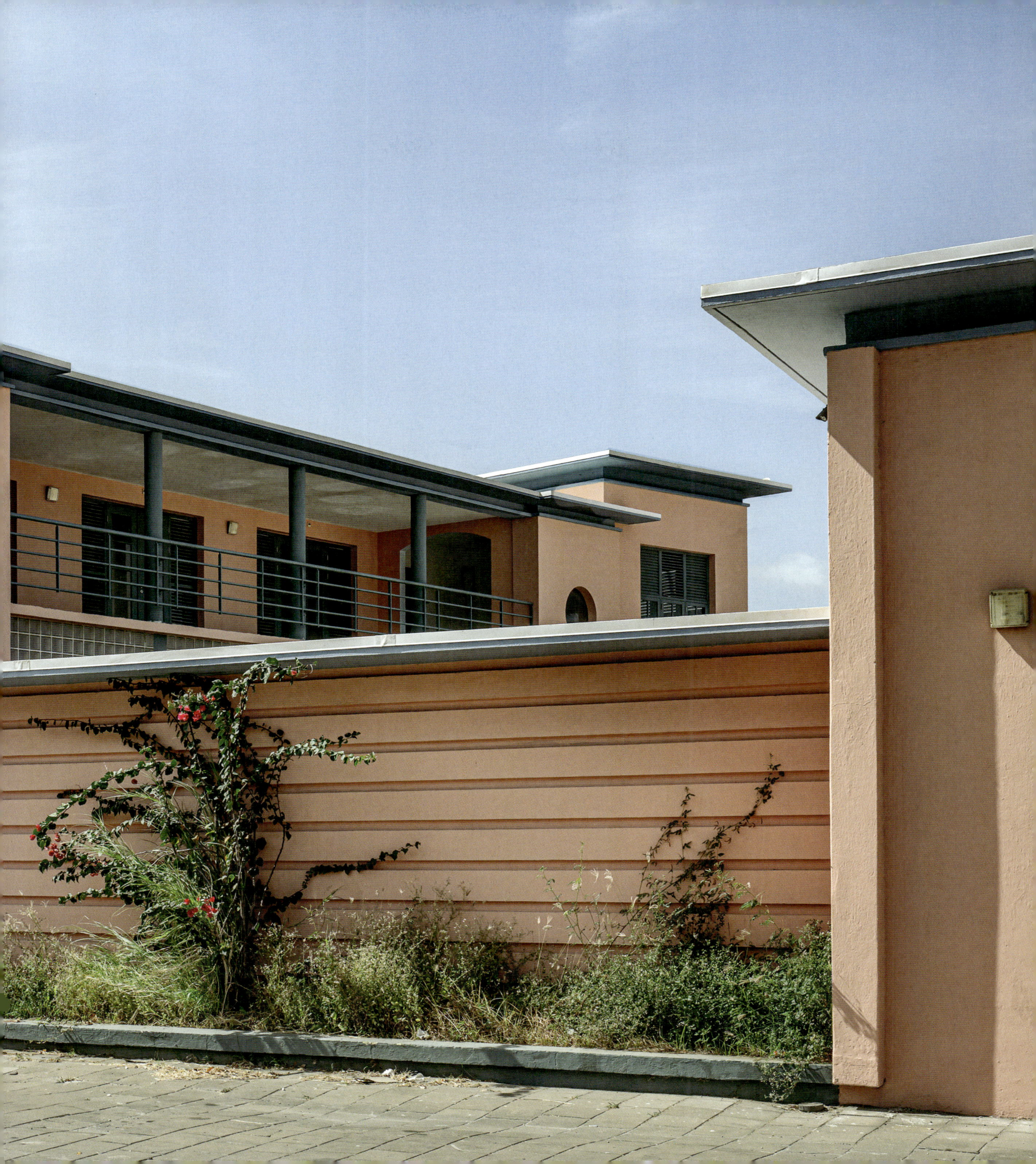

ENTRADA ADC
MRC
RENTAL
738-1700
MRC
738-1700
power.cummins.com

National grid reference: **12°06'40.5"N 68°56'26.0"W**

07.
CURAÇAO TRADING COMPANY_

ROODEWEG

National Archive Curaçao / Coll. Fisher

Originally built as a hardware store, its design is clearly utilitarian.

Historic Background_

The Curaçao Trading Company N.V. (CTC), a subsidiary of the Curaçaosche Handel Maatschappij N.V. founded in 1890, was a well-known trading company in Curaçao. The CTC had offices and agencies around the Caribbean, Central and South America, as well as in New York, Amsterdam, London, and Hamburg. The company focused primarily on import and export but was also active in shipping. In the first decades of the twentieth century, it had its own quays on both the Scharloo and Otrobanda sides of the St. Anna Bay. A new main office of the CTC was opened in 1952 at the Handelskade and Heerenstraat. This modern construction remains a very striking, large building because of its unplastered brown brick.

A few years earlier, in 1946, the CTC building on the Roodeweg in Otrobanda opened. The company already had a timber yard and a sawmill at the back where they sold wood for construction. In the front, on the street side, the new building was erected. It was built as a hardware store where CTC sold all kinds of hardware like nails, screws, toilets, and other building material. Apparently, it was not the best location for such a store since in June 1965 this CTC branch was closed. Another reason for its closure was the fact that the main street in Otrobanda, Breedestraat, became one-way in 1951, making the store more difficult to reach. The building was sold and transformed into a bookstore and stationary shop, Van Dorp, which opened in June 1967. The building was completely modernized with the addition of air conditioning. Since the beginning of this century, it has been a branch of the ADC, the governmental medical laboratory, Analytisch Diagnostisch Centrum N.V.

Architectural Design_

The building was designed in 1946 by Cornelis Marinus (Kees) Bakker (born 1903), a Dutch architect who received his education at the Technical University in Delft. He came to Curacao in 1940 to work for the Department of Public Works, where he designed various buildings, including the Public Reading Room and Library in Pietermaai. Bakker left the Department in 1944 and worked for the SHELL refinery for a few years before continuing his career as an architect until 1952 when he immigrated to Canada. He passed away there in 1989.

Description_

Originally built as a hardware store, its design is clearly utilitarian. The constructions at both ends of the façade are striking. Narrow rounded protrusions extend above the roof surface, incorporating vertical glass blocks to allow natural light entry. The slightly sloping roof is supported by seven rows of concrete columns, with the first row situated outside the front façade. Behind the columns, a series of shop windows spans the entire width of the front façade, with the entrance in the middle. The front façade is the characteristic feature of the building. Behind this façade lies a simple rectangular shed.

References:

- Gill, Ronald G. (2008) *Een eeuw architectuur op Curaçao*. Curaçao: Ronald G. Gill, (Original work published 1999)
- Monsanto, Christel (2022) Ir. Cornelis Marinus (Kees) Bakker, architect (1903 Hilversum – 1989 Toronto). *De Archiefvriend, december 2022*
- ONS ZEEWEZEN (1961) Orgaan van de Koninklijke Nederlandse Vereniging 'Onze Vloot', januari 1961, Antillennummer, p. 51 – 52

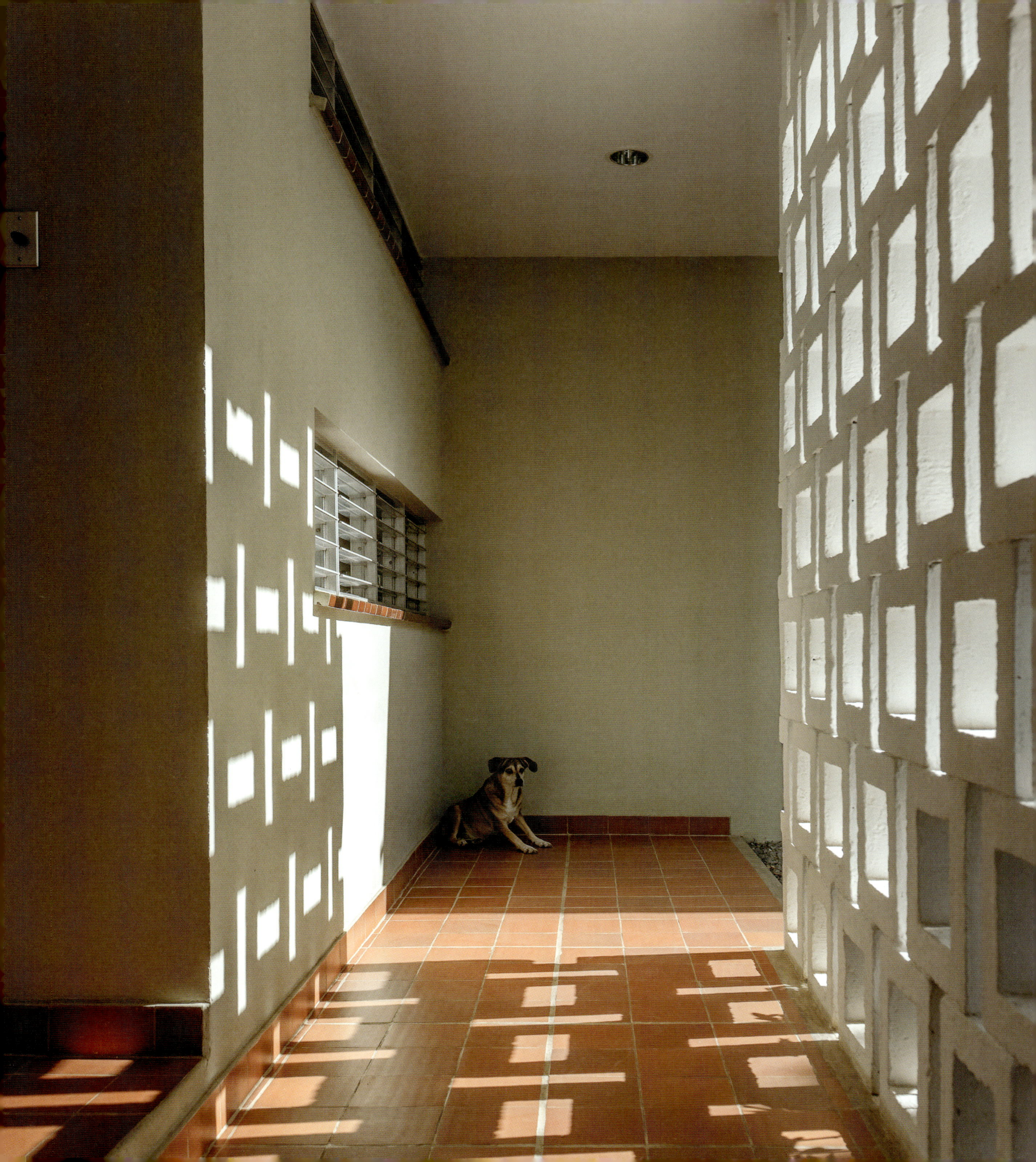

National grid reference: **12°07'20.7"N 68°53'54.1"W**

08.
BEN SMIT RESIDENCE_

ANGLOWEG 9

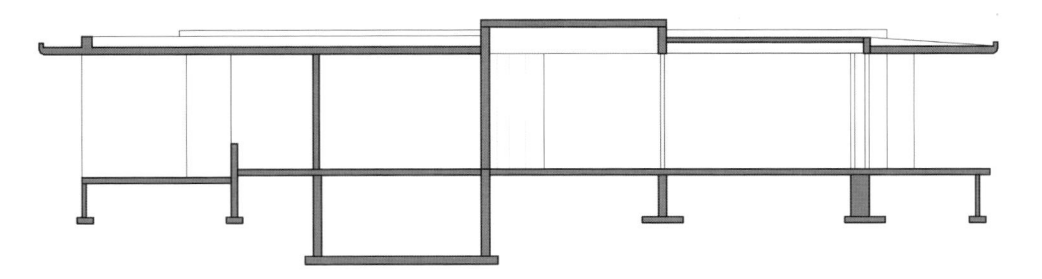

Angloweg 9. Drawing: Ben Smit, c. 1948, 1958 / Rosberg Engineering, 2016

Historic Background_

The architect Ben Smit built the house as his own private residence. It was built in the new neighborhood of Mahaai, where the well to do of the island constructed their residences after World War II.

Ben Smit was born in the Netherlands in 1922 and established himself in Curaçao in 1943. After working for the Department of Public Works for three years, he founded his own firm, one of the first local architect's offices, in 1946. He designed an impressive record of buildings on the island, making him an influential architect from the 1940's until the 1960's.
In 1969 he returned with his family to the Netherlands.

Having studied in France, he was initially inspired by the architecture of Le Corbusier. Later, living and working in a tropical environment, he was also influenced by the Brazilian modern architecture movement, especially by the architect Oscar Niemeyer. Smit became known for designing private dwellings in a natural, tropical style. His commercial buildings followed the typical Modern Movement style. Due to his adoption of these architectural styles and his numerous projects, he was very influential during his career of almost thirty years in Curaçao. Notably, Ben Smit often used the vertical 'sun-breakers', the 'brise-soleil', a technique borrowed from Le Corbusier, to prevent direct sunlight into the interior of the buildings.

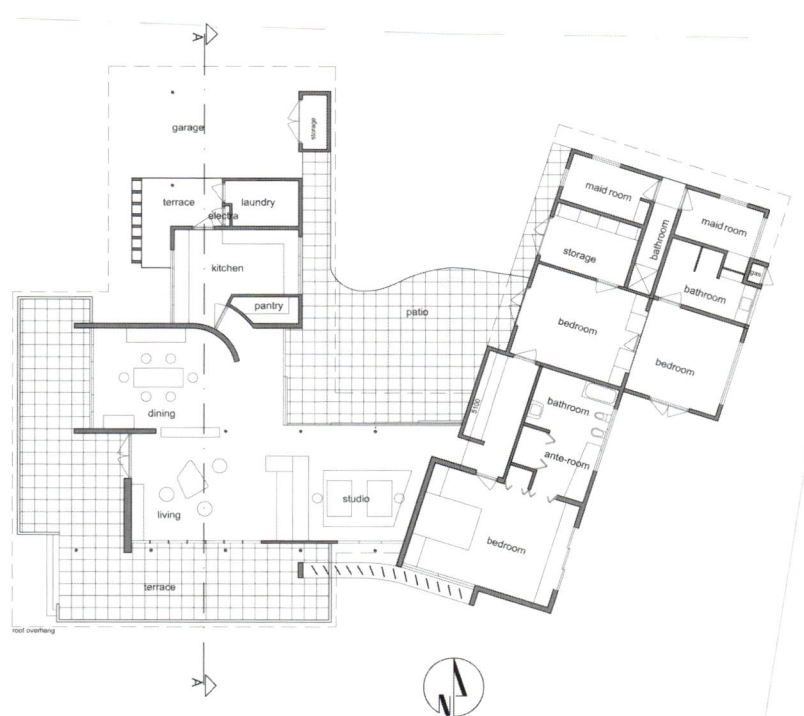

Angloweg 9. Drawing: Ben Smit, c. 1948, 1958 / Rosberg Engineering, 2016

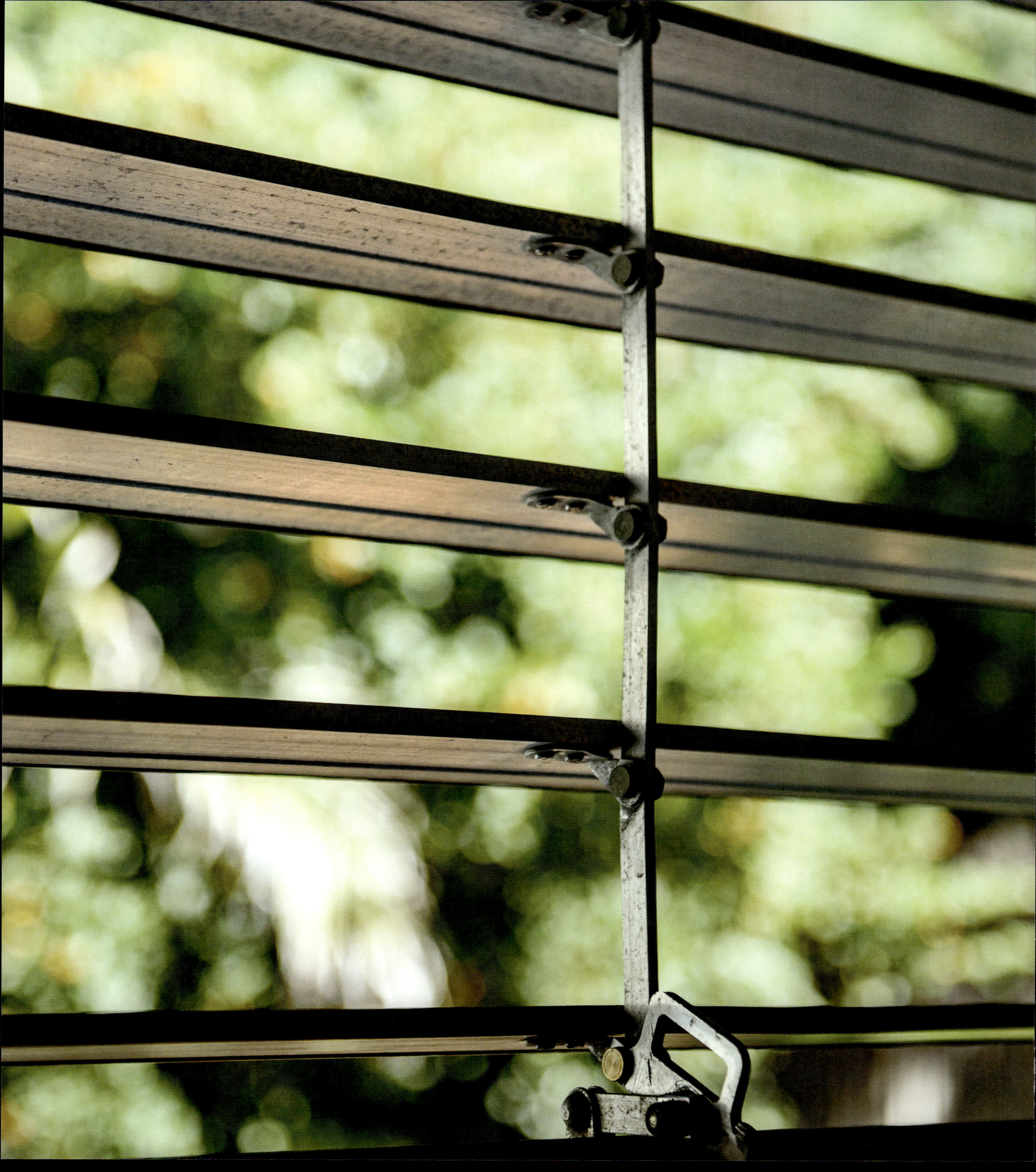

An early example of a residence built in the spirit of the Modern Movement

Architectural Design_

Built in 1948, the house is an early example of a residence built in the spirit of the Modern Movement, adapted to suit the tropical climate.

Characteristic architectural elements include the large flat roof overhangs and the incorporation of 'brise-soleil'. Both were intended to keep out the sun. In 1958, the house was extended on the north-eastern side with a bedroom and a bathroom. In 2015, Ben Smit sold the house. The new owner-resident, Sjef Visschedijk, renovated the house in consultation with the original designer. While the eastern sleeping wing was partly modified, efforts were made to restore several original elements in recognition of its historical and architectural significance, The building was officially listed as a protected monument in 2018.

74

do_co,mo,mo_curaçao

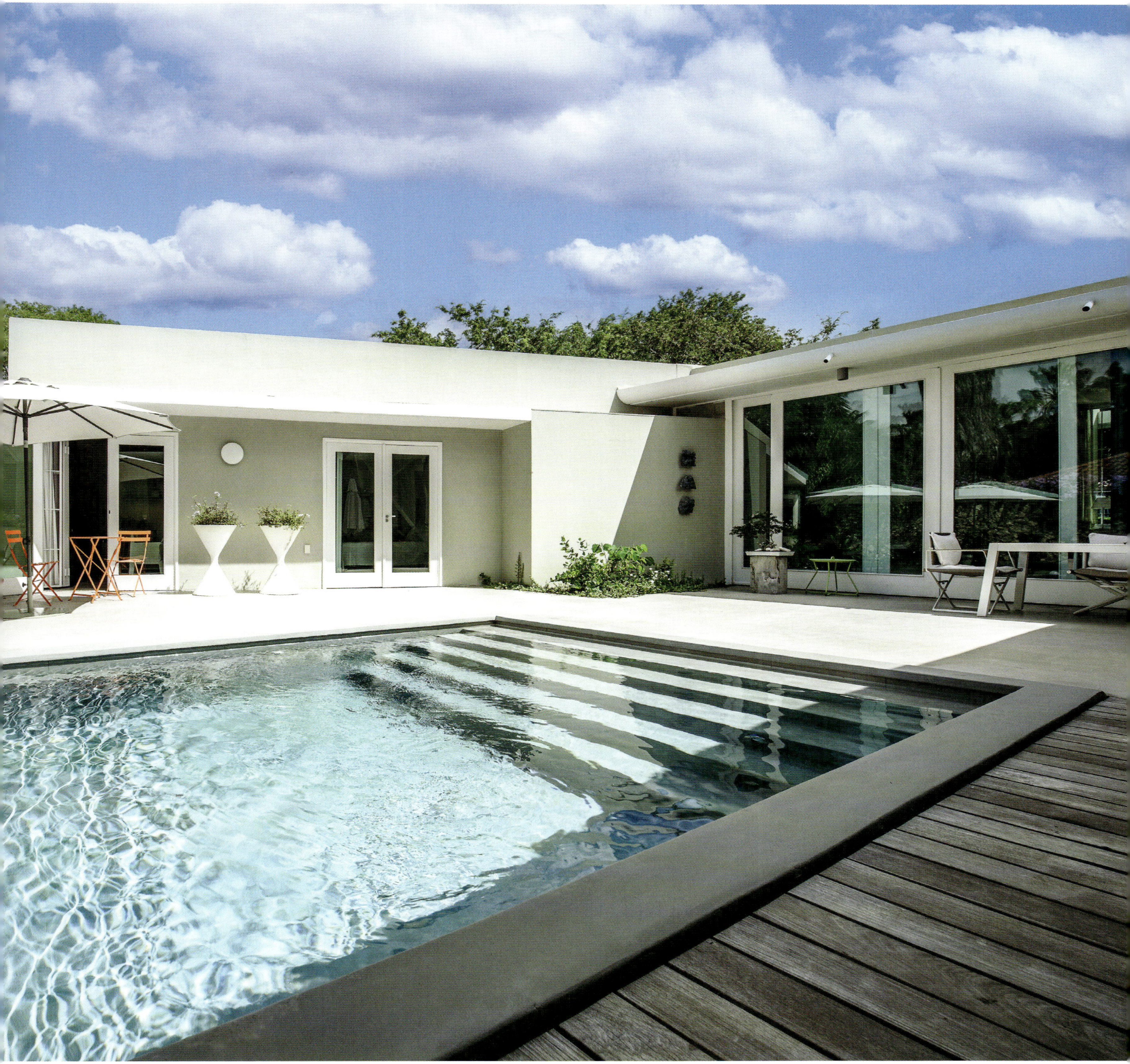

Description_

The house is built on a corner lot. The layout of the dwelling is U-shaped, with the bedrooms located on the eastern side, taking advantage of the prevailing wind direction. The living room is located to the south of the patio, with ceiling-high louvre windows and large glass sliding doors for day lighting and cross ventilation.

The large, covered terrace on the front, the living room in the middle and the rear patio can merge into one large area when all the sliding glass and louvered walls are opened.

The house has a "floating" flat concrete roof with large overhangs, accentuating the Modern Movement principle of lightness. Thin steel columns provide support for the roof, which consists of cantilevered concrete beams designed to be concealed from the exterior. The building is mainly constructed of plastered concrete blocks, wooden (sliding) doors and aluminum windows. Underneath the kitchen, there is a cistern. Rainwater collected in this cistern was used for cleaning and washing purposes.

References:

- Gill, Ronald G. (2008). *Een eeuw architectuur op Curaçao*. Curaçao: Ronald G. Gill, (Original work published 1999)
- Klaus, Dennis (2009). BEN SMIT, a personal note, *The impact of Caribbean Modern Architecture, First regional DOCOMOMO seminar, hosted by the University of the Netherlands Antilles*, Curaçao, pp. 56-59
- Smit, Ben (2002). *Projecten Curaçao 1946 – 1969*. Curaçao: Ben Smit

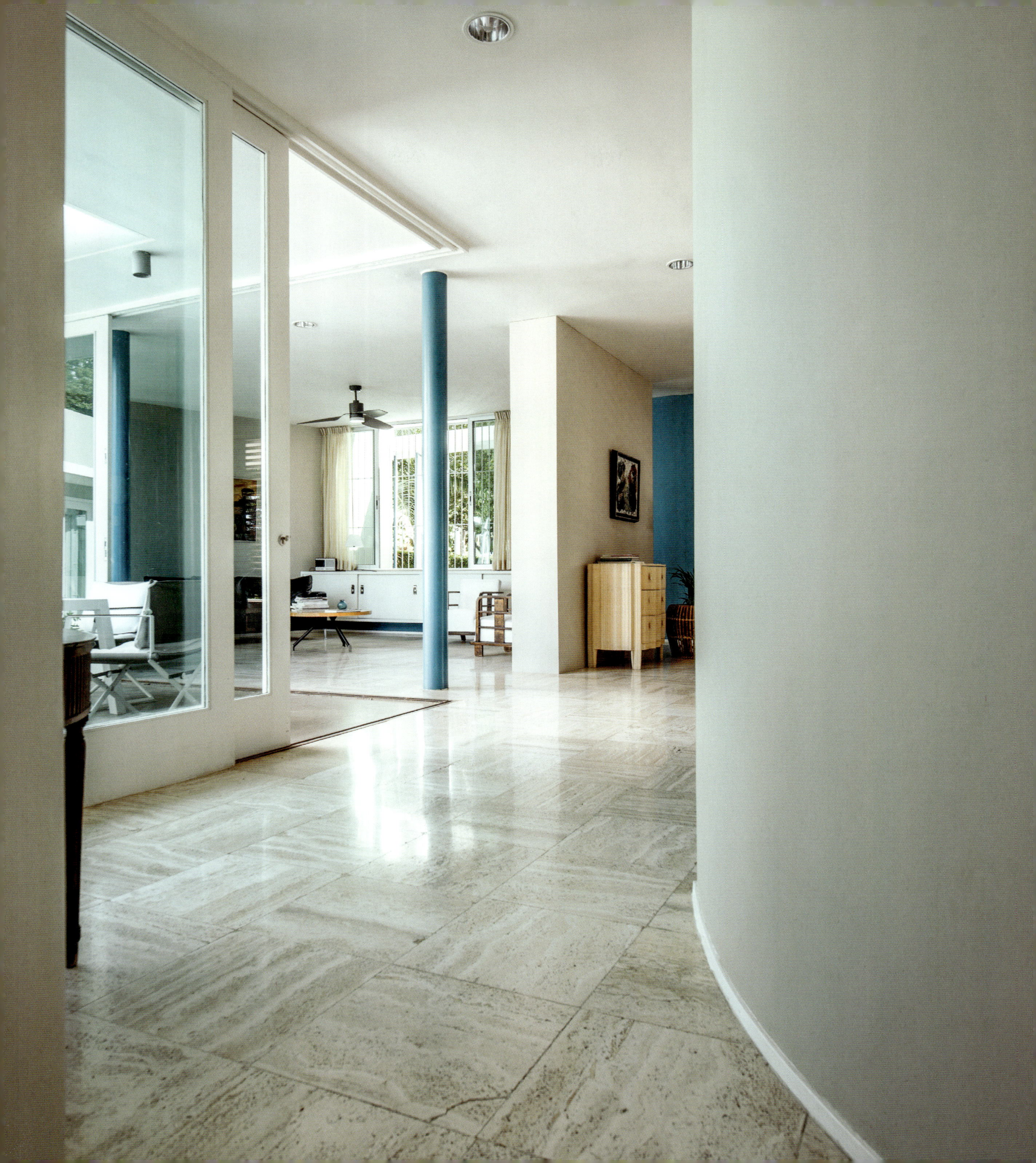

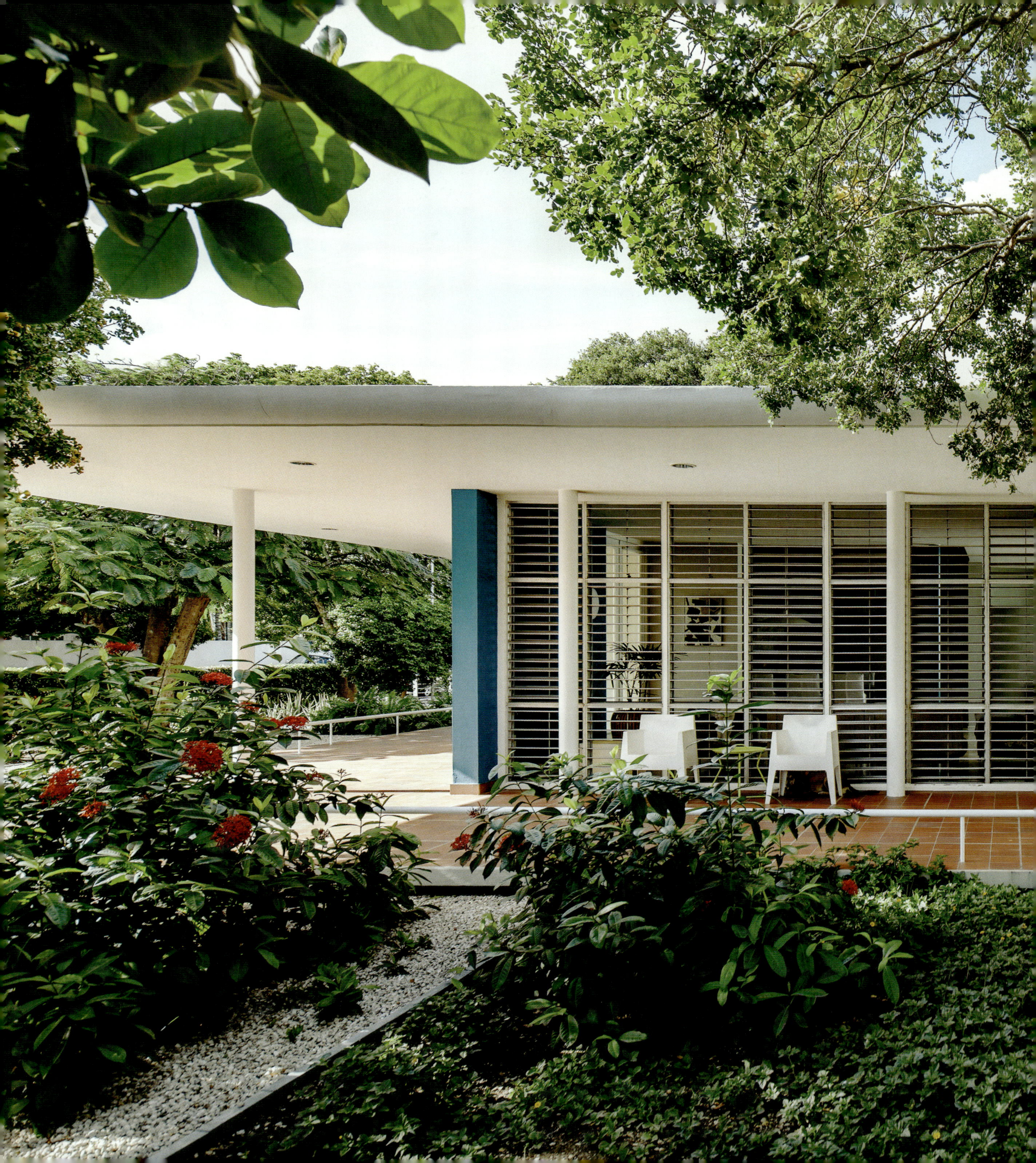

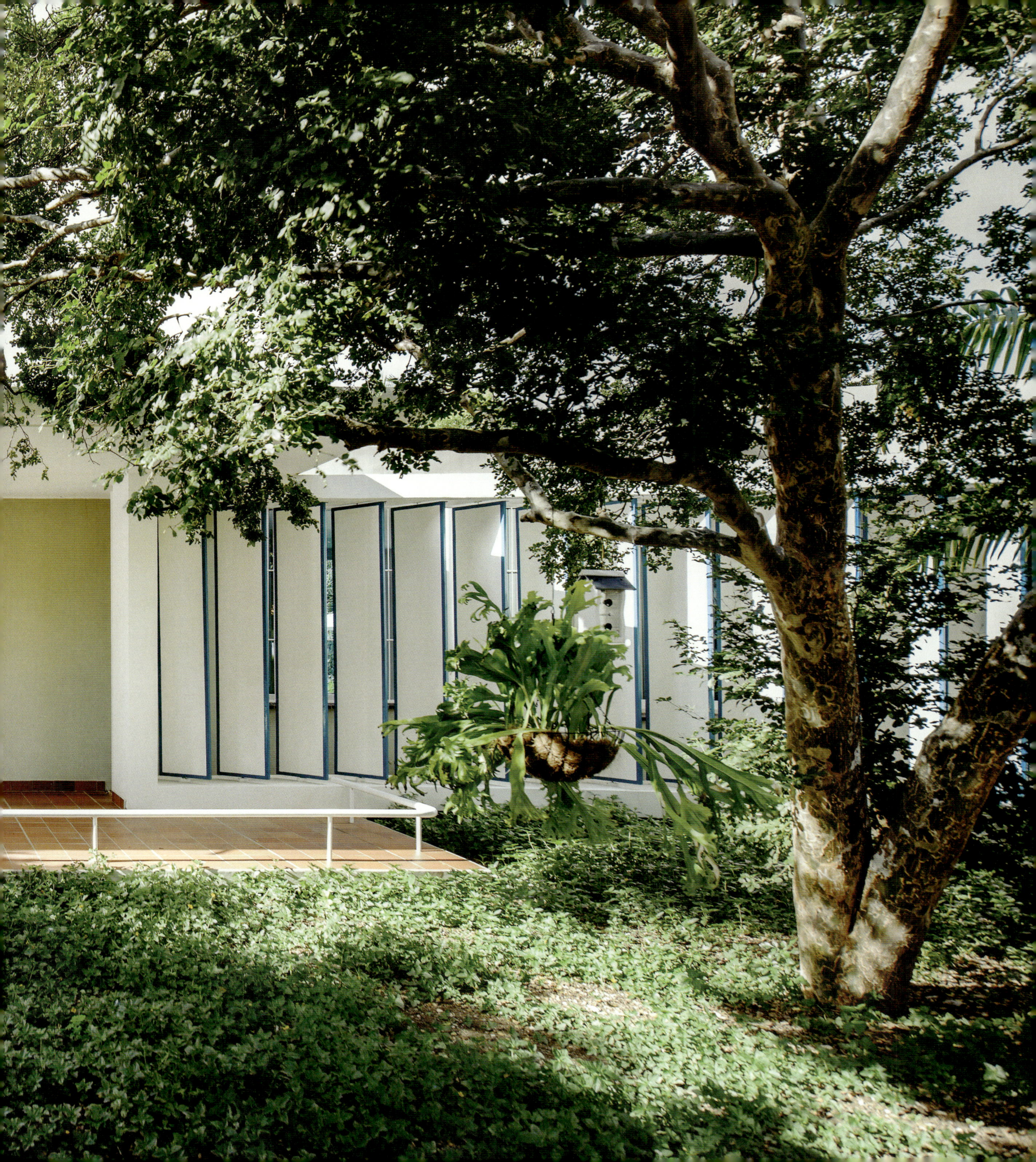

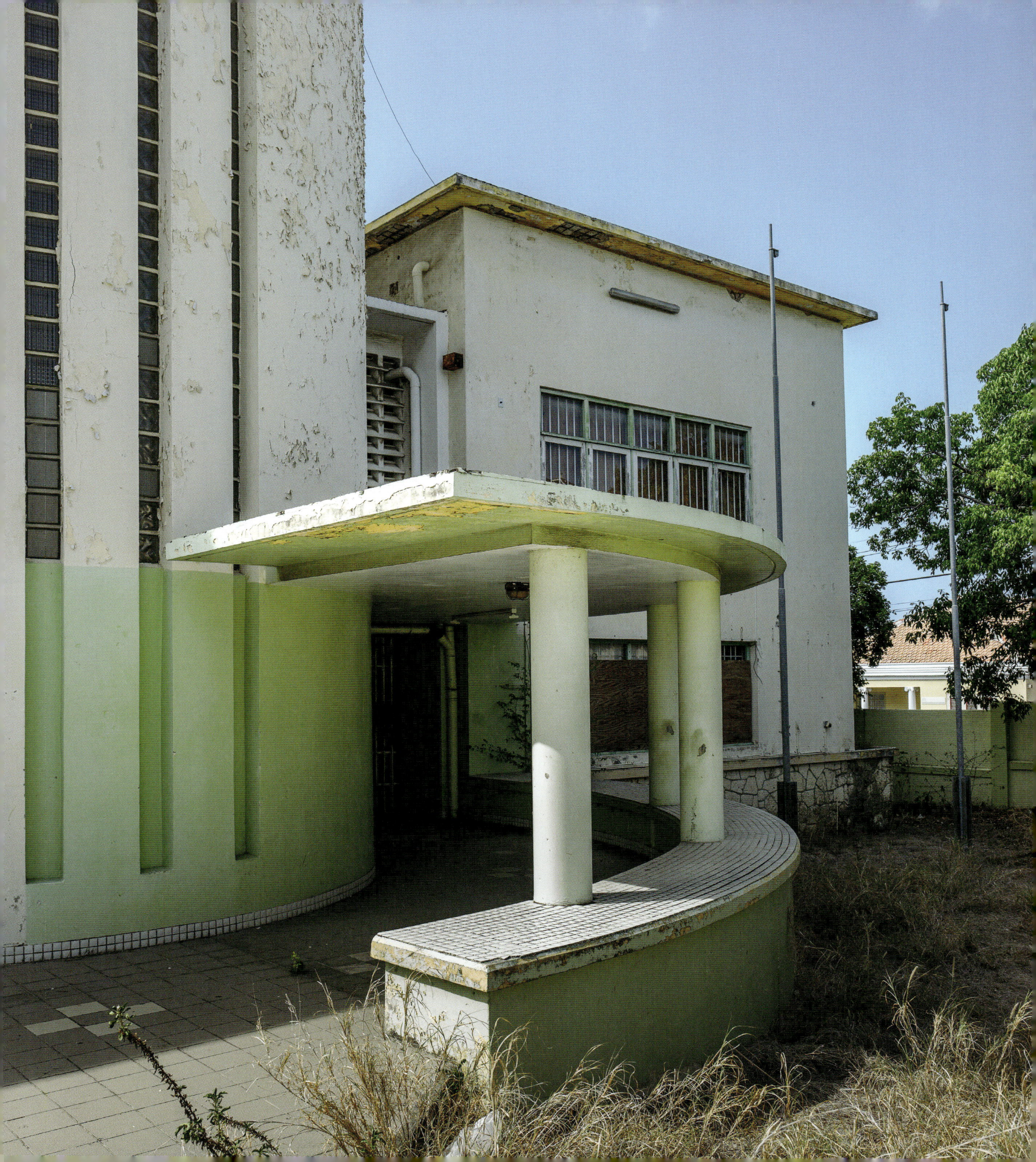

National grid reference: **12°06′40.7″N 68°56′13.4″W**

09.
ST. THOMAS COLLEGE_

L.B. SMITHPLEIN

A characteristic and prominent aspect of the building's front is the semi-circular entrance.

Historic Background_

The Catholic Sint Thomas College at the Roodeweg in Otrobanda, situated next to the St. Elisabeth Hospital, was a prestigious boys' secondary school. Instruction was given by the Brothers of Tilburg. Due to the growth of the population during the first half of the 20th century, the number of students led to a significant increase. In 1942, the St. Thomas College Foundation purchased the home of the former German consul, Mr. Fensohn, at the L.B. Smithplein in Otrobanda.

For a few years, part of the spacious house was used for several classes from St. Thomas College. In 1945, the building was demolished, and the contractor Lendering started the construction of a new, modern school for the senior classes. The lower classes remained in the main building at the Roodeweg.

The new school was inaugurated on March 7, 1950. (Amigoe, March 8, 1950). From 1994, the building housed the St. Martinus Mavo.

However, due to declining number of students in Otrobanda in recent decades, the school was eventually closed. The complex was sold some years ago and is currently awaiting redevelopment.

Architectural Design_

The new school was designed by Ir. C.M. (Kees) Bakker, a Dutch architect, who arrived in Curaçao in 1940 to work for the Public Works Department. Later, he worked for the refinery, and in 1947 he established his own architectural firm. In 1952, the Bakker family settled in Canada.

The building was U-shaped and embodied the modern Dutch architectural style known as the 'Nieuwe Zakelijkheid'. Bakker adapted this style to suit the tropical climate of Curaçao, incorporating features he had introduced elsewhere on the island. The open corridors were, in the first place, an important aspect in relation to the climate.

A characteristic and prominent aspect of the building's front is the semi-circular entrance, which includes narrow vertical slots fitted with glass blocks and the inward-turning open corridor.

Description_

The building originally had 16 classrooms, an art and science room, and a gymnasium. The classrooms have window openings in the outer façades, with an upper section of louvred shutters and glass casement windows at the bottom. Concrete awnings were installed between the louvred shutters and the glass windows to keep the sun out. Unfortunately, these awnings, which suffered from concrete rot, were removed during the renovation of the complex between 1991 and 1994. This might be due to the architect at the time not fully understanding their sun protection function.

References:

- Ditzhuijzen, Jeannette van (1995) *Monumento Habro '95 - Otrobanda, Fundashon Pro Monumento*
- Gill, Ronald G. (2008) *Een eeuw architectuur op Curaçao*. Curaçao: Ronald G. Gill, (Original work published 1999)
- Monsanto, Christel (2022) Ir. Cornelis Marinus (Kees) Bakker, architect (1903 Hilversum – 1989 Toronto). *De Archiefvriend, december 2022*
- Oirschot, Anton van, et al. (1986) *De Fraters van Zwijsen - 100 jaar fraters op de Nederlandse Antillen*; Zutphen: De Walburg Pers.

REV-00011

National grid reference: **12°06'32.0"N 68°55'31.8"W**

10.
WATER RESERVOIR LWV_

PRESIDENT ROMULO BETANCOURT BLVD - SCHARLOO

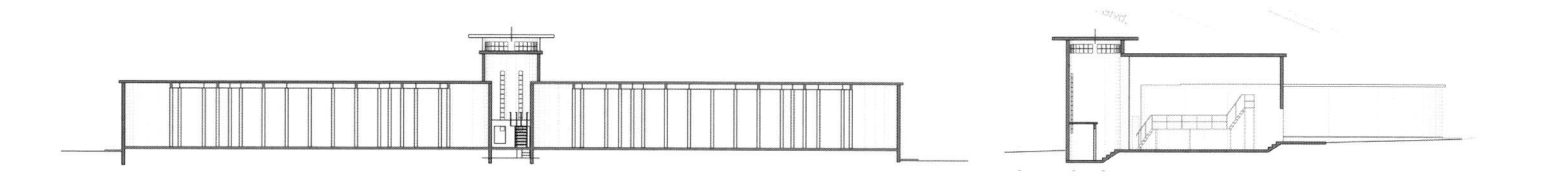

Water reservoirs Aqualectra. Drawing: Atelier Lobo & Raymann / Rosberg Engineering, 2016

Source: Landswatervoorzieningsdienst N.A. 1928 - 1953

The only original one remaining is located on the hill of Scharloo.

Historic Background_

Until the early 20th century the population of Curaçao relied mostly on rain water and well water for its daily water needs. Due to the island's arid climate, water scarcity presented a constant challenge. The establishment of the oil industry in 1915 and the accompanying increase in population forced the Government to step in.
On January 1, 1928 the "Landswatervoorzieningsdienst" – LWV, (the Governmental Department for Water Supply), was established. In 1929, the first sea water desalination factory was built east of old Willemstad in the Penstraat. The Department was also responsible for the distribution of the water. A water distribution network was established.

On various hills spread across the island water distribution reservoirs were built. On the hill north of the Scharloo district - Seru Arrarat - the reinforced concrete reservoir was built in 1949-1950.

Although about five of these large double reservoirs were constructed on the island, the one on the hill of Scharloo is the only original one remaining. The others have been demolished in the course of the past few decades and replaced by larger single round steel tanks. The present owner of the water reservoir is the government-owned company 'Aqualectra', the present producer and distributor of water and electricity on the island. The building was officially listed as a protected monument in 2011.

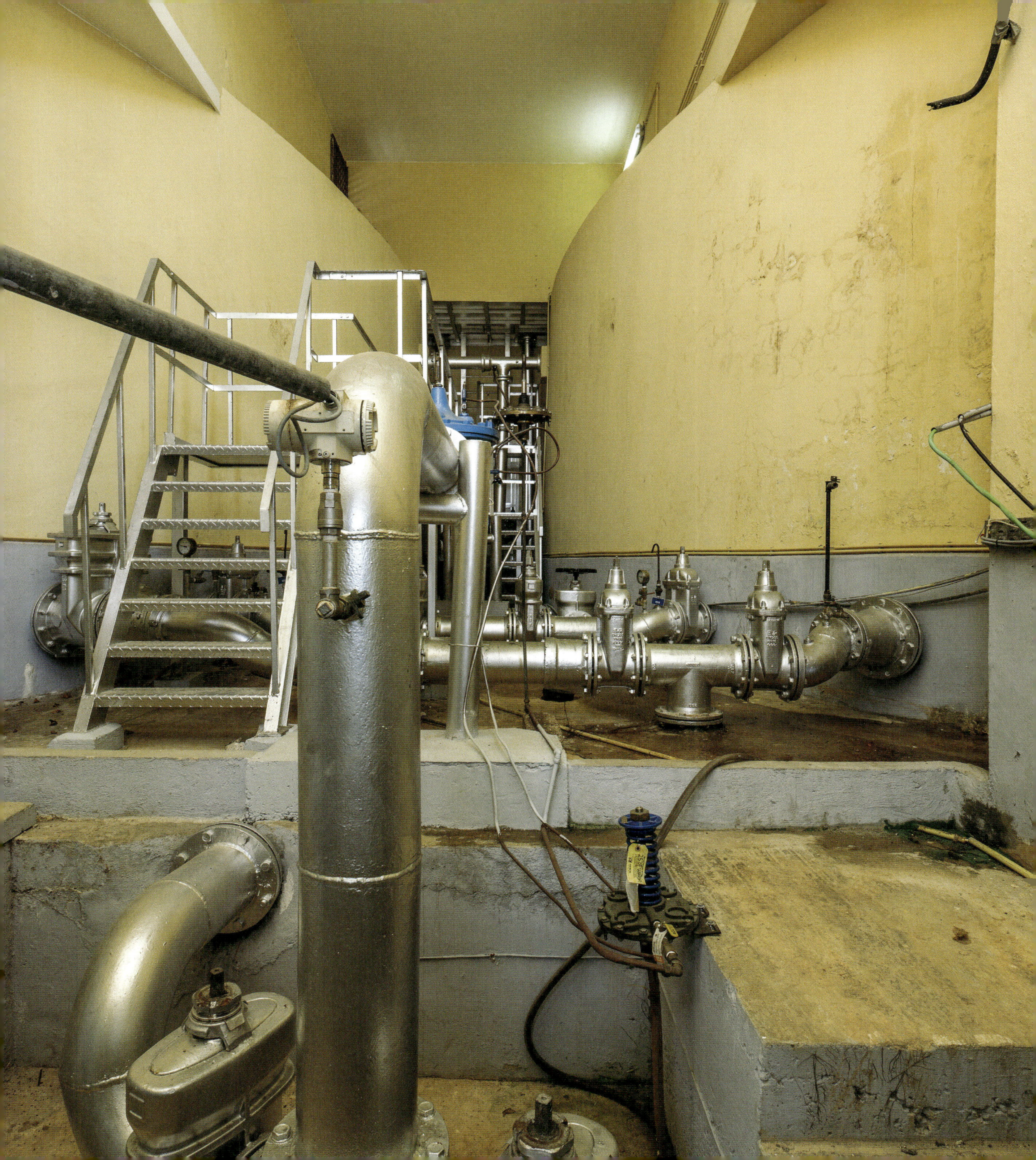

Architectural Design_

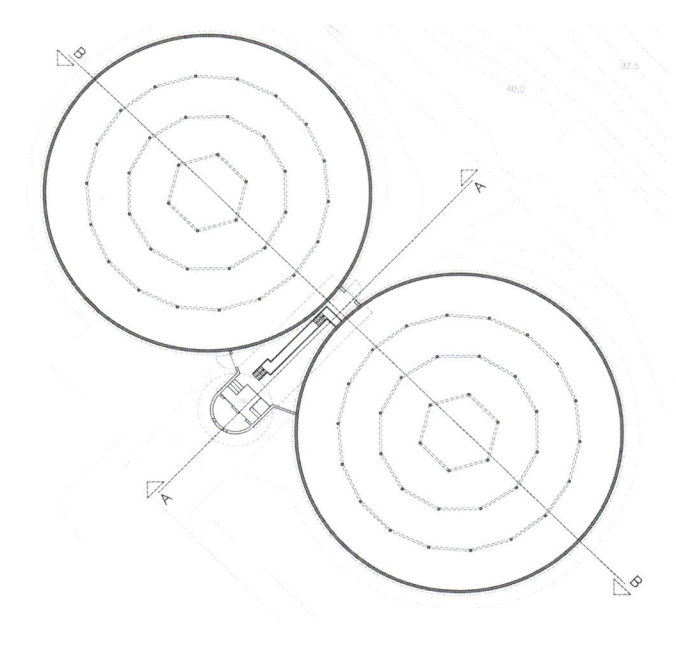

All of the structures of the LWV were designed in house. Most of them were the work of Pieter A. van Stuivenberg, a Dutch engineer who had been a manager with the Technical Department of the LWV shortly after its establishment in 1928. In 1948, he would become the director of this Department.

Although the buildings Van Stuivenberg designed for the LWV were purely utilitarian, his designs were also esthetic and often inspired by Art Deco architecture; especially the so-called Miami Beach Art Deco of the 1930's.

Water reservoirs Aqualectra. Drawing: Atelier Lobo & Raymann / Rosberg Engineering, 2016

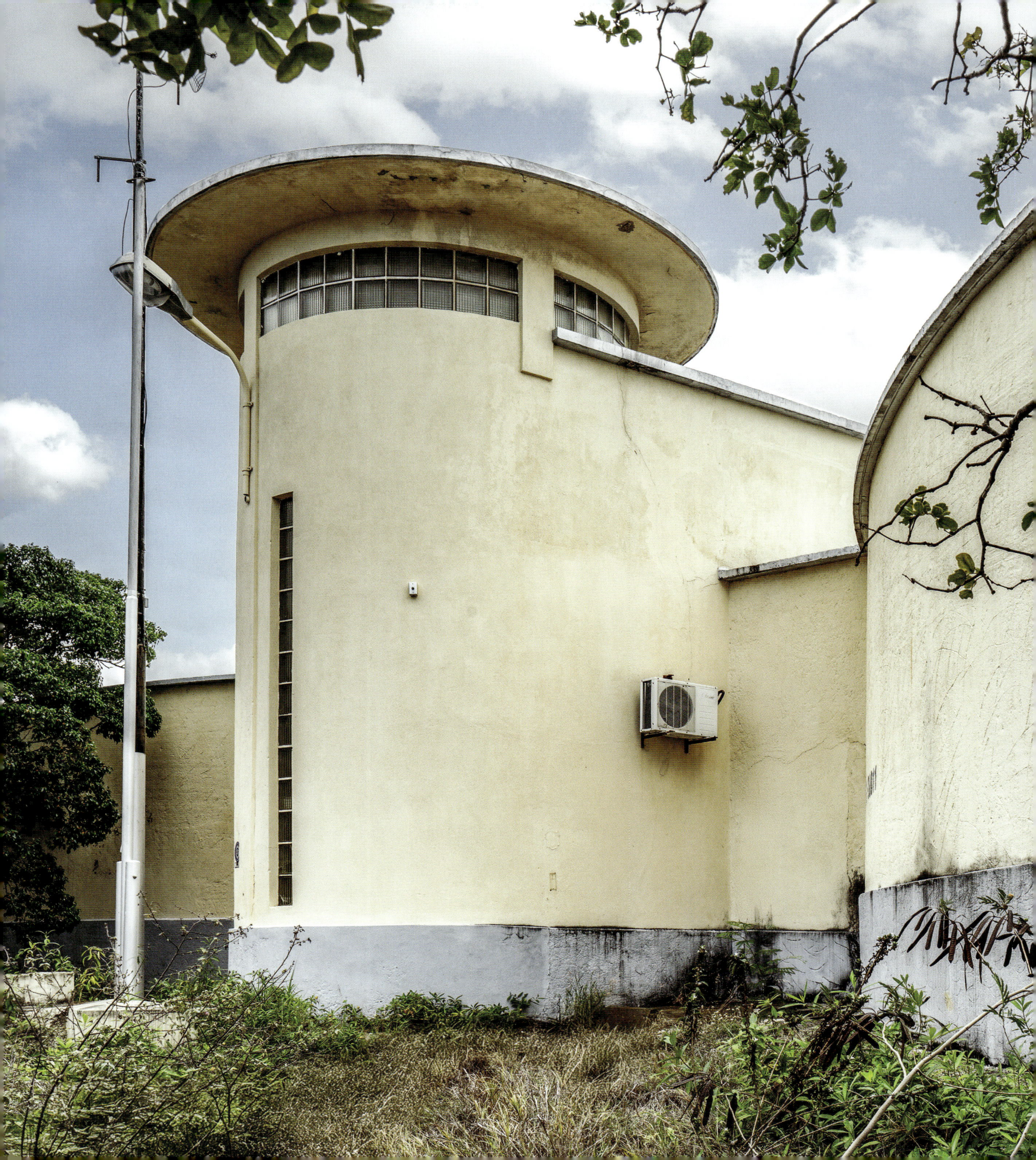

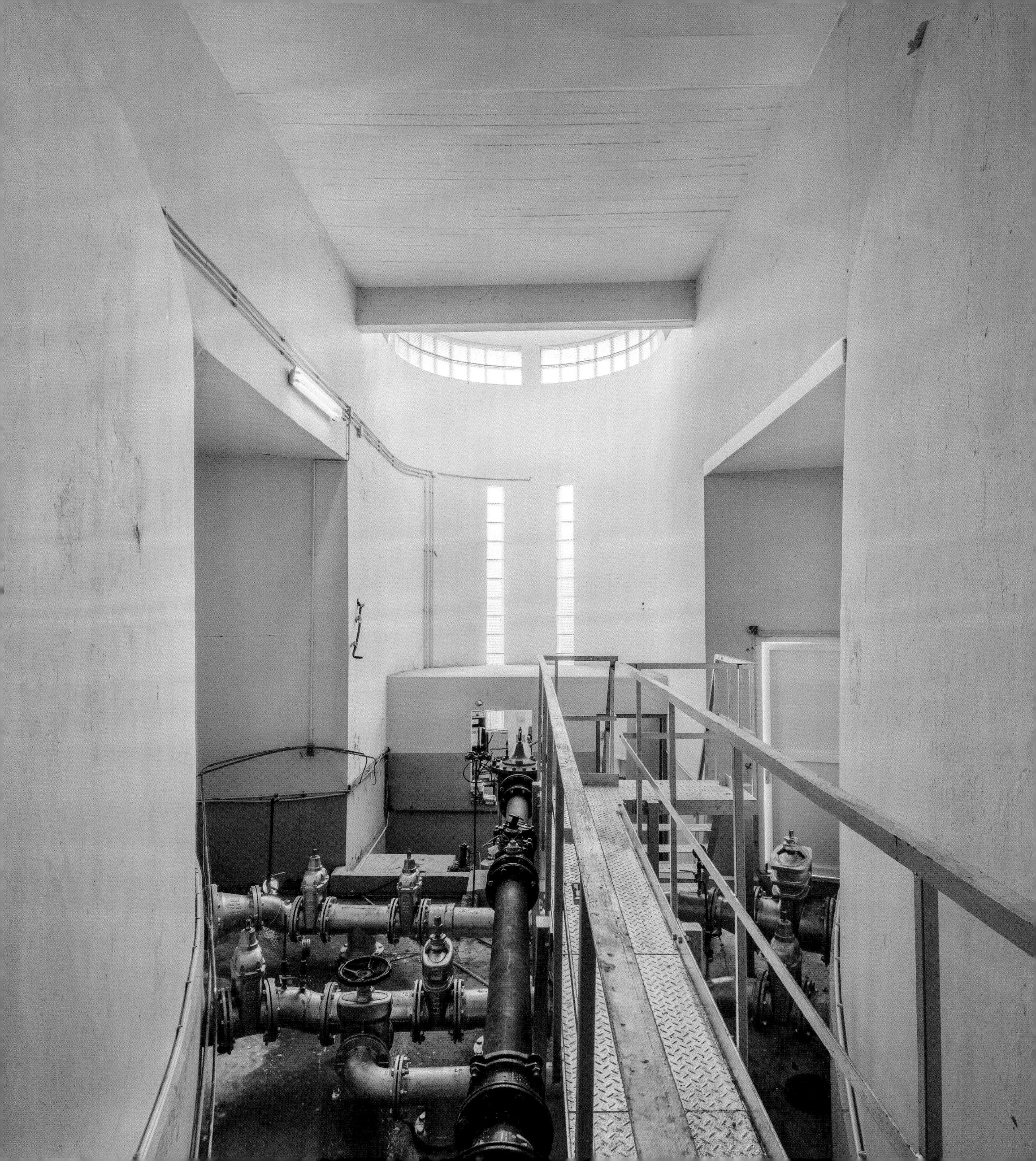

Interior concrete construction
LWV Water Reservoir on Trai Seru.
Demolished in 2010 . Photo M.A.Newton

Description_

The water reservoir complex consists of two round tanks with a diameter of approximately 25 meters each, a height of about 4 meters, and built some 2 meters from each other. The total water content of the reservoir is 4000 m3. The floor, walls, and roof of the tanks are all made of reinforced concrete. The concrete roof is supported by a circular grid of 36 concrete columns. Between the two tanks, there is a higher narrow building with a rounded front. It is constructed of plastered concrete blocks with a cantilevered concrete flat roof. In this building, the water valves are situated. Daylight reaches this valve house through horizontal and vertical rows of glass construction blocks, a building material often used by P. van Stuivenberg.

References:

- Gill, Ronald G. (2008). *Een eeuw architectuur op Curaçao*. Curaçao: Ronald G. Gill, (Original work published 1999)
- Landswatervoorzieningsdienst (1953) *Gedenkboek Landswatervoorziening in de Nederlandse Antillen: 1 januari 1928 – 1 januari 1953*, Curaçao
- Monsanto, Christel (2022) Pieter Antonie van Stuivenberg, architect. *De Archiefvriend, september 2022*

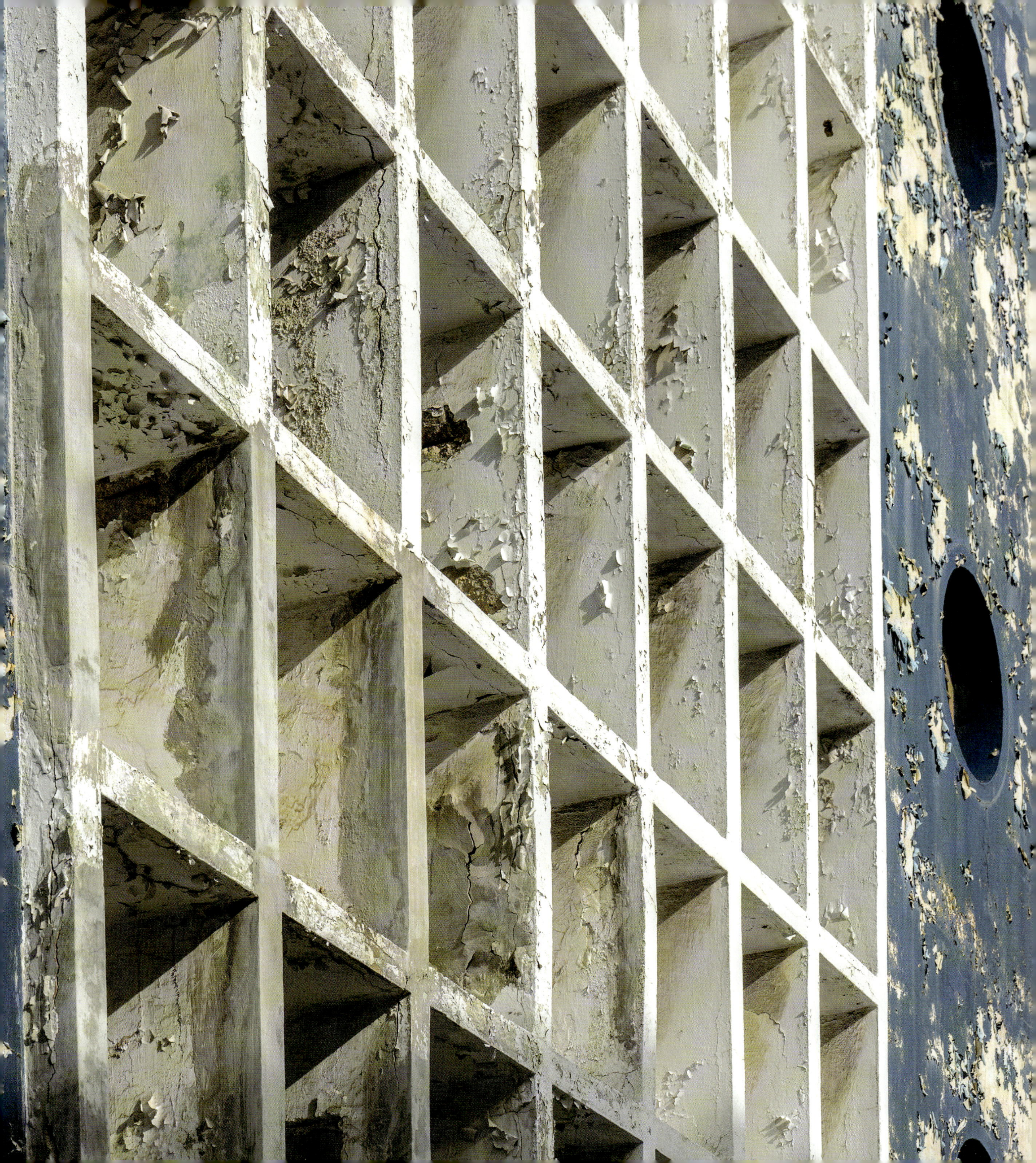

National grid reference: **12°06′12.8″N 68°55′47.1″W**

11.
CURACAOSCHE COURANT_

THEATERSTRAAT

The windows are set back in a concrete grid within the façade to limit the entry of the morning sun.

Historic Background_

Of the land that was created in the last quarter of the 19th century by filling in the inland water, the Waaigat, a small part was still undeveloped in the 1940s, located at the corner of De Ruyterkade and Theaterstraat.

In the late 1940s, two complexes were built here almost simultaneously: the business premises of Prospero Baiz, designed by the architect Ben Smit, and the other the building of the printing company Curaçaosche Courant, designed by the architect Kees Bakker.

Founded in 1812, the Curaçaosche Courant was originally located in the center of Willemstad. The new building opened on January 16, 1950 (Amigoe di Curaçao, January 17. 1950), and was at that time the largest printing house in the Netherlands Antilles. In the first decade of the 21st century, the Curaçaosche Courant vacated the building, and permanently closed in 2019. The building was sold and is currently awaiting redevelopment.

National Archive Curaçao / Coll. Fisher

Architectural Design_

The building was designed by Cornelis Marinus (Kees) Bakker, a Dutch architect, who received his education at the Technical University in Delft. Bakker came to Curaçao in 1940, where he worked for the Department of Public Works until 1944. After working for the SHELL refinery for a few years he established himself as a private architect in 1947. In 1952, he emigrated to Canada.

The complex consists of a three-storey corner block on Theaterstraat and William Leestraat, with a shop and offices above it. Adjacent to this, and visually interlocking, is a two-storey block for the printing department.

Description_

The building is a clear example of Modern Movement Architecture in a tropical environment. On the eastern front side, the windows are set back in a concrete grid within the façade to limit the entry of the morning sun. Next to these windows, in a vertical line, are round window openings in the stairwell. On the southern side, facing William Leestraat, and the western back side, the façades are characterized by an elongated rhythm of window openings. In the three-story block, these openings are equipped with operable jalousie windows, while the adjacent two-story building has fixed blinds surmounted by glass blocks.

Unfortunately, the ground floor façade of the main building block is now almost completely closed off and looks uninviting. The light color that this block had for quite some time, characteristic of Modern Movement Architecture, has now been changed to bright red and dark blue.

References:

- Gill, Ronald G. (2008) *Een eeuw architectuur op Curaçao.* Curaçao: Ronald G. Gill, (Original work published 1999)
- Monsanto, Christel (2022) Ir. Cornelis Marinus (Kees) Bakker, architect (1903 Hilversum – 1989 Toronto). *De Archiefvriend, december 2022*
- Verschoor, J.A.J. (1962) *Gedenkboek ter gelegenheid van het 150-jarig bestaan van drukkerij " DE CURAÇAOSCHE COURANT" N.V.* ; Curaçao: Curaçaosche Courant

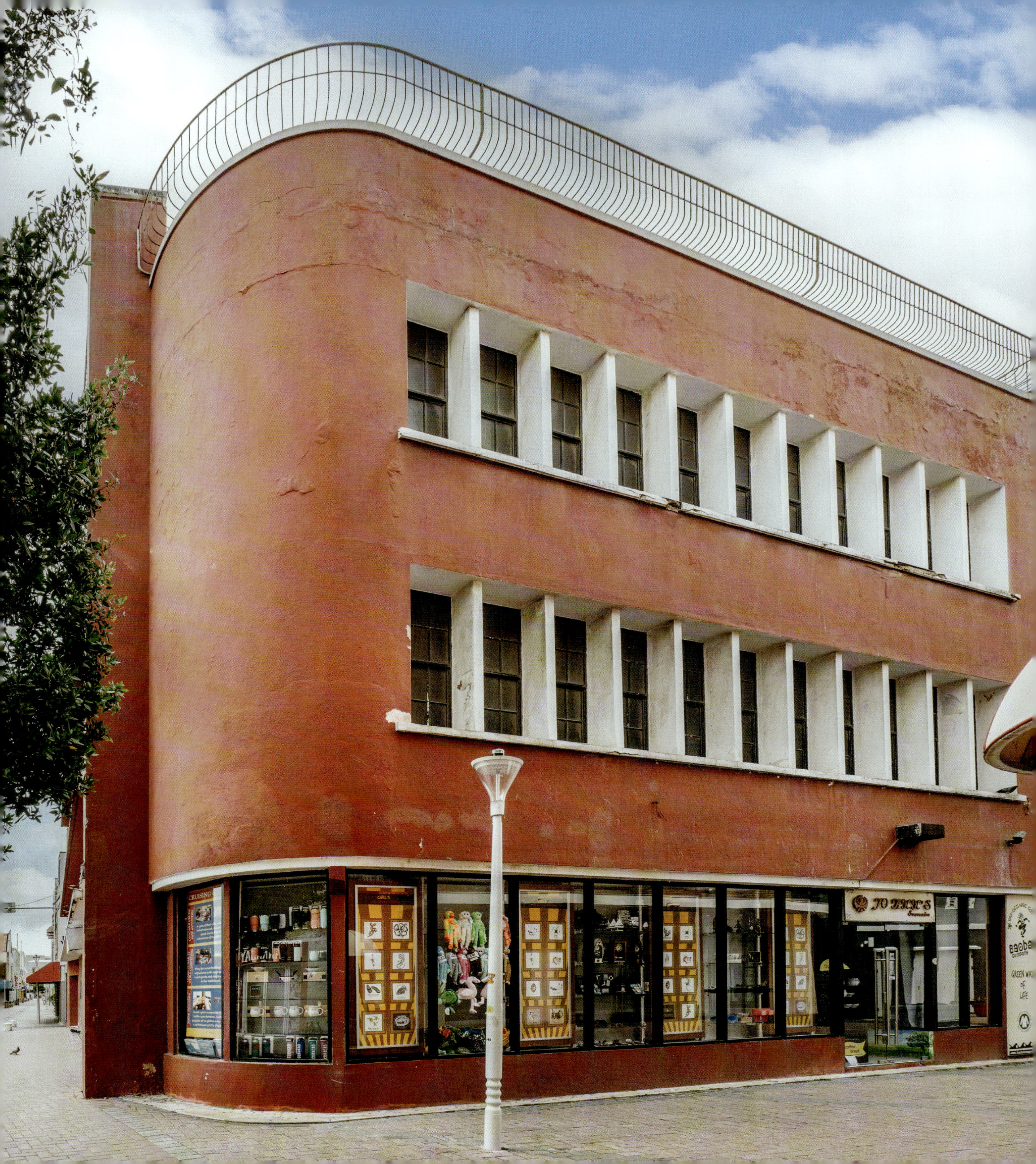

National grid reference: **12°06'23.0"N 68°55'59.9"W**

12.
ALEX BUILDING_

PLAZA JOJO CORREA

National Archive Curaçao / Coll. Fisher

The corner location is accentuated by the curved façade on the Heerenstraat side.

Historic Background_

In the 1950's Curaçao was doing well economically. The oil industry provided significant income for both the government and the residents, which was also reflected in the retail sector. New, modern properties were built in the inner city, often with an increase in scale compared to the old shops, which were frequently demolished. The Alex building was built around 1950 on the site of a demolished 18th-century building.

A few years later, the new building was bought by Ruben and Alex Irausquin. On January 20, 1954, they opened the new pharmacy, Botica Nueva (Amigoe di Curaçao, 20 January 1954). In addition to the pharmacy, the large building also housed the La Favorita shop and the Linea Aeropostal Venezolana travel agency on the ground floor. The insurance company "Nieuwe Eerste Nederlandsche schadeverzekering", N.E.N, (the later ENNIA), was located on the first floor. Eventually, the name of the Botica was changed to ALEX.

Architectural Design_

The building was designed by Cornelis Marinus (Kees) Bakker (born 1903), a Dutch architect. He received his education at the Technical University in Delft and moved to Curaçao in 1940 and worked for the Department of Public Works until 1944. He subsequently worked for the SHELL refinery and as a private architect till 1952, when he emigrated to Canada.

The three-storey building has been adapted to the tropical climate to a limited extent. Originally, it featured jalousie windows on the upper floors to provide necessary ventilation. Later, these windows were replaced with glass sash windows, likely to facilitate air conditioning. The thin, slightly protruding vertical slats that divide the interconnected windows provide some protection against sunlight. Ventilation in the stairwell is achieved through perforated blocks and the flat roof appears to have been designed as an open terrace.

Description_

The building is located at the end of a block, enclosed by Heerenstraat, the current Plaza Jojo Correa and Keukenstraat. The corner location is accentuated by the curved façade on the Heerenstraat side. On the corner of Keukenstraat, the front façade ends with an openwork stairwell. At the top of the façades, there is a characteristic surrounding steel balustrade, likely intended for a roof terrace that is not used as such.

Unfortunately, the ground-floor facing Plaza Jojo Correa is now almost completely closed and uninviting. The original light color, which the building had for quite some time, and is characteristic of Modern Movement Architecture, has now been changed to bright red.

References:

- Gill, Ronald G. (2008) *Een eeuw architectuur op Curaçao*. Curaçao: Ronald G. Gill, (Original work published 1999)
- Gomez Casseres, Charles (2004) *PUNDA PUNDA*. Curaçao: Charles Gomes Casseres
- Monsanto, Christel (2022) Ir. Cornelis Marinus (Kees) Bakker, architect (1903 Hilversum – 1989 Toronto). *De Archiefvriend, december 2022*

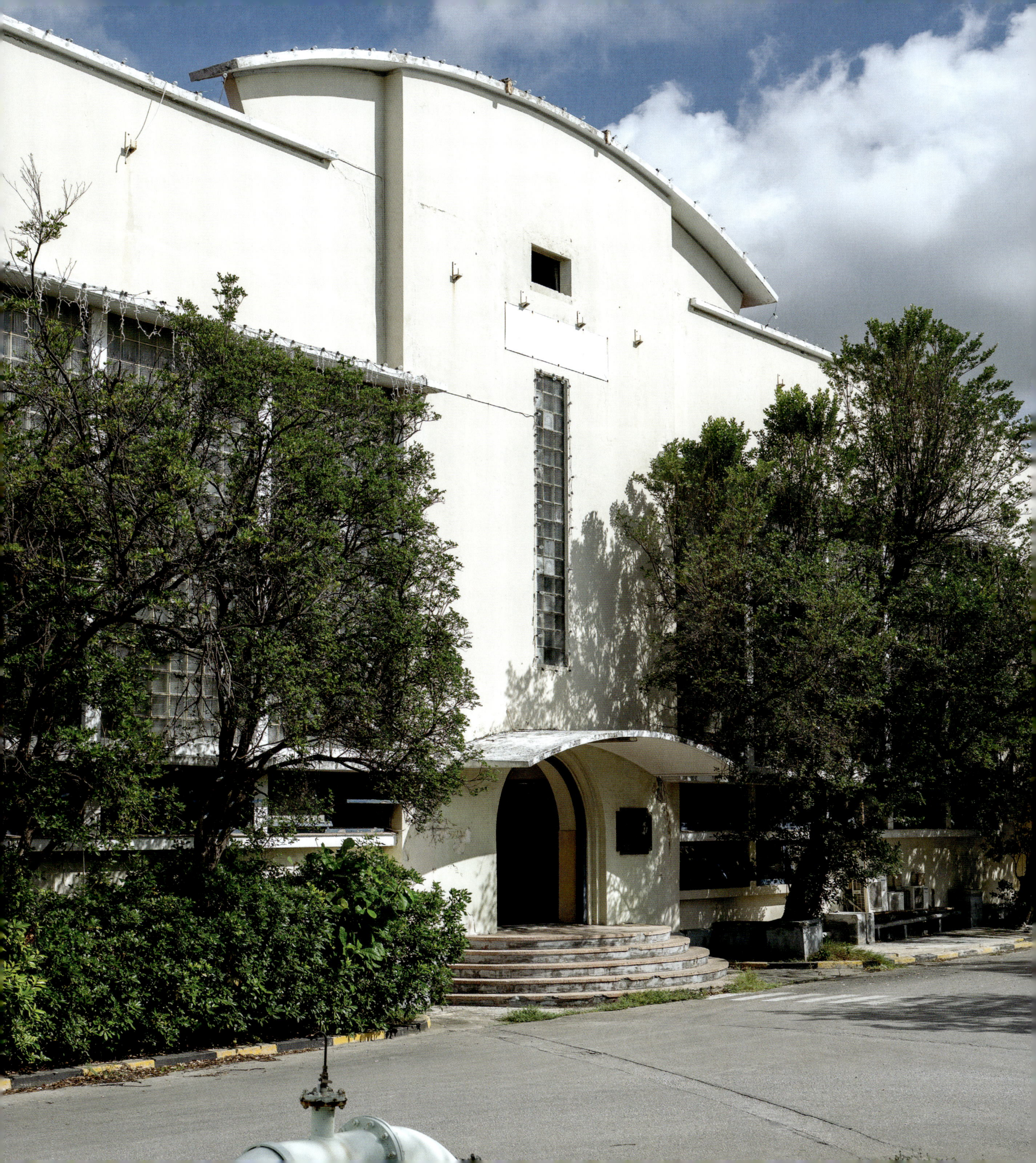

National grid reference: **12°06′37.5″N 68°57′01.0″W**

13.
WATER FACTORY LWV_

MUNDO NOBO

National Archive Curaçao / Coll. Fisher

Large parts of the façade are made of glass blocks, arranged in rectangular or circular openings.

Historic Background_

Until the early 20th century, water scarcity was a common challenge in Curaçao, due to the island's arid climate. The population relied mostly on rainwater and well water for its daily needs. The increase in population during the first decades of the 20th century forced the Government to intervene. In January 1928, the "Landswatervoorzieningsdienst" (LWV), the Governmental Department for Water Supply, was established.

In the course of subsequent decades, the LWV constructed necessary infrastructure such as seawater desalination plants, water reservoirs, and a distribution network across the island. In 1929, the first seawater desalination factory was built east of old Willemstad, in Penstraat. A few years later, in 1931/32, the second factory was constructed next to the Riffort in Otrobanda. Then, on January 1, 1953, exactly 25 years after the LWV was founded, the large factory at Mundo Nobo was put into use. The present owner of the factory and the water distribution network is the government-owned company 'Aqualectra'.

Architectural Design_

All constructions of the LWV were designed in-house, with most of them by the Dutchman Pieter A. van Stuivenberg. He was employed in March 1928 as a technical officer and later became manager of the Technical Department. In 1948, he succeeded the first director of the company, Mr. R. Beaujon. Although the buildings designed by Van Stuivenberg for the LWV were primarily utilitarian in nature, his designs also possessed aesthetic qualities and were often inspired by Art Deco architecture, in particular the so-called Miami Beach Art Deco style of the 1930's.

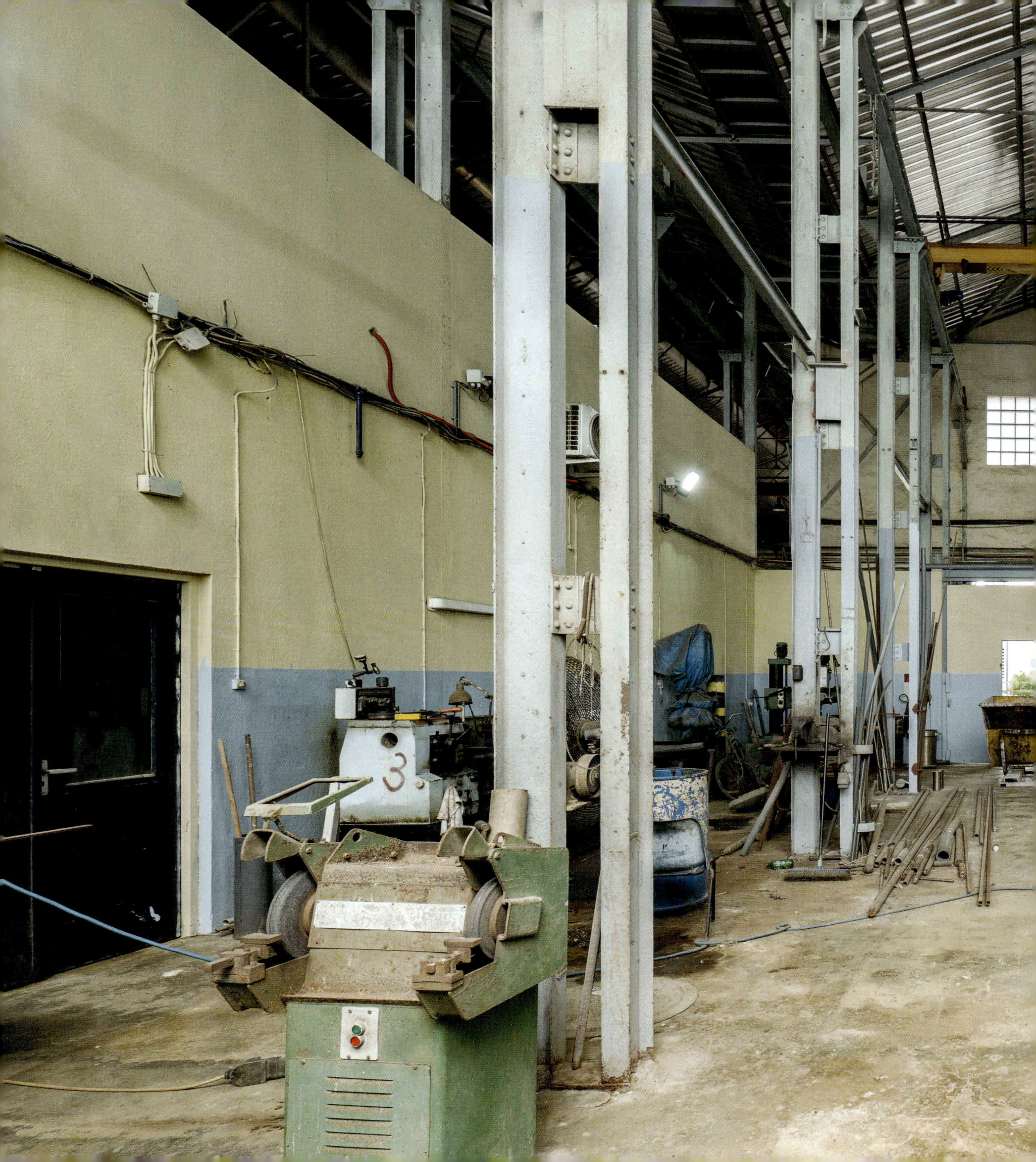

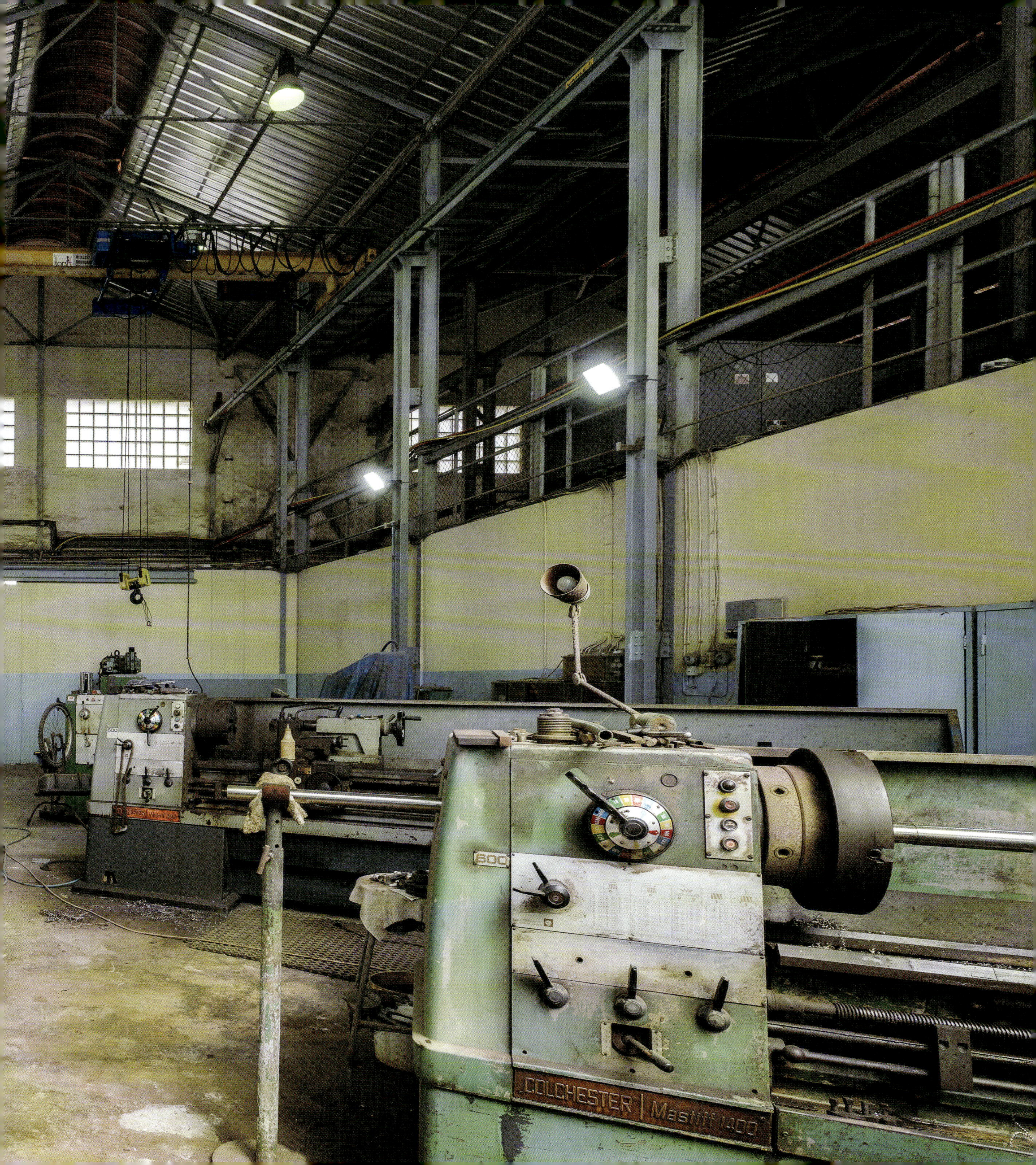
600
COLCHESTER | Mastiff 1400

Description_

The wide front of the main factory building is completely symmetrical. Large parts of the façade are made of glass blocks, arranged in rectangular or circular openings, a building material frequently used by Van Stuivenberg to improve internal natural lighting. The central section of the front façade slightly protrudes and is capped by a curved concrete edge at the top. Originally, the facade bore large letters spelling "LWV" atop, along with a clock at the top center of the front. At some point both were removed. The entrance door is also accentuated by a concrete, slightly curved canopy.

Behind the simple Art Deco front, a series of factory halls exist, most of them also incorporating glass blocks into the outer walls. The structural support of the buildings consists of a slender high steel structure, still visible from the interior.

Most of the buildings are still in use, although the entire factory will eventually be dismantled.

References:

- Gill, Ronald G. (2008) *Een eeuw architectuur op Curaçao*. Curaçao: Ronald G. Gill, (Original work published 1999)
- Landswatervoorzieningsdienst (1953) *Gedenkboek Landswatervoorziening in de Nederlandse Antillen: 1 januari 1928 – 1 januari 1953*, Curaçao
- Monsanto, Christel (2022) Pieter Antonie van Stuivenberg, architect. *De Archiefvriend, september 2022*

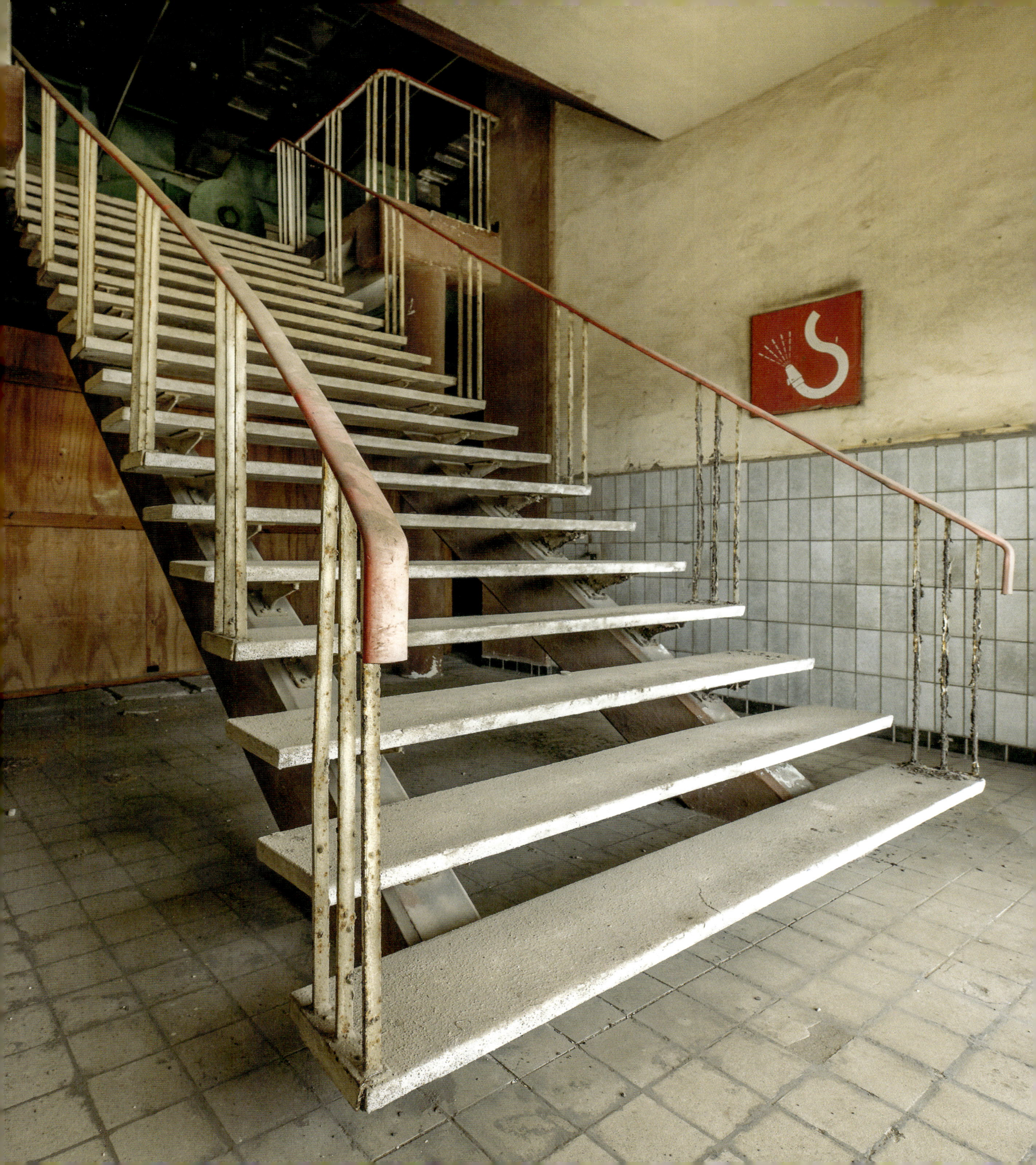

do.co.mo.mo_curaçao

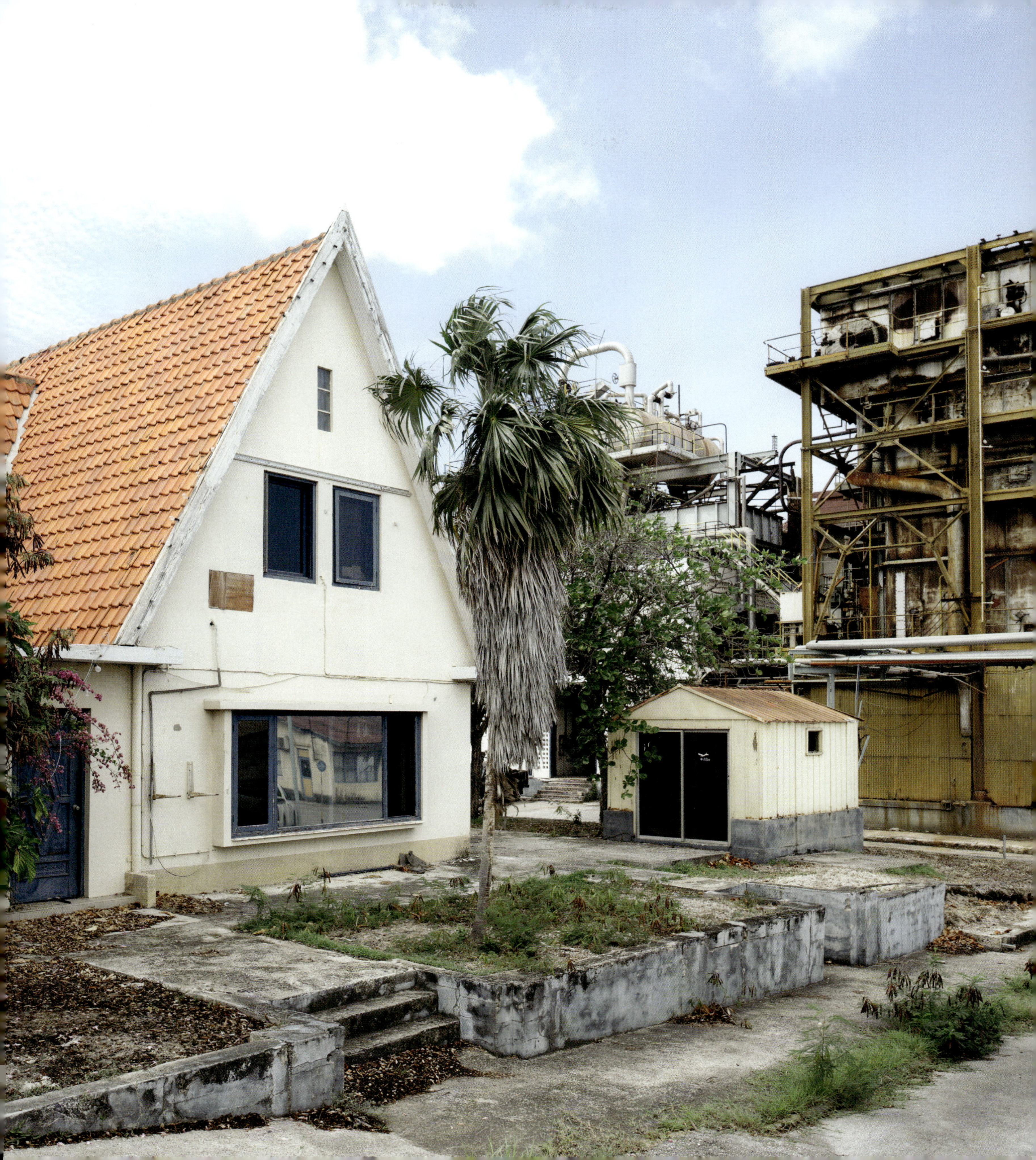

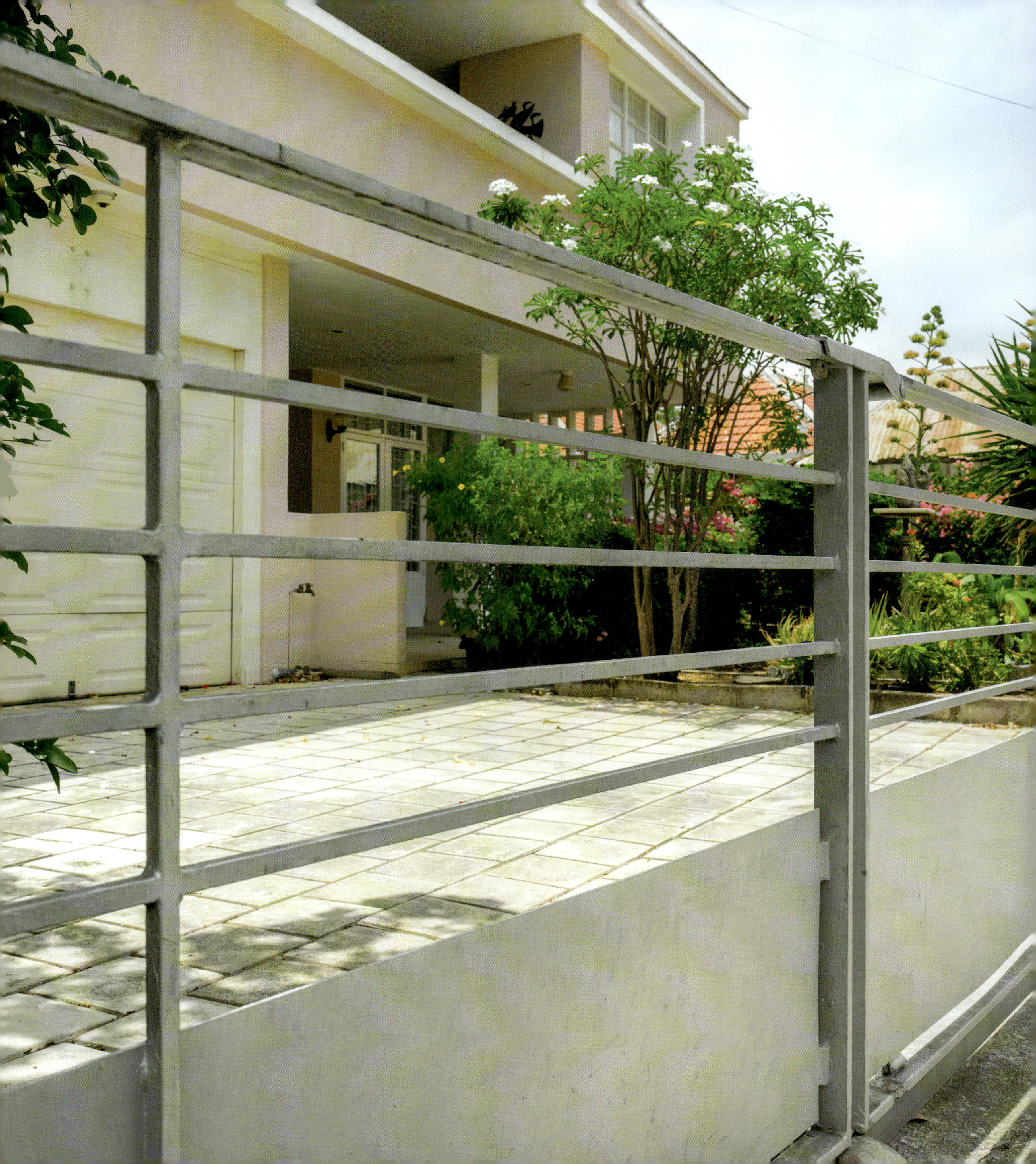

National grid reference: **12°06′00.6″N 68°55′11.5″W**

14.
BENESCH RESIDENCE_

PENSTRAAT 105

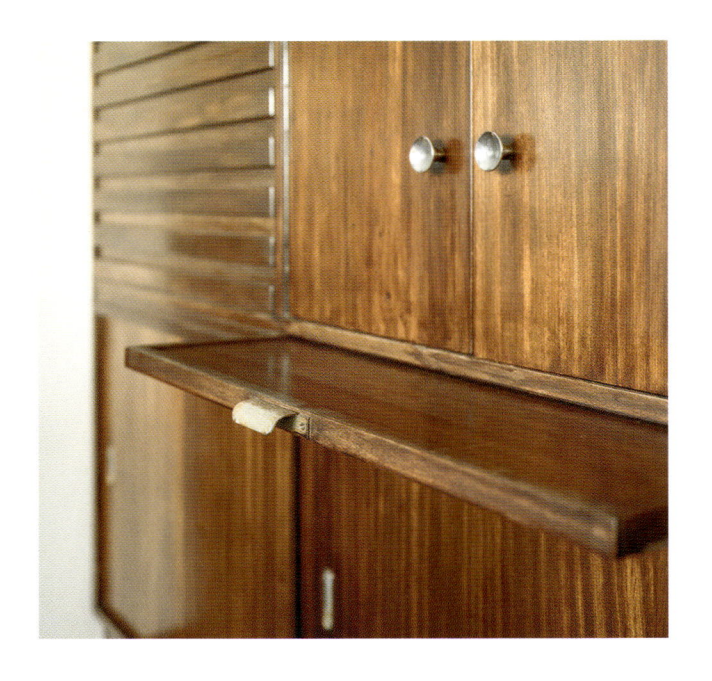

In the interior, the drawing room on the second floor boasts mahogany furniture consisting of wall units along two walls and a sideboard.

do_co_mo_mo_curaçao

Historic Background_

Dr. Julius Benesch was a medical doctor who practiced on Curaçao until his passing in 1962. Born in 1892 in Bohemia, he was of Jewish descent and pursued his medical education in Vienna. After arriving in Curaçao in 1922, he served as a government physician, working on Curaçao, Saba, and Sint Eustatius. In 1928, he returned to Vienna, where he married Melanie Berger. Due to Austria's incorporation into Nazi Germany in 1938, Dr. Benesch, had to leave his homeland once again. On July 22, 1938, he and his wife Melanie arrived in Curaçao aboard the SS Simon Bolivar, settling at "Pyrmont House", Penstraat 24, owned by the Levy Maduro family (currently known as "Kas di Pueblo"). Following Germany's invasion of the Netherlands, Dr. Benesch and his wife were arrested by the police on the night of May 10, 1940. The former government physician, who was anti-Nazi and a Jewish fugitive from Austria, was considered a dangerous individual to the state. He and his wife, Melanie, were interned in Bonaire during World War II. The deed of sale for the house he purchased at Scharlooweg 37 was declared null and void in 1944 and he remained under supervision until 1947.

In 1951, Dr. Benesch commissioned architect Ben Smit to design a new residence on Penstraat. Dr. Benesch utilized the ground floor for his practice, while he and his wife occupied the upper level. Esteemed by his patients, especially those in need whom he often treated without charge, Dr. Benesch passed away childless in 1962. He was interred with honors at the Jewish cemetery on Berg Altena. His wife, Melanie Berger, remained in the house until her own passing. Their housekeeper, Bernadine from St. Kitts, still resides at Penstraat 105, diligently preserving the home's original character to the best of her ability.

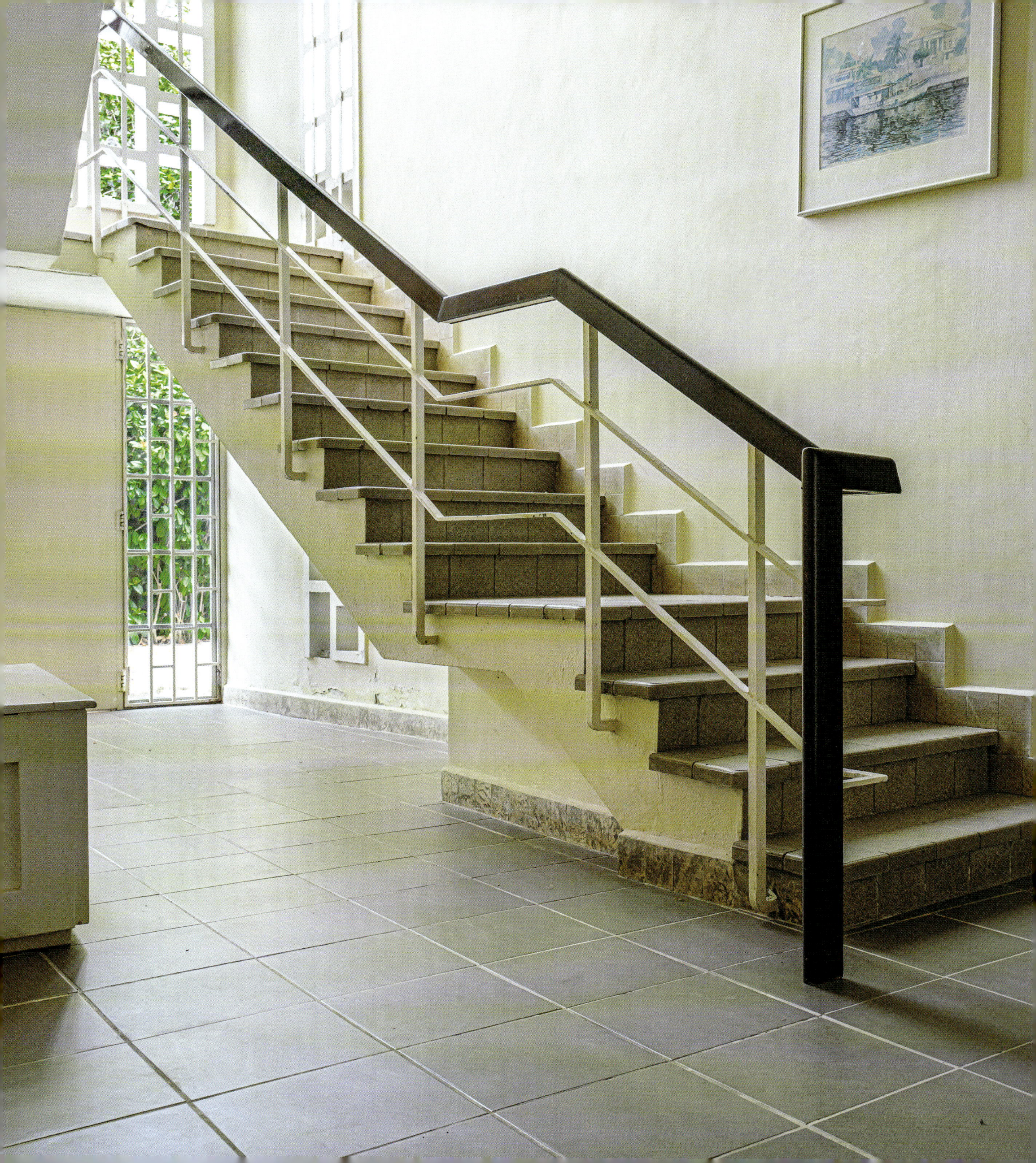

Architectural Design_

Benesch's residence is an example of Modern Movement architecture by Ben Smit. Clean lines, integration of indoor and outdoor spaces, and adaptation to the climate correspond with the principles of the Modern Movement. Notable features include a flat roof, protruding concrete canopies, a recessed balcony, and an open gallery along the rear part of the western facade. Utilizing perforated building blocks ensured efficient ventilation, while vertical concrete slats controlled sunlight entry. The striking metal door at the main entrance, crafted from corrugated metal sheets, and the steel window frames reflect a preference for sleek materials. A unique ventilation system was created to optimize airflow in the main rooms on the second floor, utilizing the prevailing Trade Winds. Additionally, Ben Smit created the interior design of the drawing room, giving the Benesch residence a special personal touch.

Description_

The house is situated on a narrow, deep plot on the north side of Penstraat. It comprises two floors and a flat roof with a terrace. The front façade presents a deep recessed balcony, with a strikingly simple staircase leading to the rooftop terrace. In the interior, the drawing room on the second floor boasts mahogany furniture consisting of wall units along two walls and a sideboard. A centrally placed large arched settee with a high back and no armrests is a prominent feature. The floor is elegantly adorned with mahogany parquet. Along the south side of the drawing room, folding glass doors open up onto the recessed balcony at the front of the house.

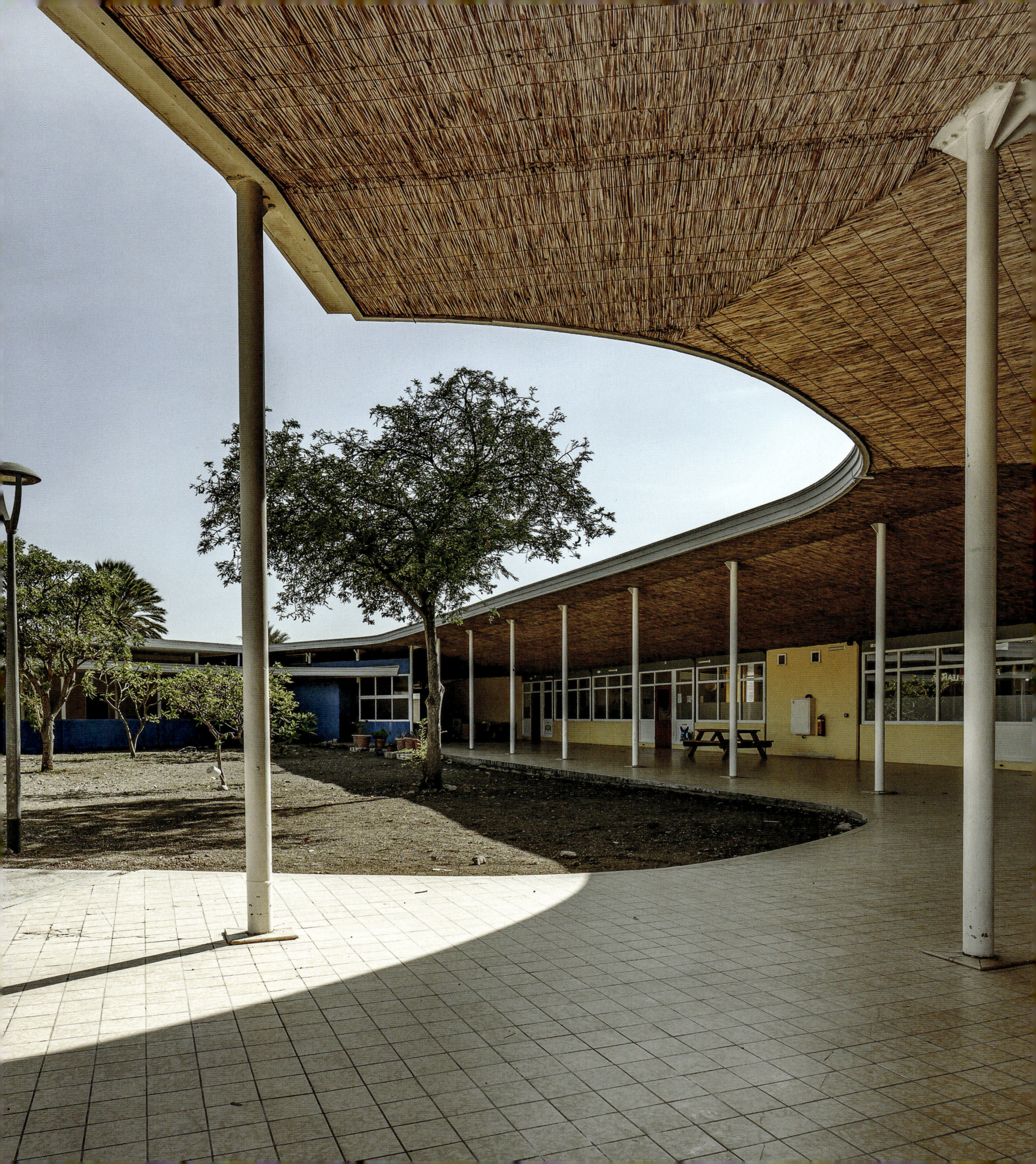

National grid reference: **12°09'31.5"N 68°56'38.1"W**

15.
MGR. VERRIET INSTITUTE _

SALSBACHWEG 20

Mgr. Verriet Institute. Drawing: Project Planners & Designers, 2006 / Rosberg Engineering, 2016

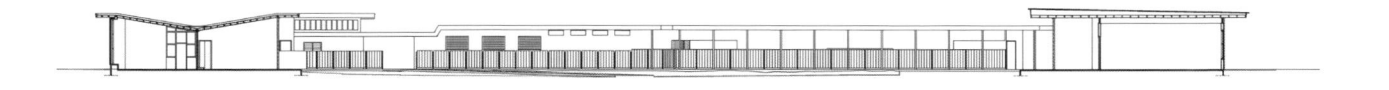

Source: R. Gill - Een Eeuw Architectuur op Curaçao

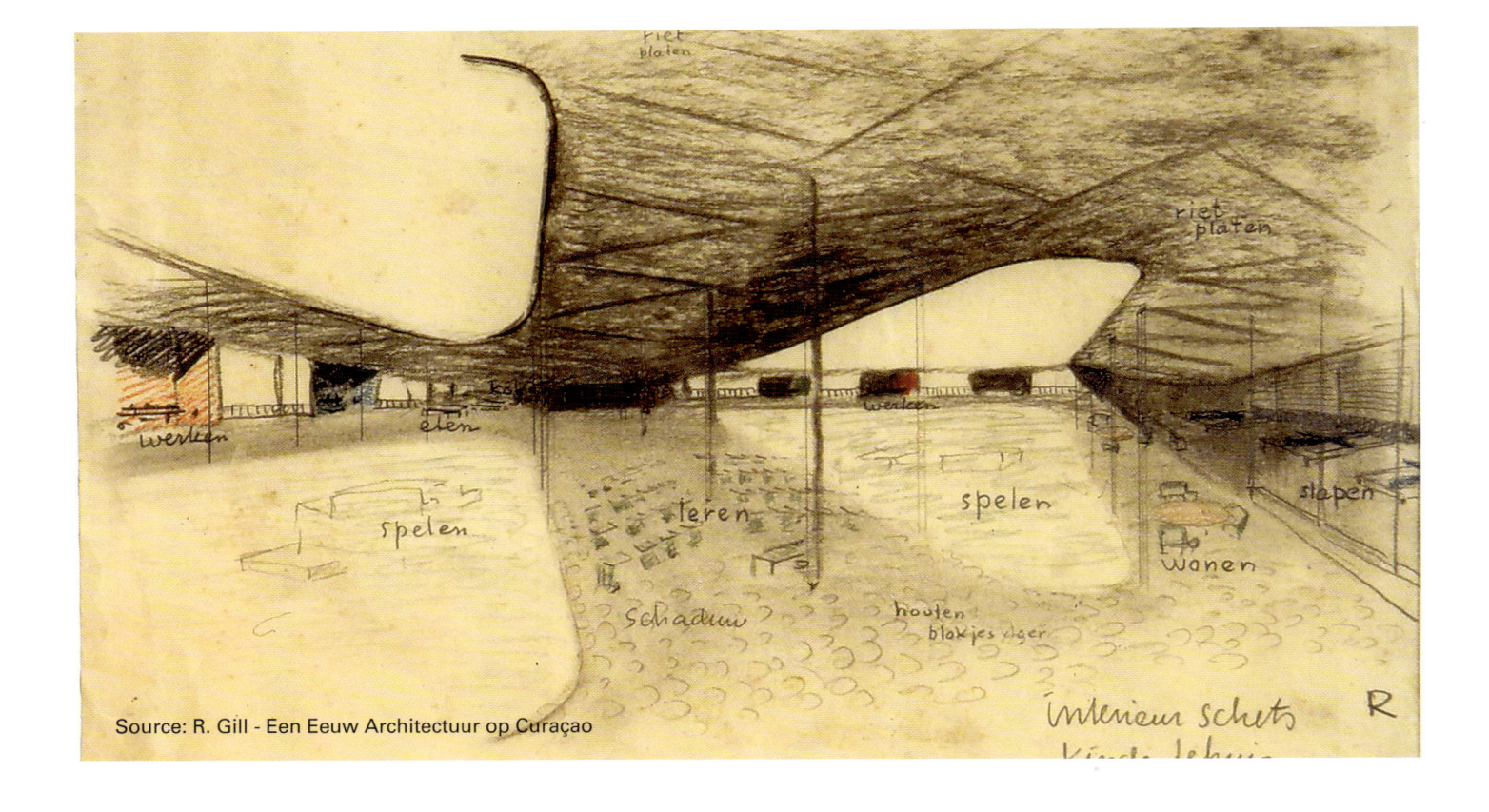

He believed that "the interior space should be separated from the outdoor space as little as possible".

Historic Background_

The 'Wit Gele Kruis' (White Yellow Cross) was a Catholic institution in Curaçao that was involved in medical and social care. Today, the WGK mainly focuses on providing home care. At the end of the 1940s, the organization planned to build a home for disabled children. Dr. Chris Engels, the medical advisor of the WGK, was not happy with the design, feeling it resembled an asylum and not very 'friendly'.

During a visit to the Netherlands, Dr. Engels met the renowned Dutch architect Gerrit Thomas Rietveld and invited him to come to Curaçao to provide advice on the design. Rietveld also expressed reservations about the plan and was commissioned by the WGK board to develop a new design. During his brief stay on the island in October 1949, he created successive sketches to discuss with the client. By the time he returned to the Netherlands to finalize the plan, the main concept for the Monseigneur Verriet Institute in the Santa Maria neighborhood on the outskirts of Willemstad had been established. The young local architect Henk Nolte of the Curaçao Public Works Department was responsible for executing the detailed drawings and overseeing the construction. The official opening took place in November 1952.

In 2004, the section of the building originally designed by Rietveld was officially designated as a protected monument.

do.co.mo.mo_curaçao

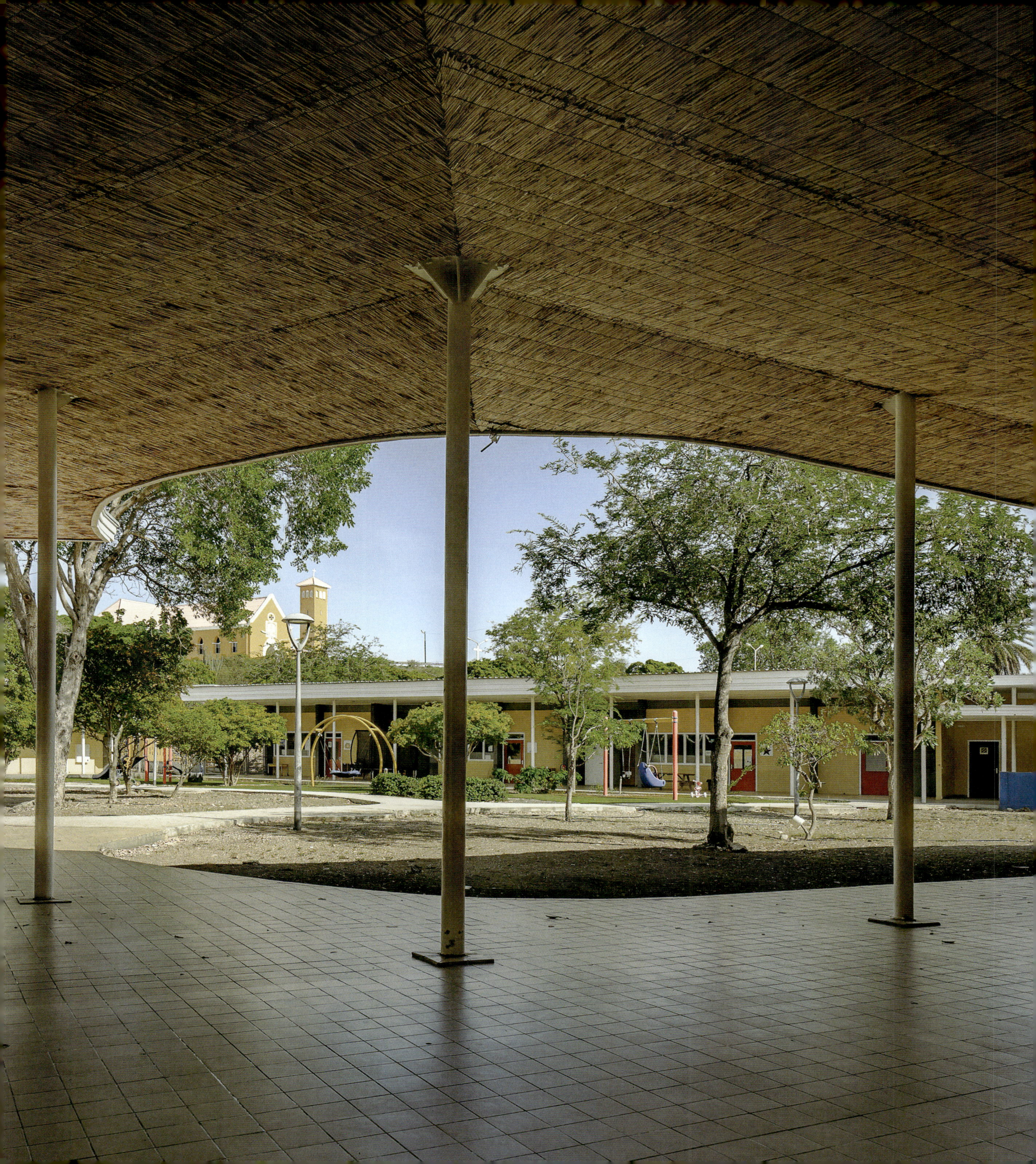

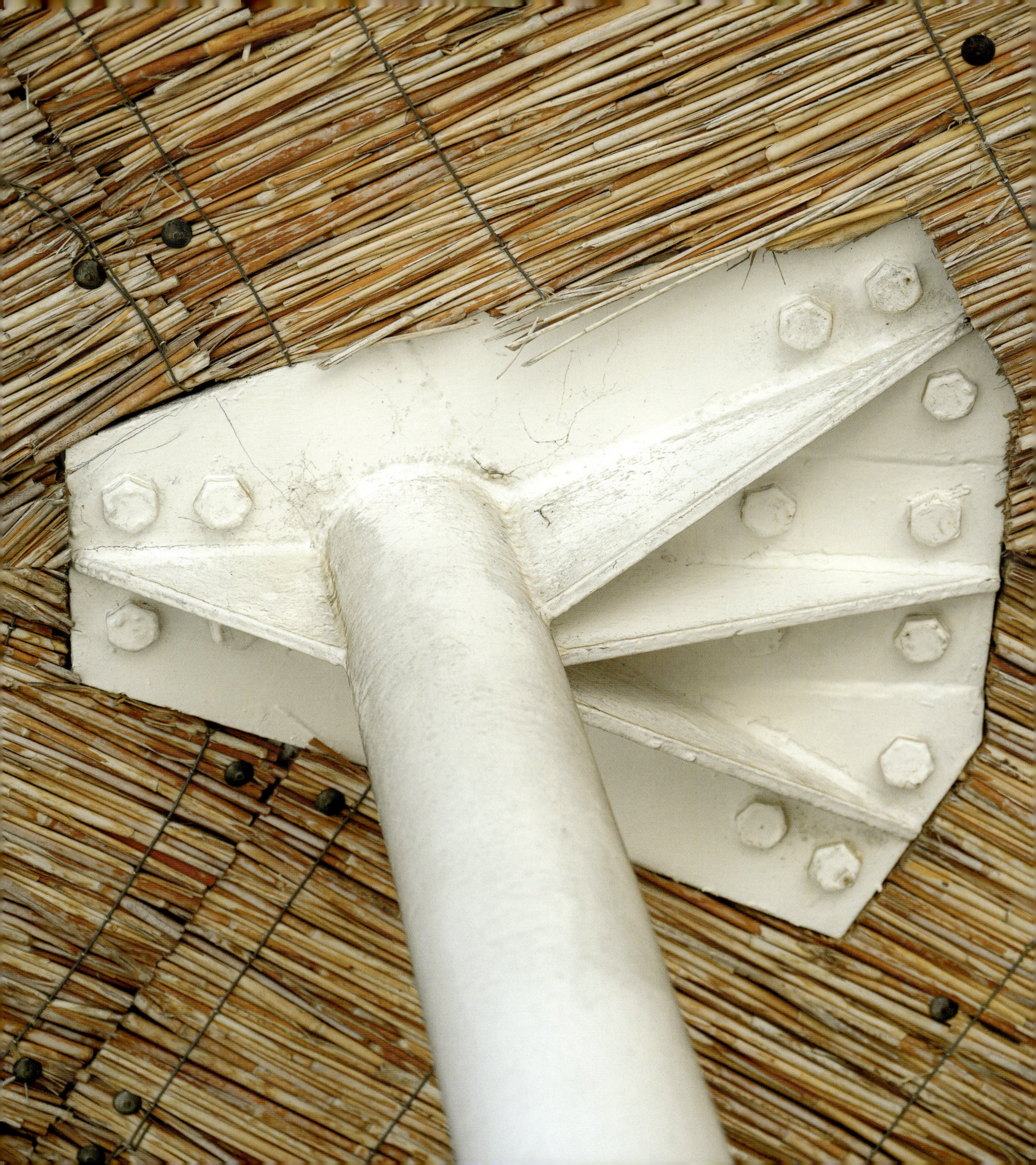

Mgr. Verriet Institute. Drawing: Project Planners & Designers, 2006 / Rosberg Engineering, 2016

Architectural Design_

Although Rietveld stayed on the island for only a short time, he quickly understood the need to adapt to the tropical climate, which he achieved by minimizing the use of walls to allow for natural ventilation.

This concept aligned with his design philosophy from the famous Rietveld Schröder House in 1924, a UNESCO World Heritage site since 2000, where he believed that "the interior space should be separated from the outdoor space as little as possible". In the tropics, he was able to fully implement this.

According to Rietveld, the design featured an enormous thatched roof supported by numerous slim columns with two large skylights. The most striking element of the interior is the thatch, composed of reed mats, which forms the ceiling beneath the roof structure.

The idea of using reed mats for the ceiling likely came from Dr. Engels (HEER, Jan de (2011), p. 43). This concept references traditional cornstalks used for the roofs of slave huts on plantations in earlier times. Rietveld adapted this idea by using reed mats, known as Oosterhoutsche dakplaten in the Netherlands, typically used as an underlayer for stucco ceilings.

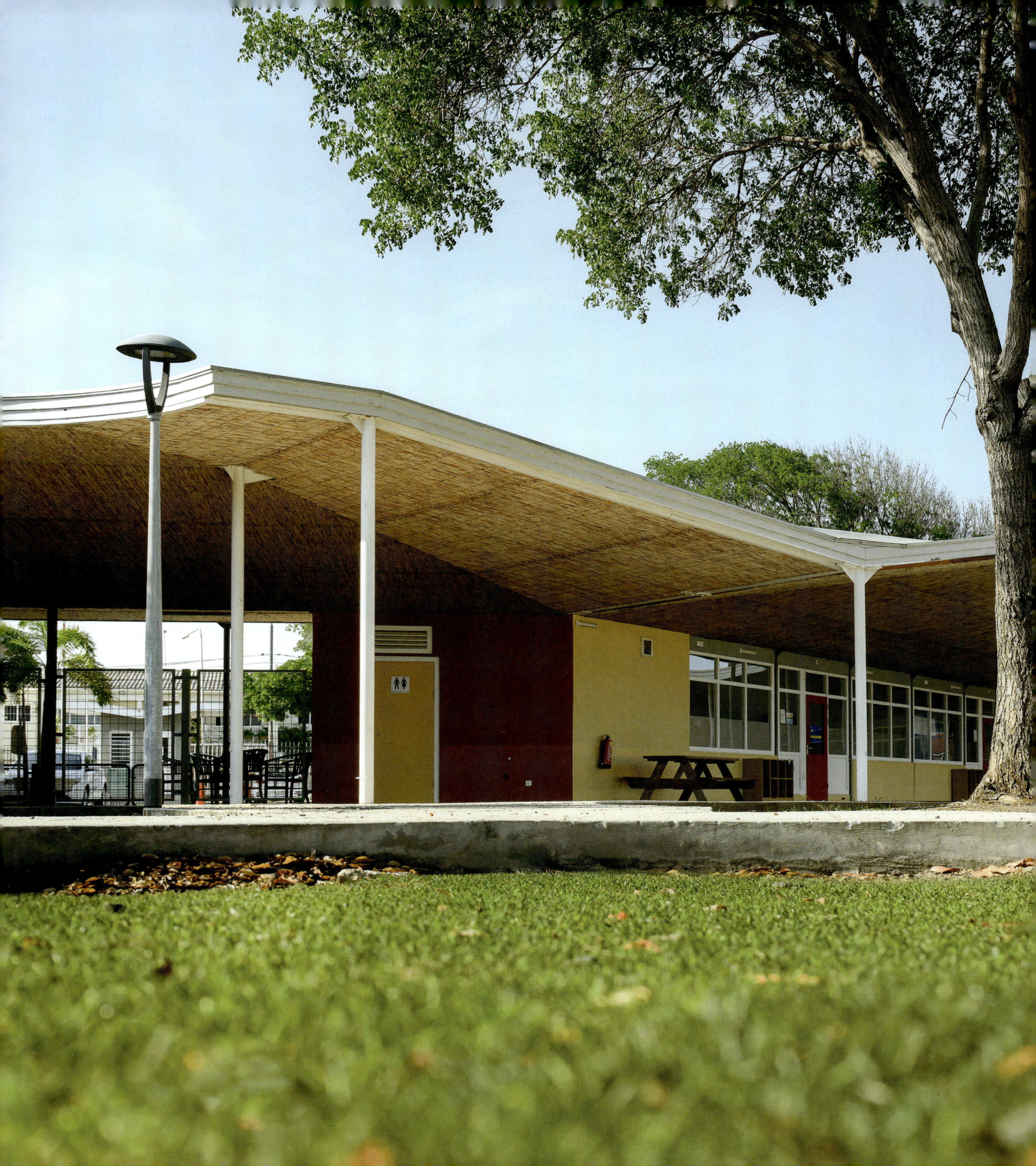

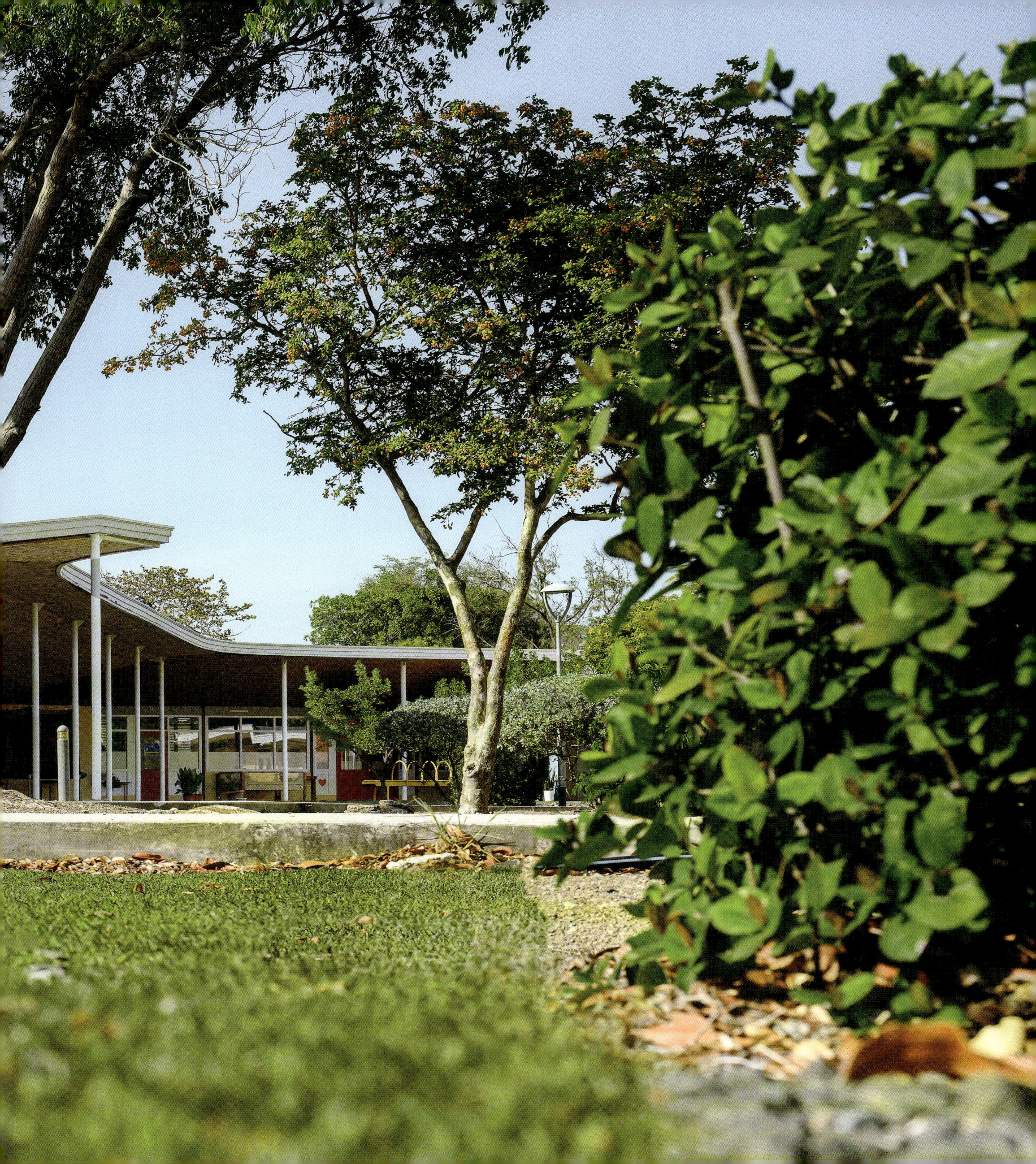

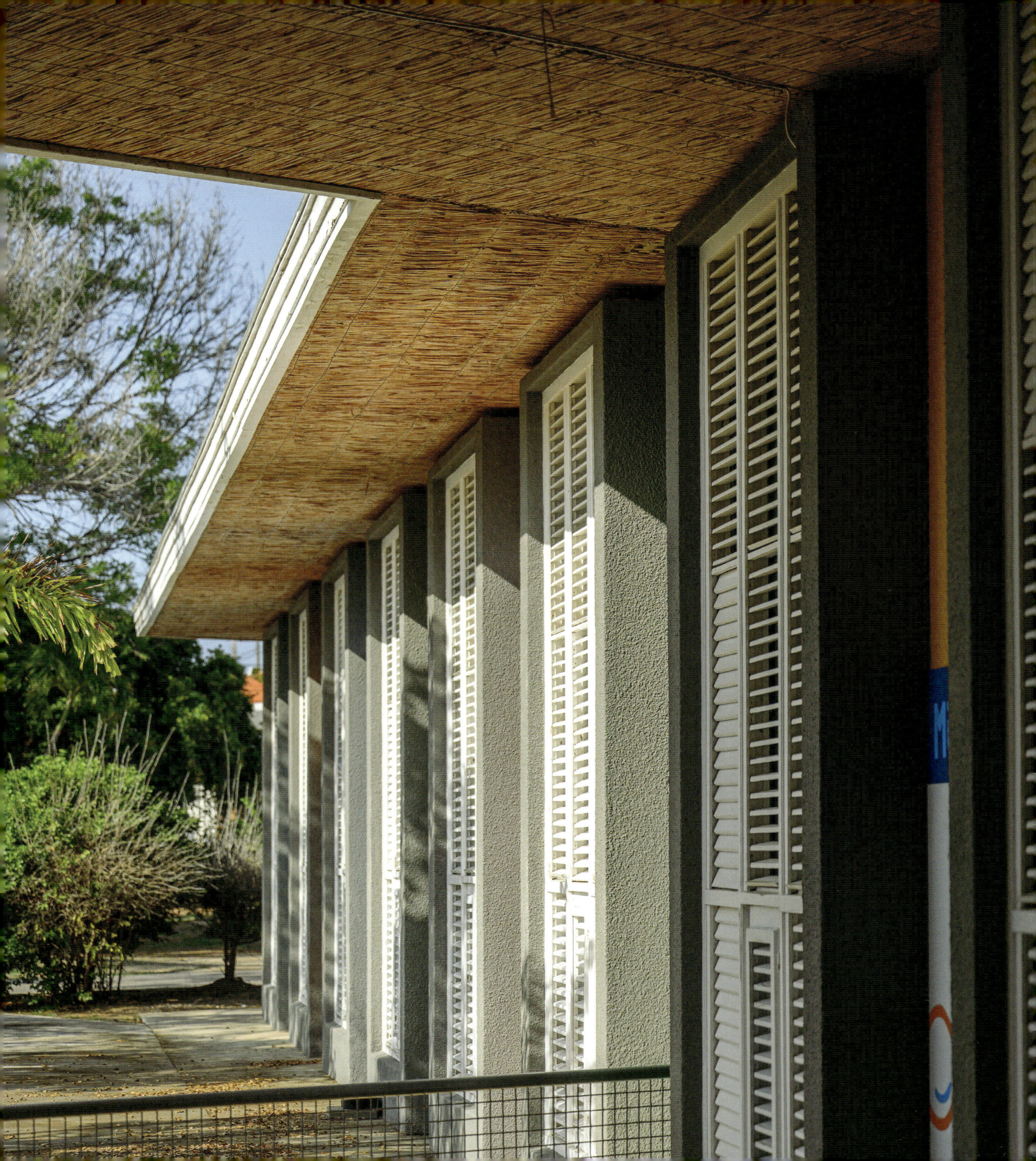

Description_

Rietveld's design was a completely sheltered compound. He described it as a large roof for shade and rainwater collection, with a floor where children could crawl, walk, play, learn and work. Additionally, there were two smaller wings on the periphery, connected by a diagonal central gallery wing. The wings were essentially wide-open galleries covered by large V-shaped cantilevered roofs, supported by a prefabricated steel structure on round steel columns. The V-shaped wings housed the children's sleeping and living quarters, with the sleeping gallery on the outer side of the compound and an open living gallery facing the open inner space. The central wing served as an open classroom, while the two peripheral wings contained the handicraft workshops. The external walls of the complex were composed of floor-to-roof wooden louvers, allowing for cross ventilation that provided optimal cooling at all times of the day.

Shortly after the design was completed, it became clear that the budget would be insufficient to build the entire complex. Rietveld himself proposed constructing the institute in phases, beginning with the two V-shaped wings. Unfortunately, the second phase of Rietveld's design was never realized.

A few years later, the peripheral wings were added by the executive architect Henk Nolte, although not exactly as designed by Rietveld.

The outline of the diagonal central gallery wing, which was projected but never built, can still be recognized.

In 1964, Nolte designed pavilions adjacent to the main building for children with severe disabilities.

From 2014 to 2016, the current owner, the Fundashon Verriet, part of the Stichting voor Gehandicapten- en Revalidatiezorg (SGR group), had the building renovated by the architect's office Project Planners and Designers.
Since the building was only used for day-care and the disabled children did not live there anymore, the internal use was adjusted. The previously open partitions between sleeping quarters and the living gallery were closed off for the new functions and to accommodate the installation of air-conditioning. The reed mats in the former sleeping quarters were covered with gypsum board as the reed had deteriorated. In the open galleries facing the inner garden, the characteristic reed mats were renewed.

Rietveld initially proposed using various colors on the exterior. This was rejected at the time, especially by the executive architect. During the most recent renovations, various colors were applied to the exterior, inspired by Rietveld's proposals from more than 60 years earlier.

References:

- Gill, Ronald (1990) The architecture of Rietveld on Curaçao. *Building up the future from the past*. Zutphen: De Walburg Pers.
- Gill, Ronald G. (2008) *Een eeuw architectuur op Curaçao*. Curaçao: Ronald G. Gill, (Original work published 1999)
- Gill, Ronald (2009) Gerrit Rietveld's Verriet Institute for diasabled children; *The impact of Caribbean Modern Architecture, First regional DOCOMOMO seminar, hosted by the University of the Netherlands Antilles*, Curaçao, pp. 60-61
- HEER, Jan de (2011) *Rietveld en Curaçao*, Rotterdam: Uitgeverij 010.

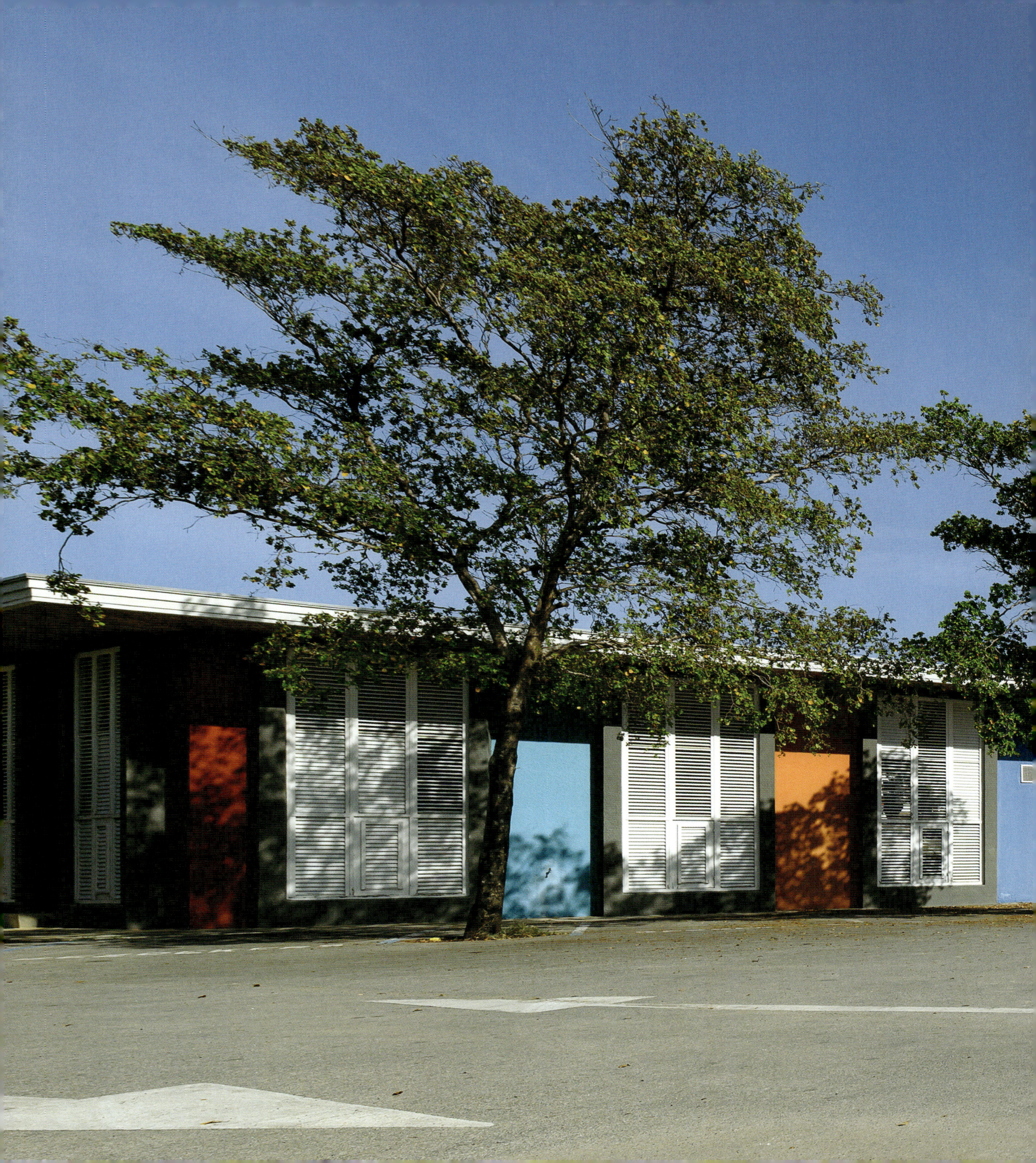

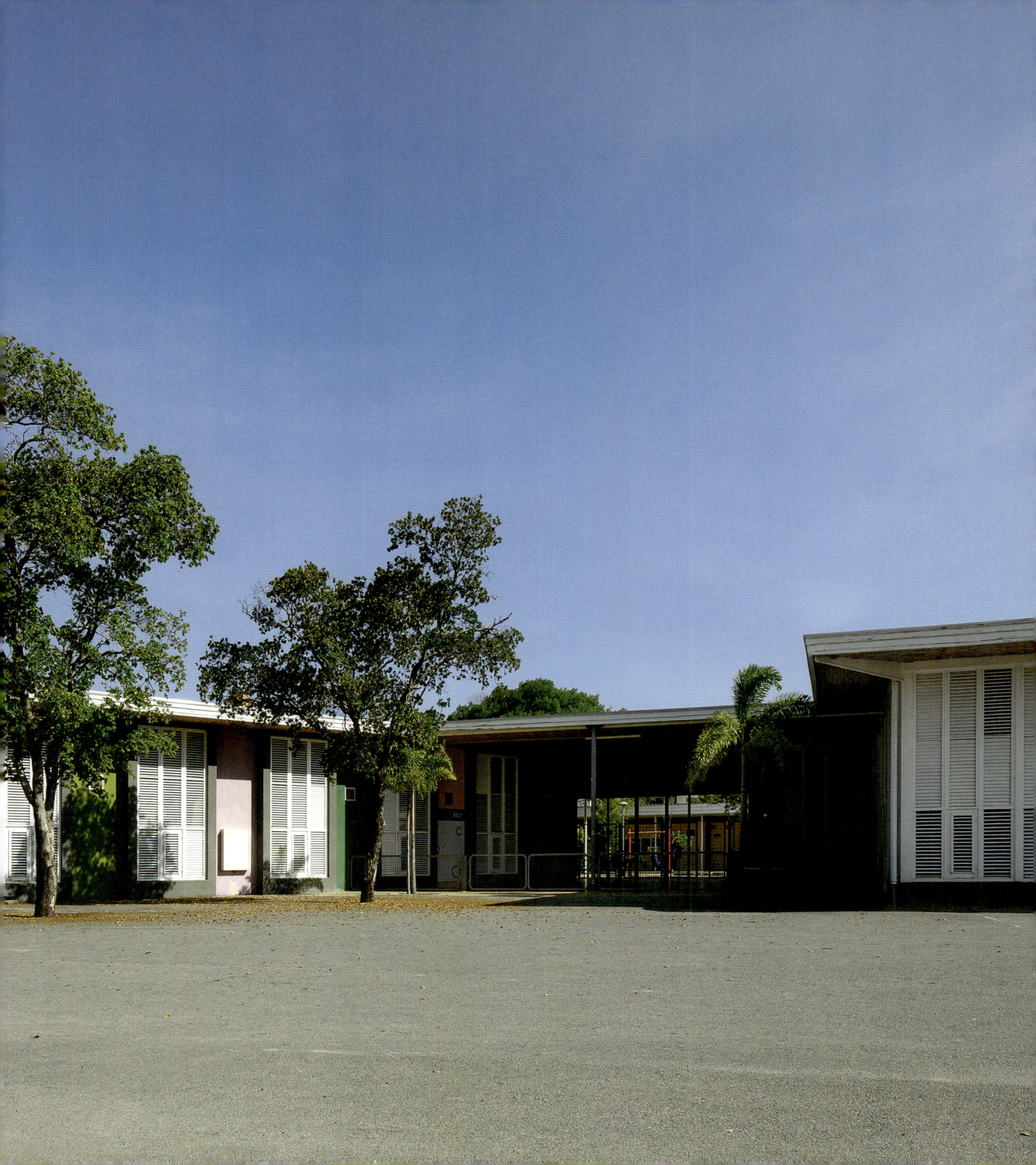

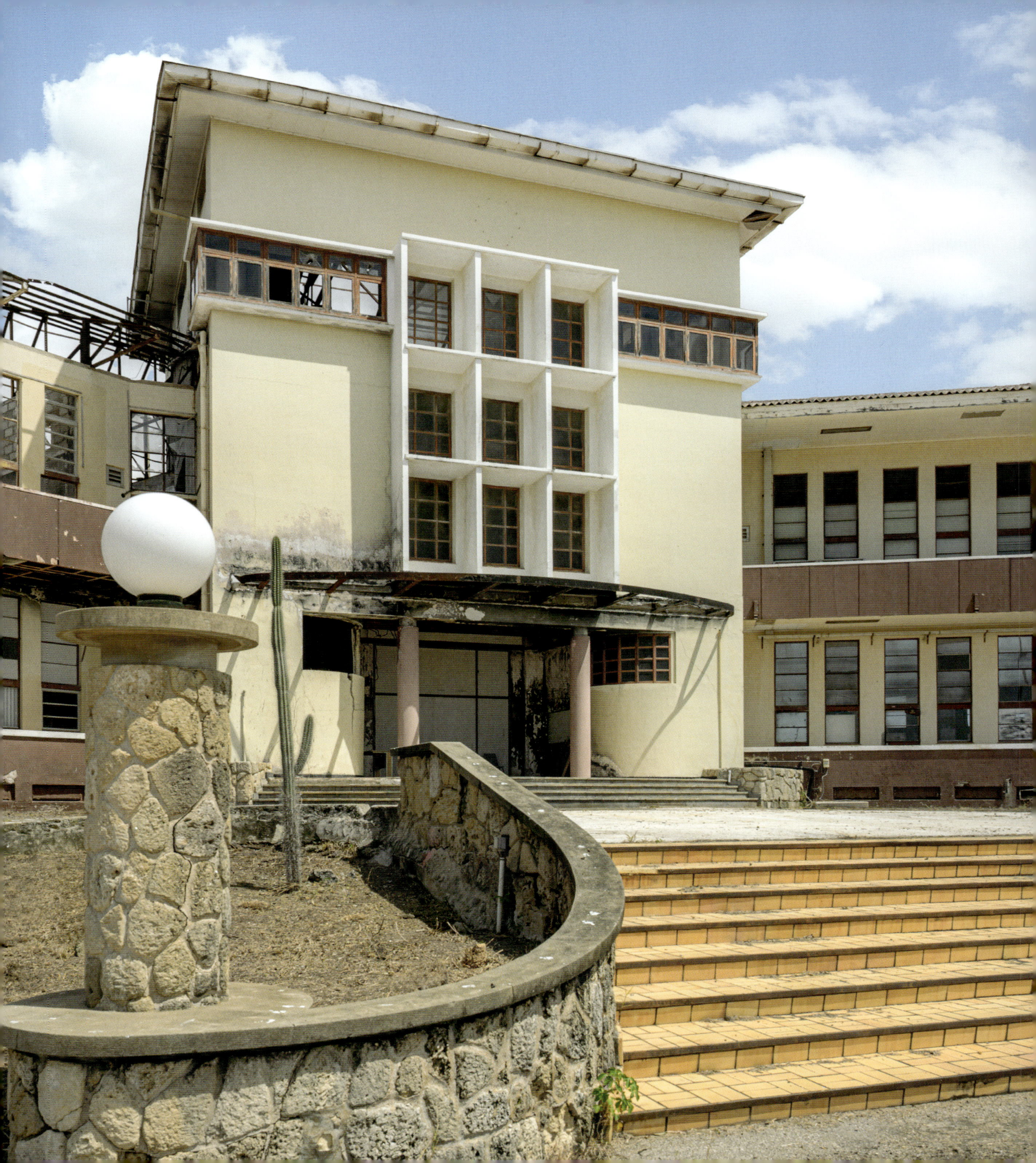

National grid reference: **12°08'06.2"N 68°55'18.2"W**

16.
CPIM
LABORATORY_

EMMASTAD

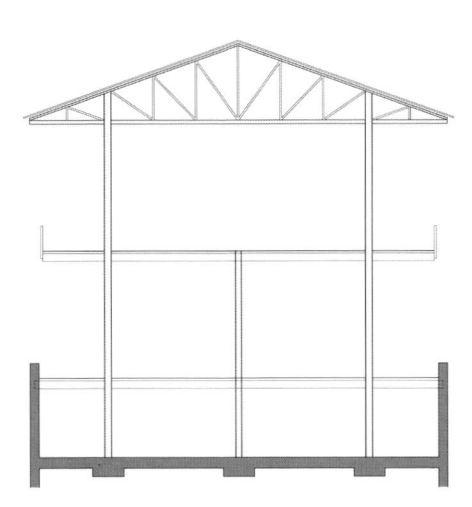

Laboratory Refineria ISLA. Drawing: Archive Ref. ISLA / Rosberg Engineering, 2016

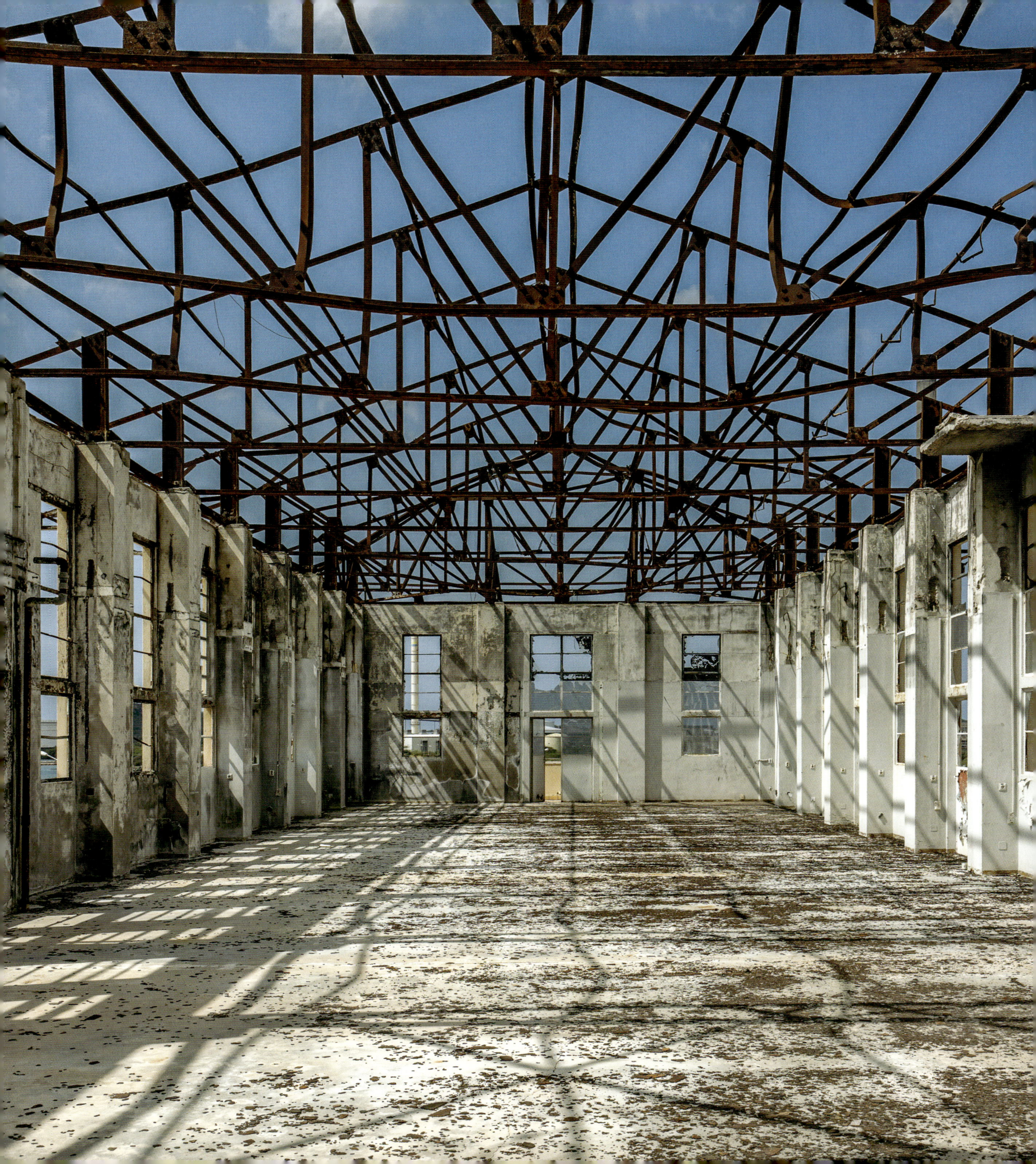

Source: Coll. Steenhuizen c. 1950

Characteristic of this building are the three wings, the large roof overhangs, and the outside galleries designed for shade.

Historic Background_

The oil industry in Curaçao was established in 1915. Crude oil from Venezuela was shipped to the island, initially for transshipment but in 1918 the Royal Dutch Shell group built an oil refinery on the Northern borders of the Schottegat, the natural inner harbour. At one point in time the company was the largest in the world in terms of its number of different oil products. During a lengthy period of the 20th century the CPIM, the Curaçaosche Petroleum Industrie Maatschappij NV, (as the Royal SHELL was called prior to 1959) was the most important employer on the island, exerting a strong influence on the rest of the economy and on the island's architecture. Thousands of people earned their income at the refinery.

At first most of buildings and constructions (industrial, offices and residential facilities) were located along the shore of the Schottegat on various peninsulas. Later, the refinery expanded inland onto former plantations north of the Schottegat, most of which the Shell had bought in the 1920's. In 1940, a new Head Office for the refinery was opened. Across from the office, the construction of the Laboratory complex was initiated in 1947 and opened on January 29, 1952. On January 24, 2022, the top floor of the west wing went up in flames. Only the twisted steel construction still stands. The owner, CRU/RdK intends to rebuild the wing.

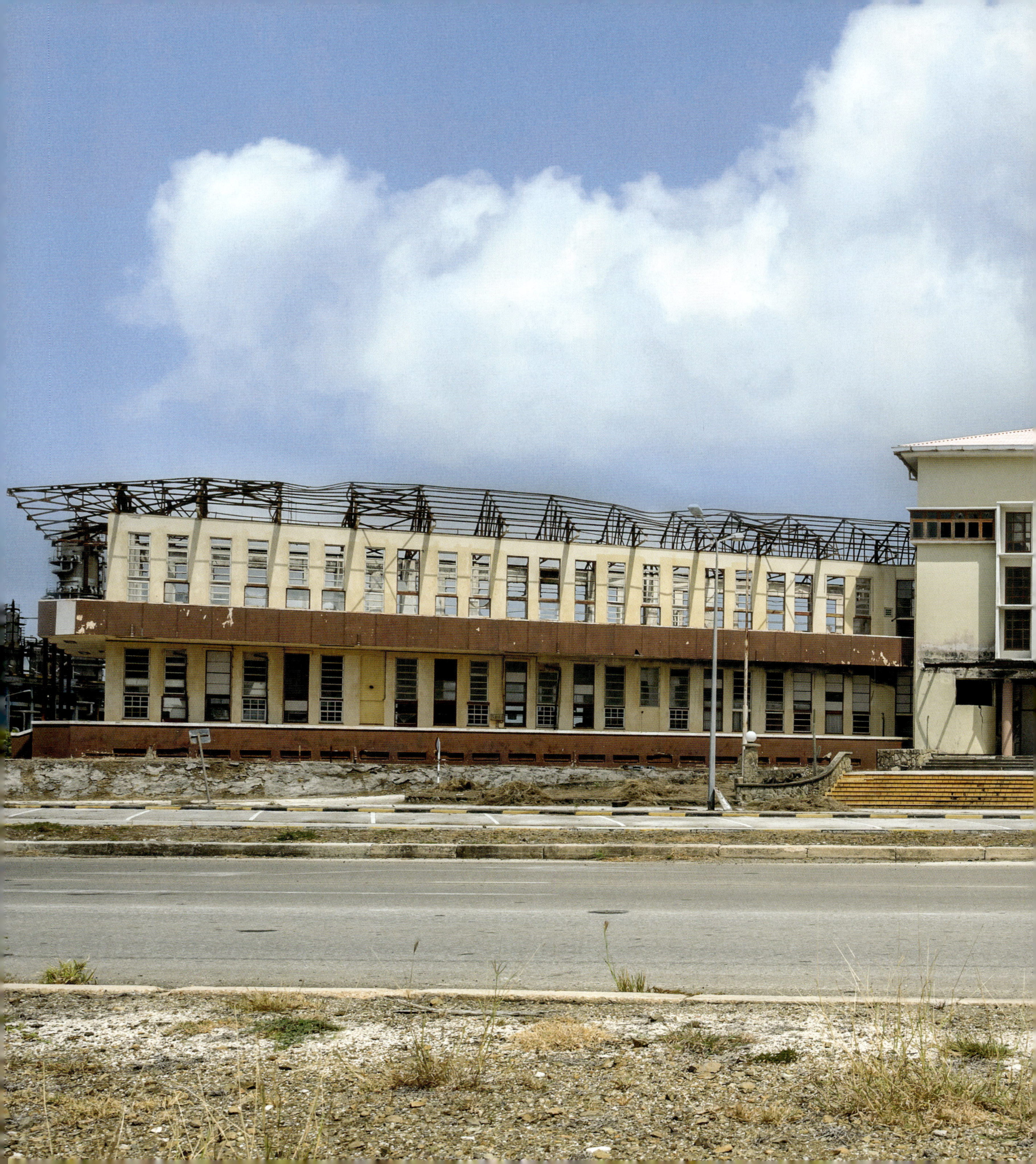

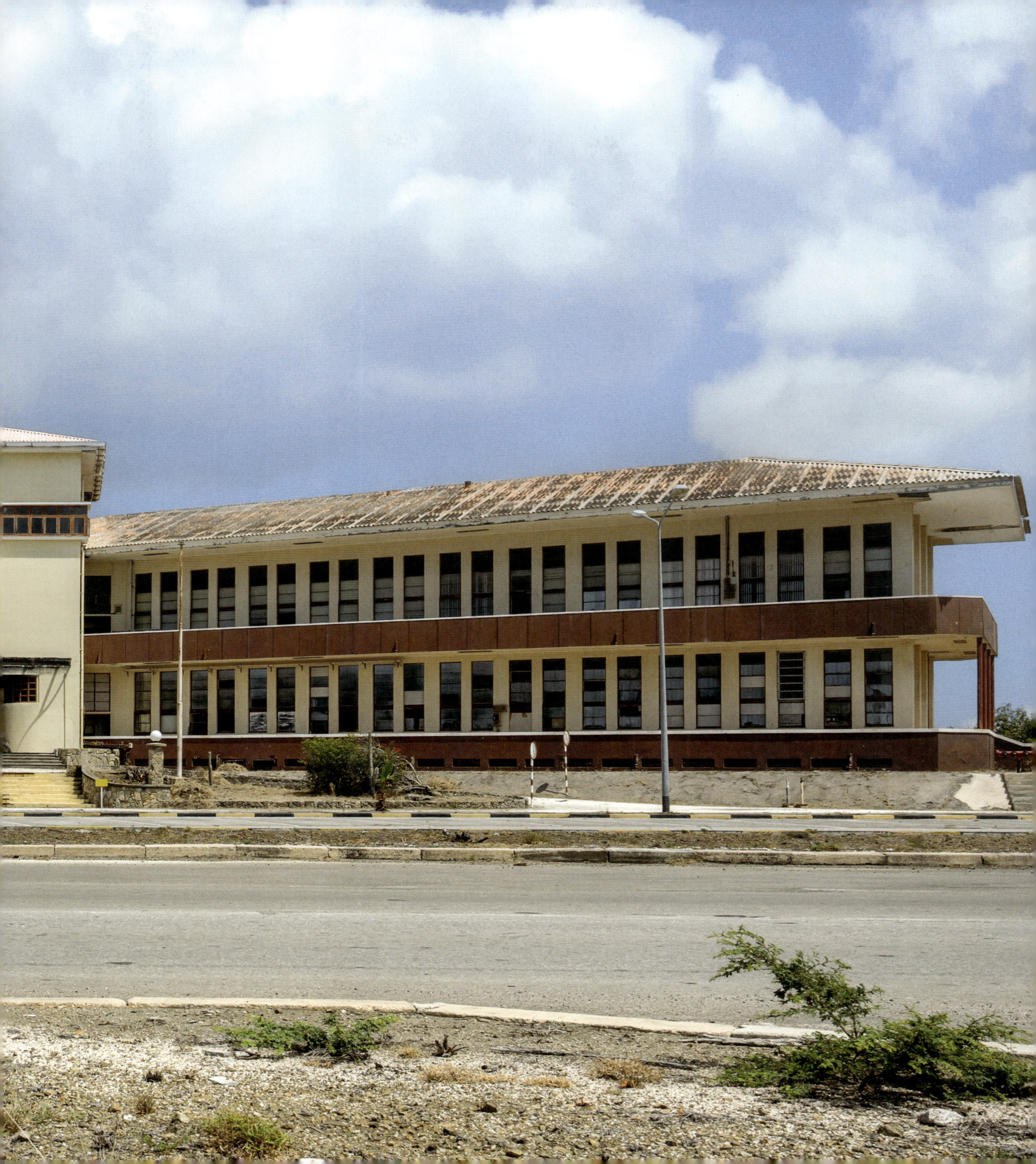

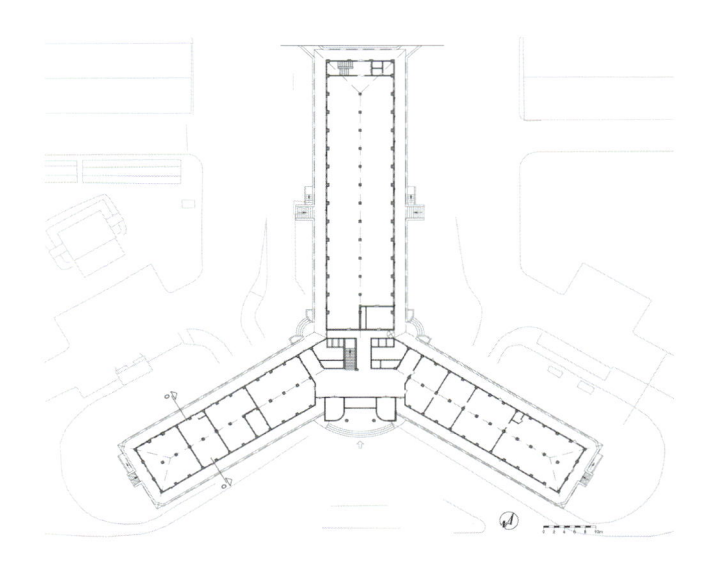

Laboratory Refineria ISLA. Drawing: Archive Ref. ISLA / Rosberg Engineering, 2016

Architectural Design_

The Head Office building and the Laboratory show strong similarities to buildings by Dutch architects in another Dutch colony, Indonesia. The buildings were well adapted to the tropical climate with large roof overhangs and elevations carefully designed for ventilation and daylight access.

The Head Office Building, opposite the laboratory, was designed in a typical tropical architectural style by Shell's architect-in residence, the Dutchman C.A. (Kees) Abspoel.

Remarkably, the Laboratory building was designed by English architects White and Trafers, yet they incorporated similar tropical design elements. The Laboratory building consists of three wings of two floors with, underneath, a basement. The wings are connected to a rectangular central building with the main entrance and a stairwell. Different types of laboratories were set up in the building, all for different types of research.

Characteristic of this building are the three wings, the large roof overhangs, and the outside galleries designed for shade. These features are typical for tropical architecture from that period.

The Head office and the Laboratory were among the largest buildings on the island and as such had an important impact on the architectural scene. The foreign architects succeeded in creating suitable buildings for new functions in a new environment.

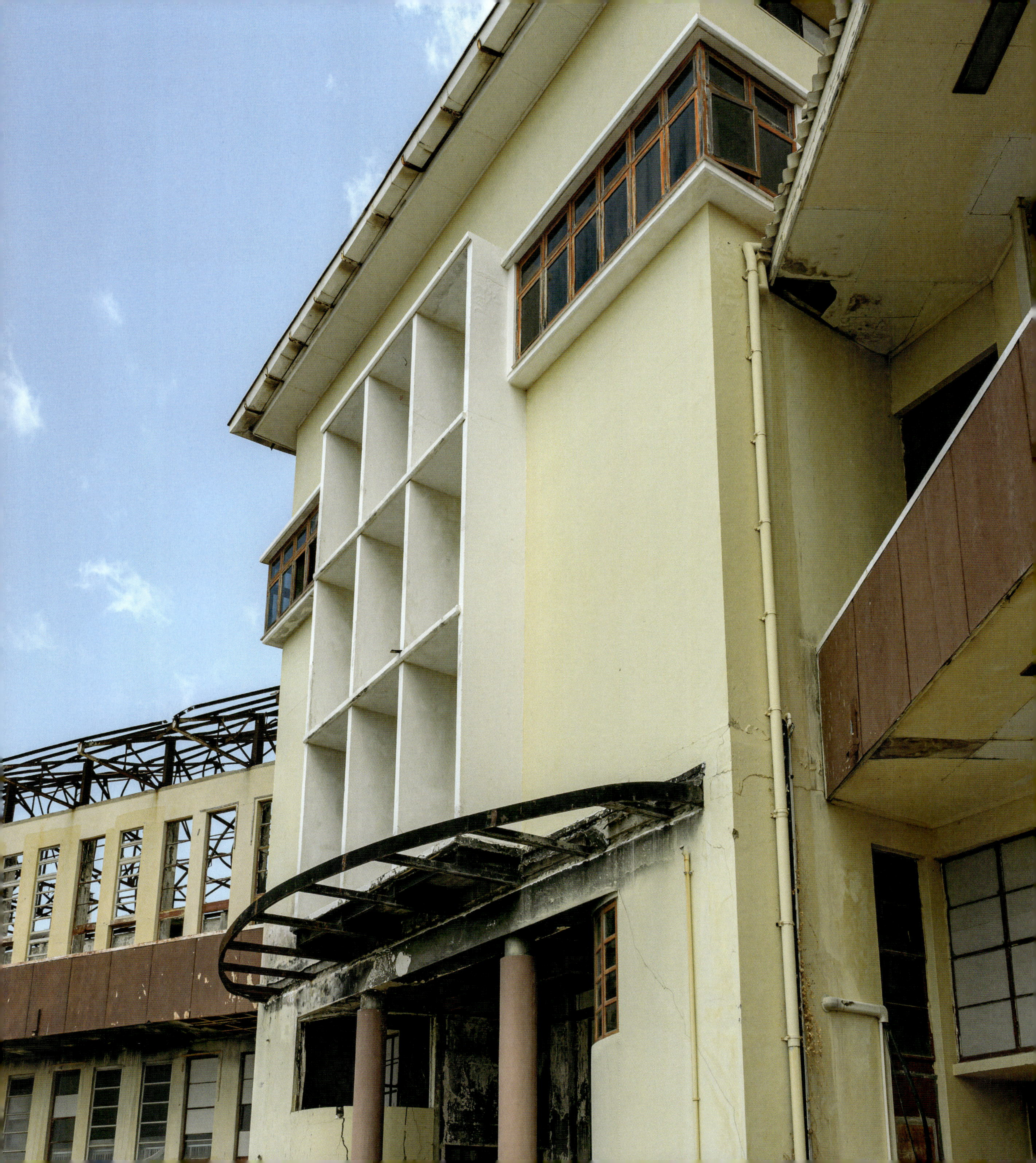

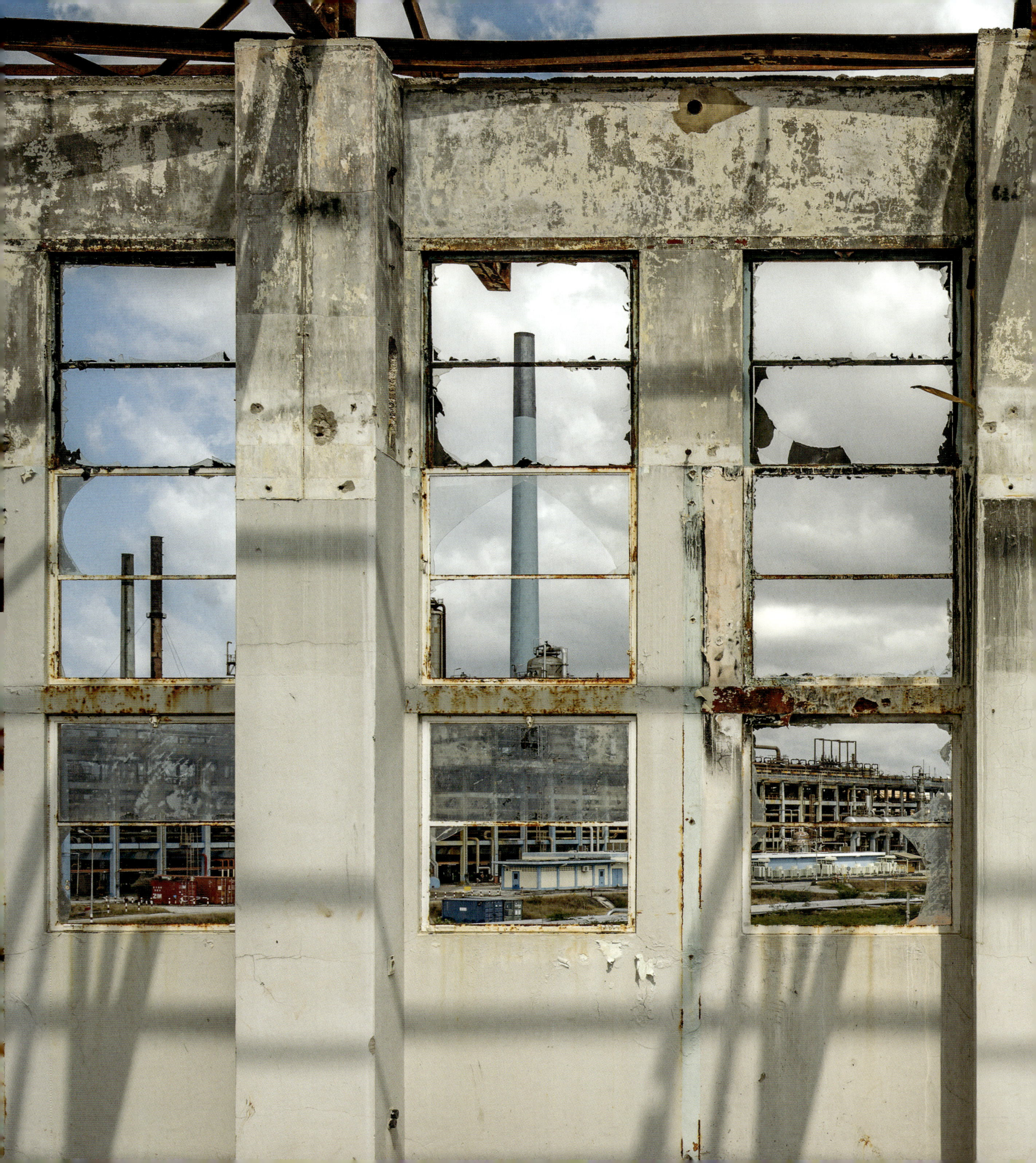

Description_

The main construction of the building is a prefabricated steel frame and, in this way, introduced a new form of construction on the island. The rectangular entrance in the center of the building, also a prefabricated steel construction, visually connects the wings. The floors are made of reinforced concrete. Within the steel framework are walls of traditional plastered concrete blocks.

The building has steel windows and doors, with thin profiles that add to the "lightness" preferred by most architects of the modern movement. The architects of the building succeeded, with high glass windows, to comply with the request of their client to create a human and friendly atmosphere with bright working areas. Thus they delivered a building constructed with influences of the Modern Movement adapted to the tropical climate.

References:

- Hartog, Dr. Joh. (1961) CURAÇAO – *Van Kolonie tot Autonomie, deel II*. Aruba: De Wit; p.912
- Lobo, Ronny (2009) Refining oil, Redefining architecture - The former Shell office and laboratories; *The impact of Caribbean Modern Architecture, First regional DOCOMOMO seminar, hosted by the University of the Netherlands Antilles*, Curaçao, pp. 66-68

LA CONFIANZA

National grid reference: **12°06′19.6″N 68°55′54.9″W**

17.
LA CONFIANZA _

DE RUYTERKADE / COLUMBUSSTRAAT

Source: Coll. Jeannette van Ditzhuijzen

A distinctive feature is the quarter-round glass bay window, situated on the curved corner of the building's first and second floors.

Historic Background_

In the 1950's, Curaçao was doing well economically, primarily due to the oil refinery and also the development of trade in the inner city, which was supported by the emerging cruise tourism industry. Retailers in the city constructed new, modern shops. Among these retailers were Ashkenazi Jewish entrepreneurs, originally from Eastern Europe, who settled in Curaçao before or during the Second World War.

Notable among these entrepreneurs were the Wiznitzer brothers Abraham, Shaya, Salomon and Mozes. In 1952, they established their new shop, La Confianza, a wholesale company and retail store, at the corner of Columbusstraat and De Ruyterkade. It opened on June 24, 1953 (Amigoe di Curaçao 25-06-1953). The shop was designed by Anton de Vries, a Dutch architect who came to the island before the Second World War to work at the refinery. De Vries later transferred to the Public Works Department, becoming head of the construction department in 1946. During his tenure at Public Works, he also designed for private clients.

do_co_mo_mo_ curaçao

Architectural Design_

The architecture of La Confianza is less focused on the tropical climate compared to the work of other architects from this period. The windows are accentuated by the outward jutting concrete borders, with marble façade panels incorporated around these edges. The ground floor façade was also completely covered with marble panels.

A distinctive feature is the quarter-round glass bay window, situated on the curved corner of the building's first and second floors. This curve on the ground floor once housed an eye-catching shop window.

References:

- Ditzhuijzen Jeannette van (2010) *Een sjtetl in de tropen*, Amsterdam: KIT Publishers
- Gill, Ronald G. (2008) *Een eeuw architectuur op Curaçao*. Curaçao: Ronald G. Gill, (Original work published 1999)
- Gomez Casseres, Charles (2004) *PUNDA PUNDA*. Curaçao: Charles Gomes Casseres

Description_

The building is situated on the corner of Columbusstraat and De Ruyterkade. It consisted of three floors: the ground floor, intended for everyday products; the first floor, for the more luxurious items, and the third floor, used as a storage area. The elevator was special for that time. Previously, shops in the city had various entrances. Nowadays, there is just one point of access.

In the beginning of this century, when the building was converted into a branch of the Girobank, the distinctive corner shop window was removed and replaced with the main entrance of the building. The other entrances and all shop windows were changed into glass windows. Previously, the building was terracotta red, with white accents around the concrete window borders. The new owner painted the building white and changed the borders to the blue of the Girobank. After the bank went bankrupt and closed its doors in 2019, the concrete borders were painted red.

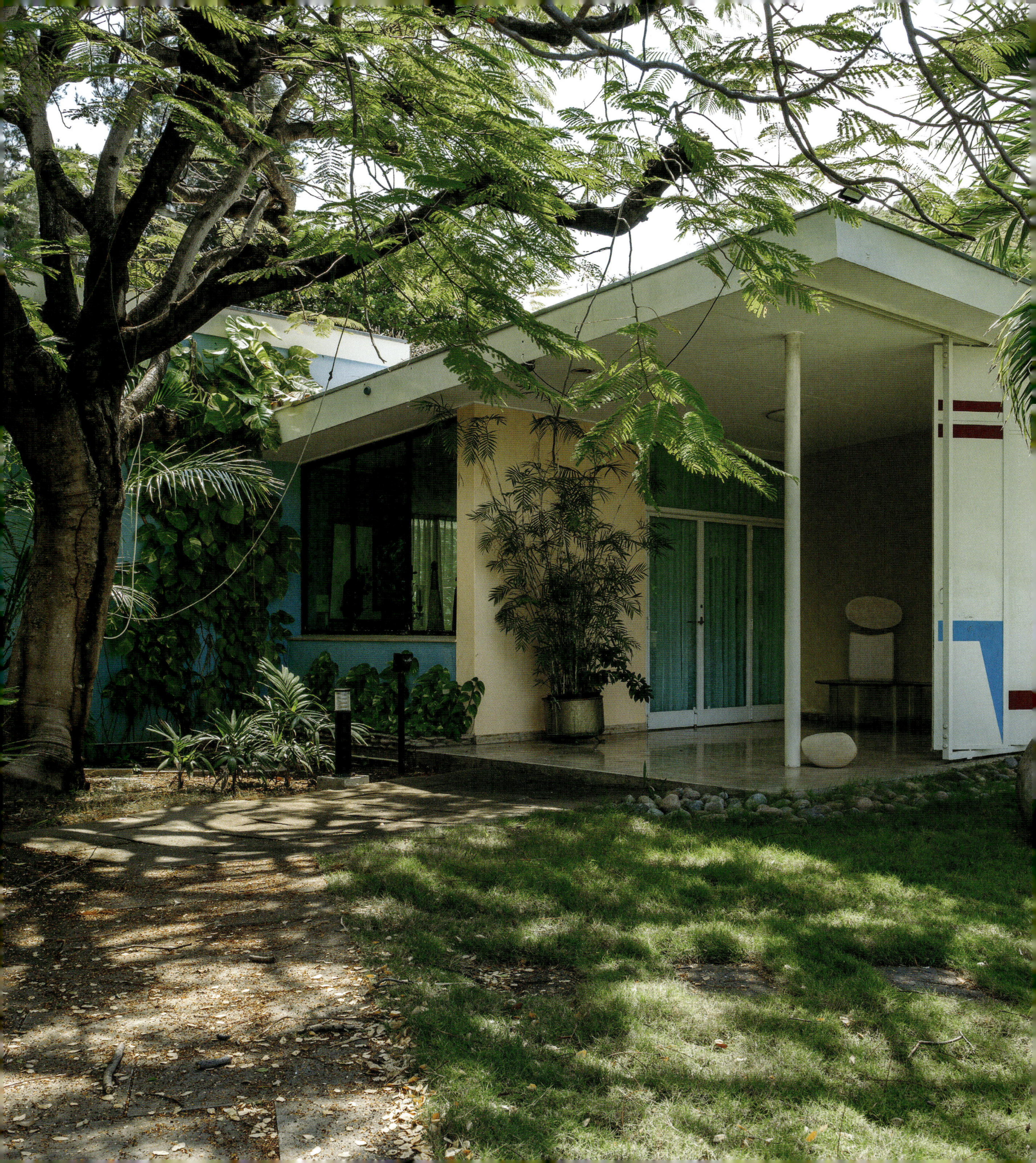

National grid reference: **12°07'44.6"N 68°53'51.5"W**

18.
SPRITZER RESIDENCE_

SCHOUT BIJ NACHT DOORMANWEG 38

Coll. Mongui Maduro Library

The movable vertical 'sun-breakers', the 'brise-soleil', are very eye-catching from the main road, feature an abstract painting by the architect

Historic Background_

The private residence was built in 1952 for the Erno Spritzer family, son of the founder of the famous Spritzer & Fuhrmann jewelry company. It is located in the Damacor neighborhood where, like the nearby Mahaai district, the well to do residents of the island built their homes after World War II. In 1958, Mr. Spritzer and his family emigrated to the Netherlands and sold the house to Mr. Frank Brandao, whose heirs still own the building.

The residence was designed by architect Ben Smit, who was born in the Netherlands in 1922 and established himself in Curaçao in 1943. After working for the Department of Public Works for three years, he founded his own firm in 1946, one of the first local architectural offices. He created an impressive portfolio of buildings on the island, making him an influential architect from the 1940's to the 1960's. In 1969, he returned to the Netherlands with his family.

do_co_mo_mo_curaçao

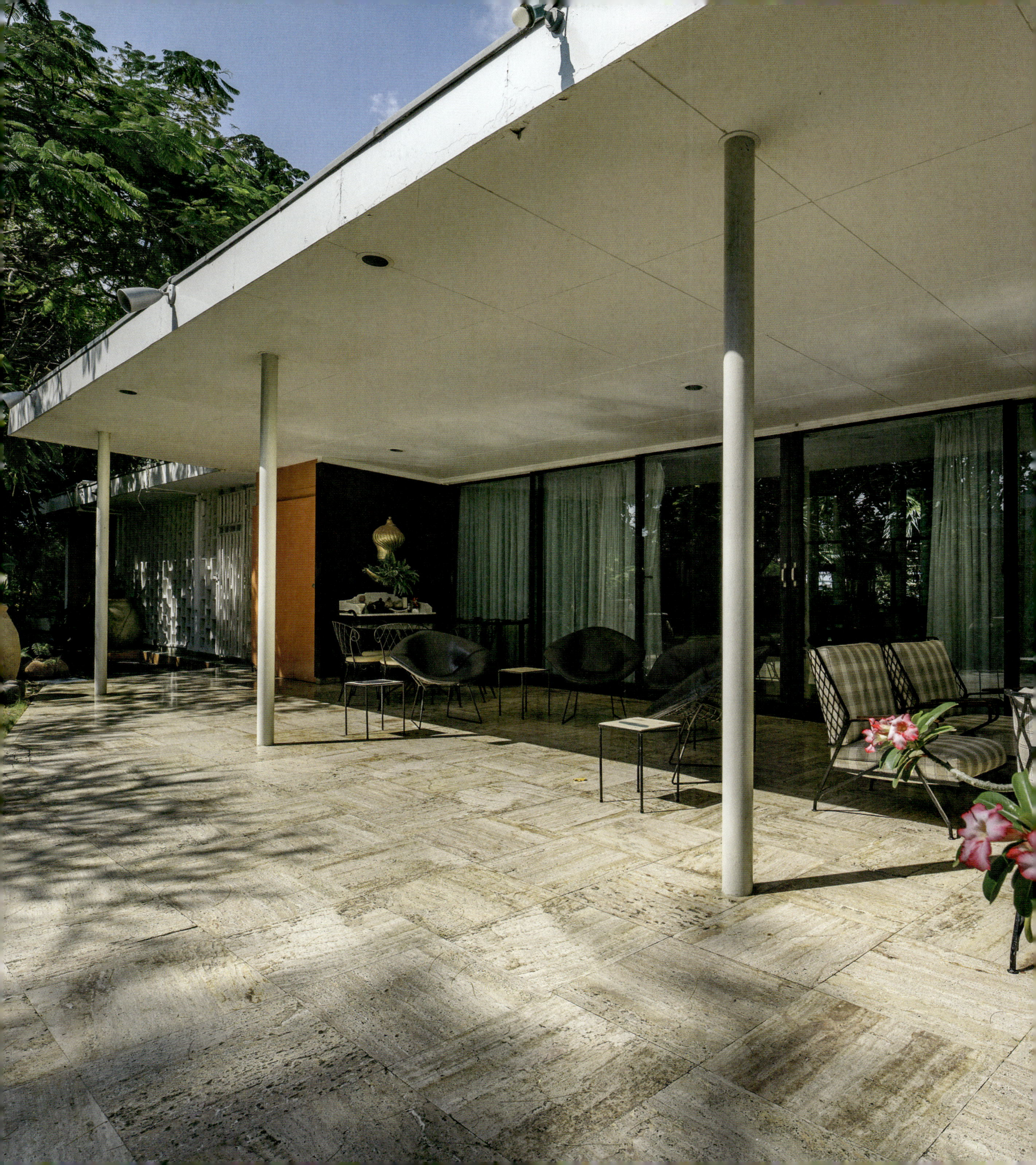

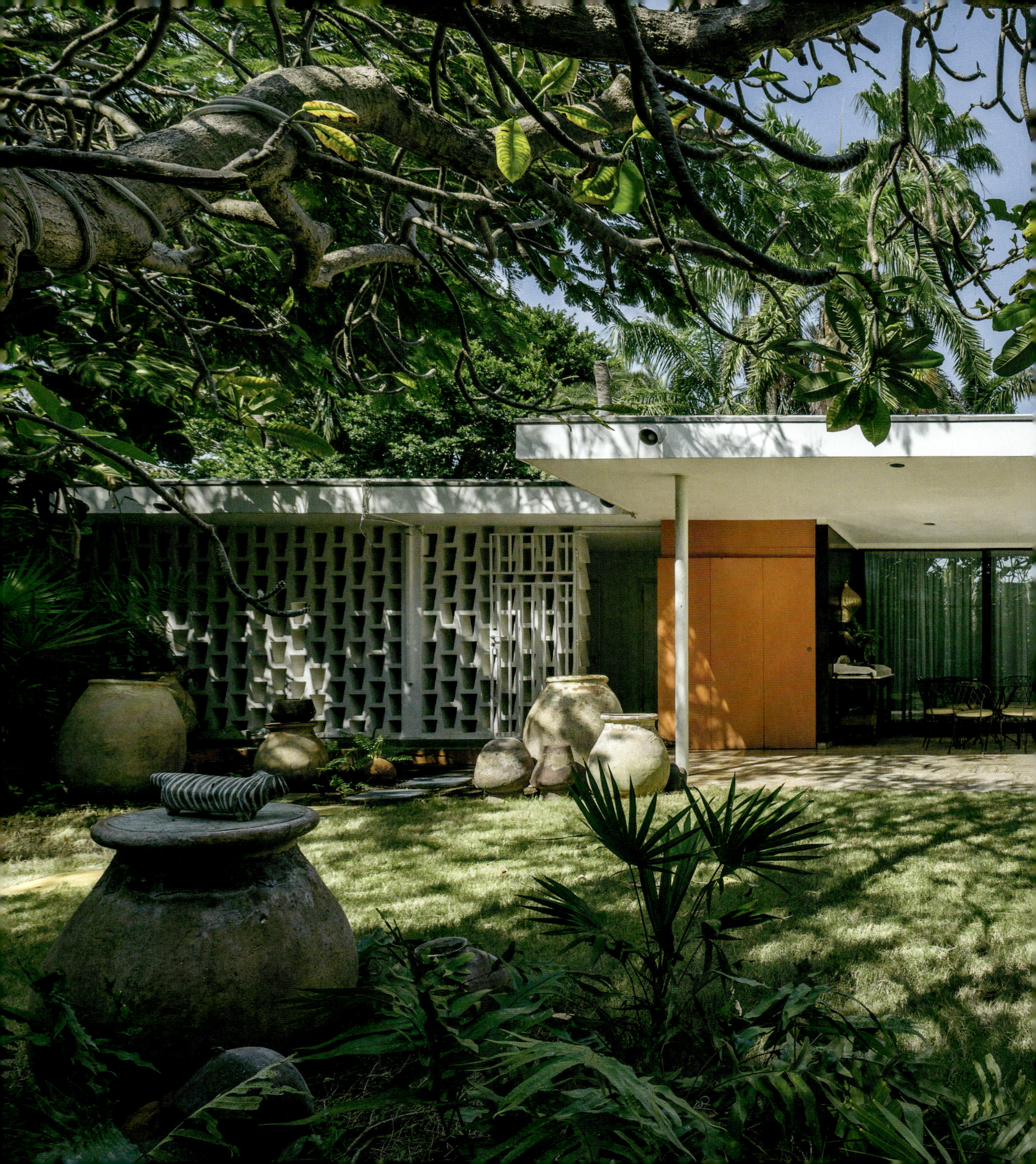

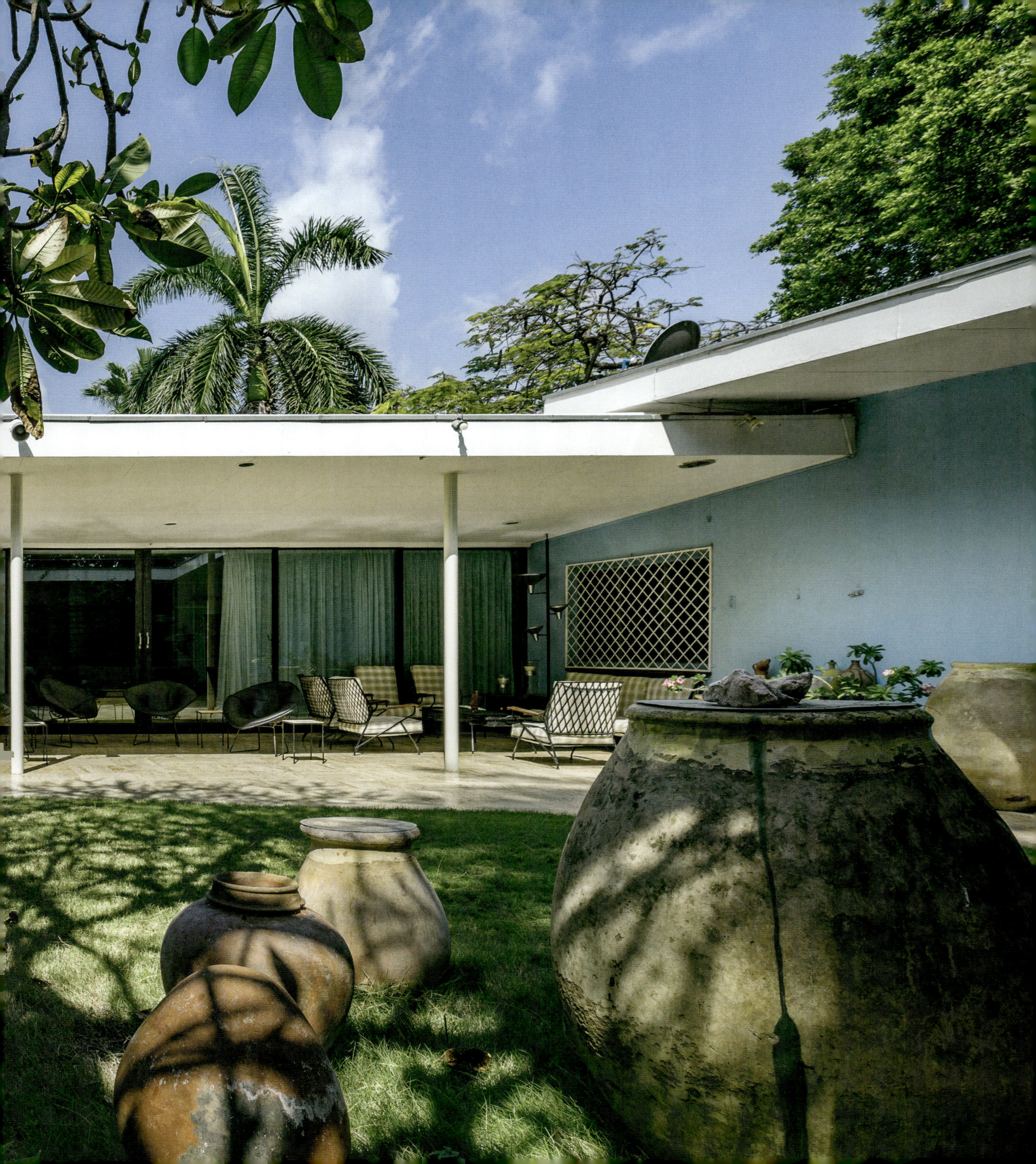

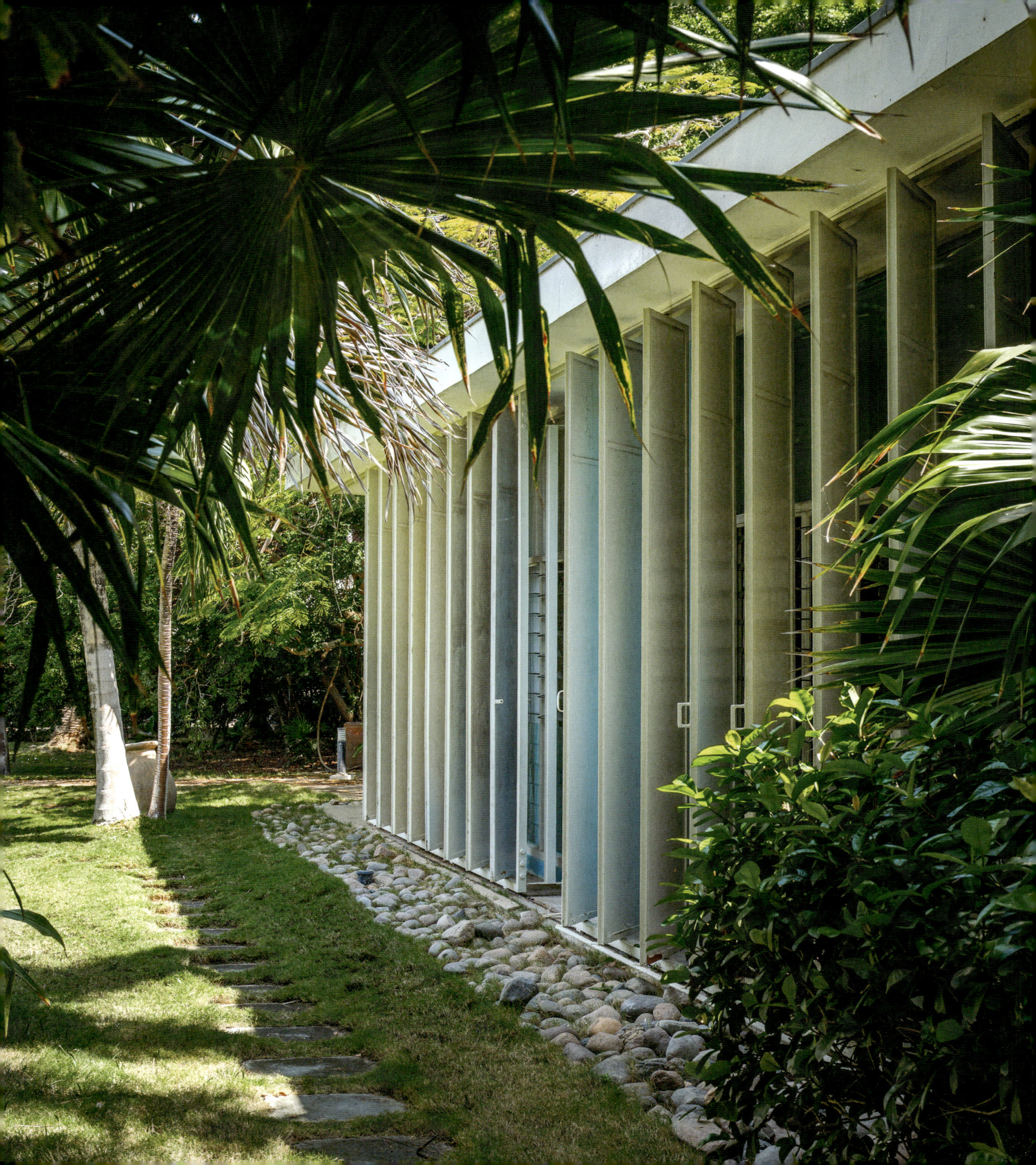

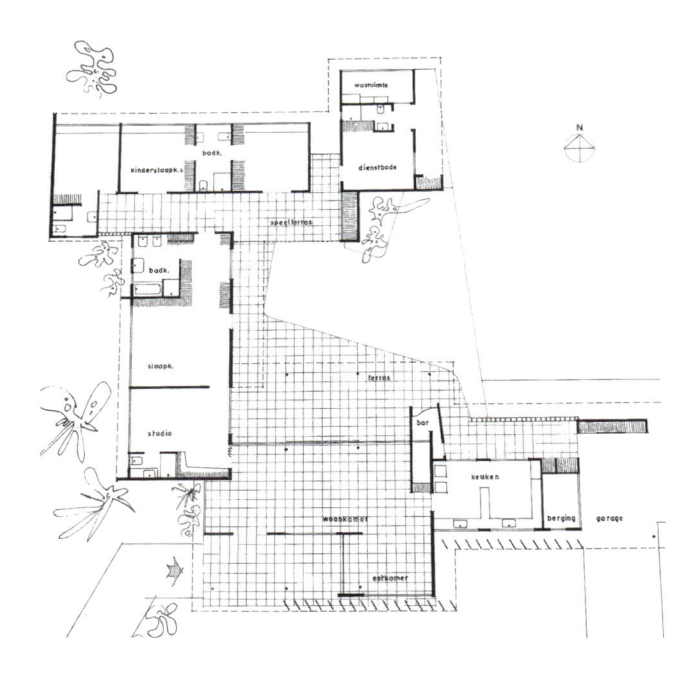

Architectural Design_

This Spritzer residence is one of Ben Smit's most successful designs and, after more than seven decades, remains largely in its original state.

Built in the spirit of the Modern Movement and adapted to the tropics, it incorporates orientation with respect to the sun and wind, ensuring optimal cross ventilation, which is of utmost importance.

The afternoon sun is kept out on the western front façade by movable vertical 'sun-breakers', the 'brise-soleil', a technique introduced by the French architect Le Corbusier. Ben Smit often used this method to prevent direct sunlight from entering the interior of the buildings. These characteristic sun-breakers, which are very eye-catching from the main road, feature an abstract painting by the architect on the exterior.

Floor Plan. Drawing: Ben Smit 1952

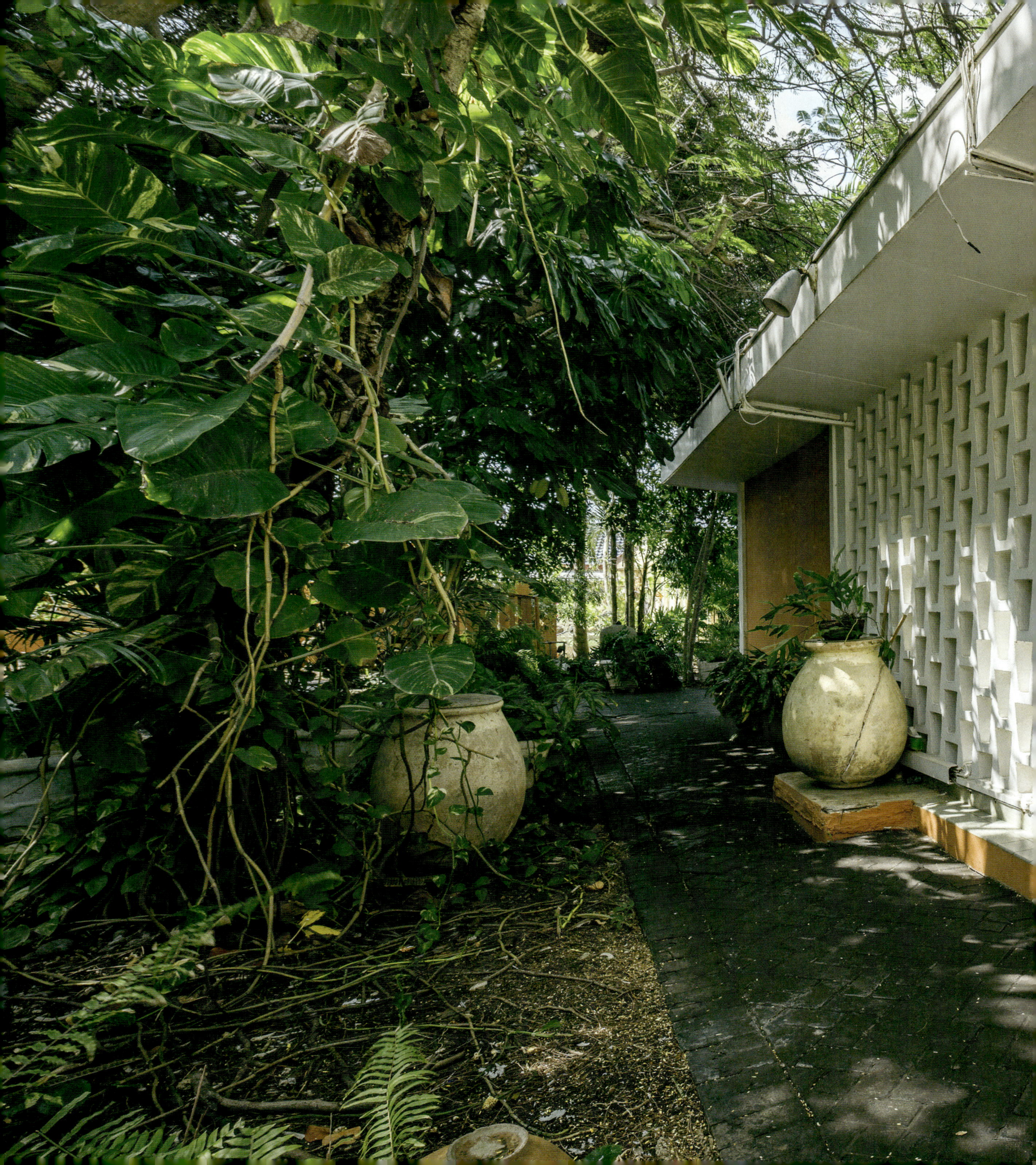

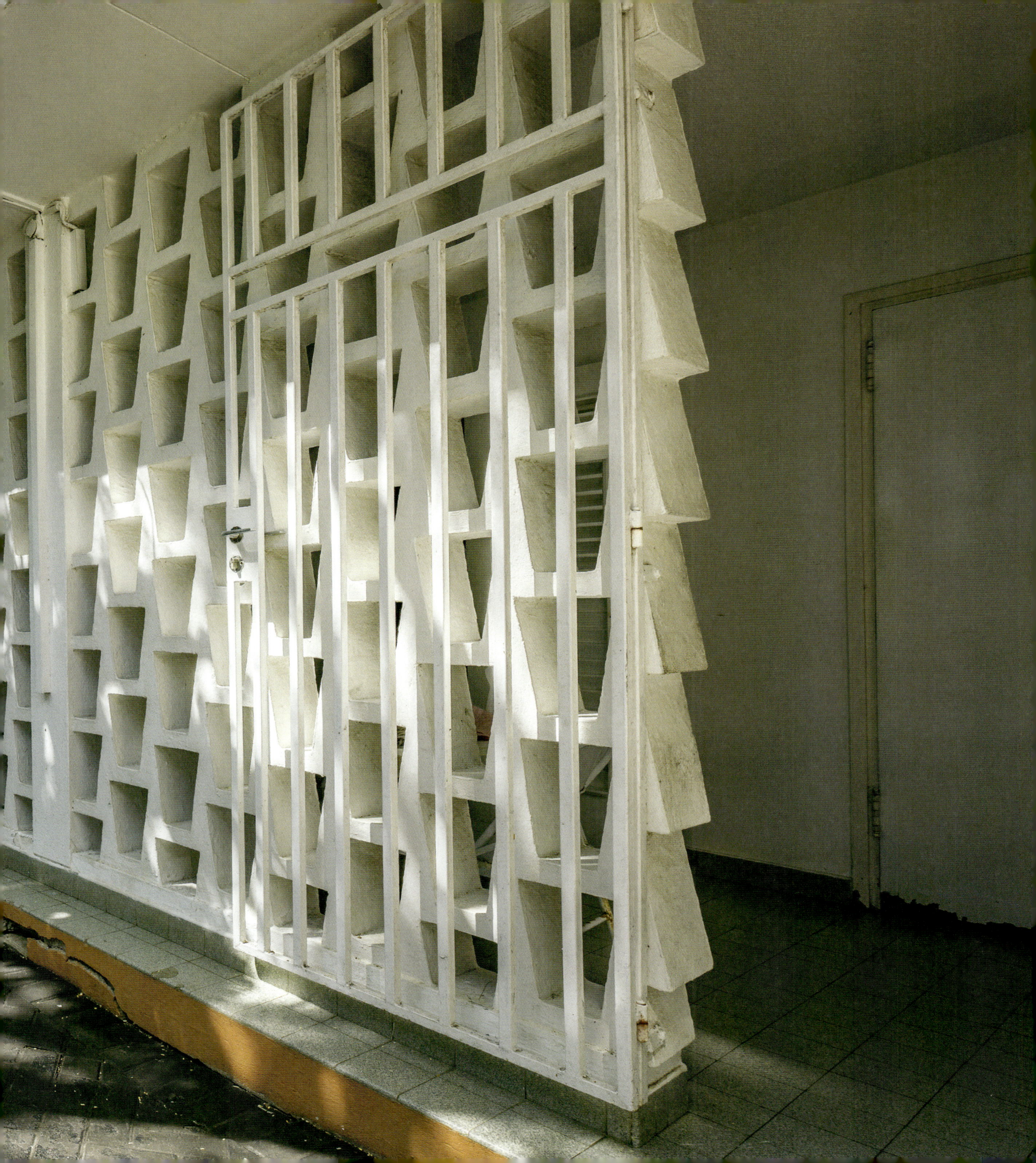

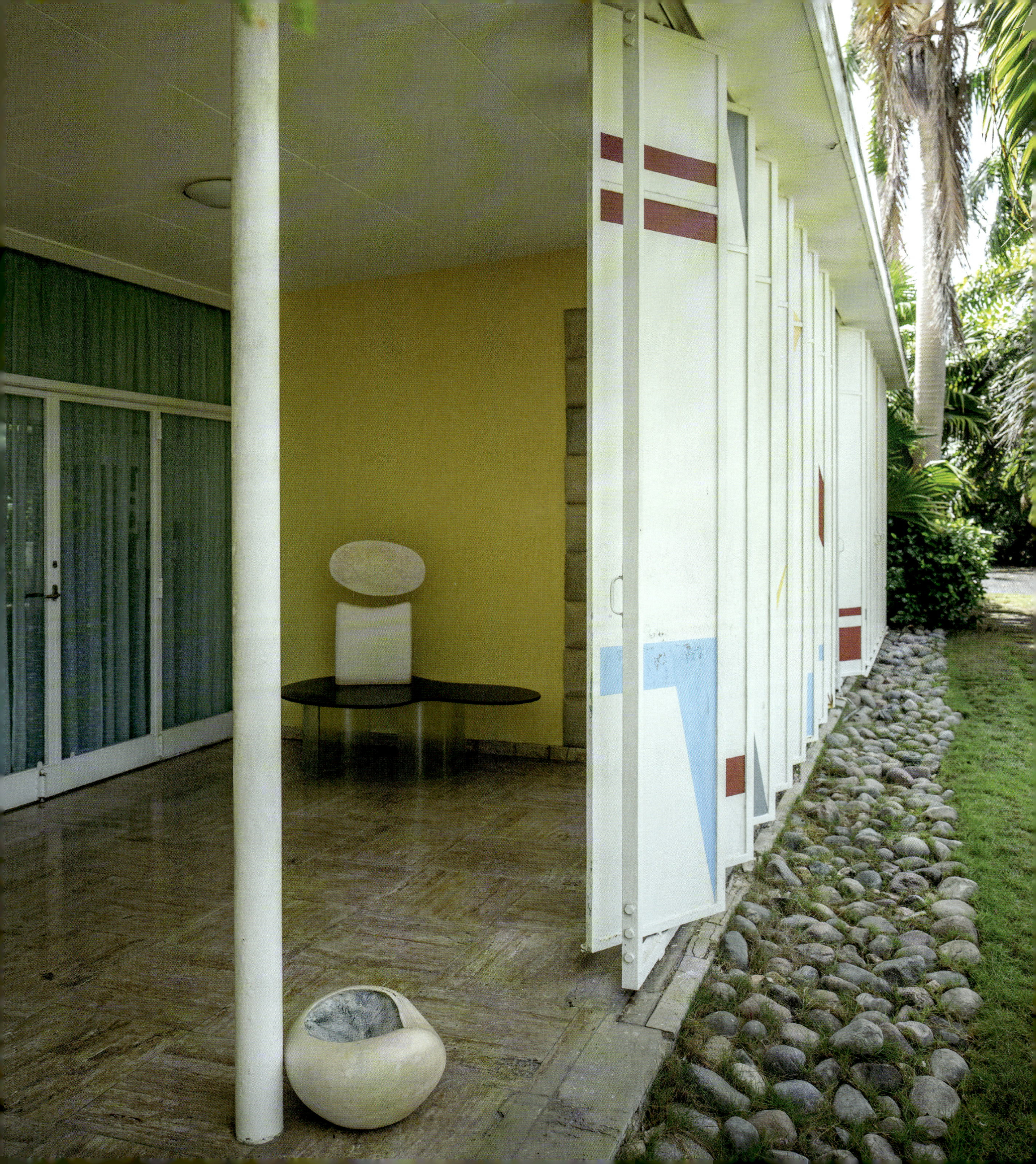

References:

- Ditzhuijzen Jeannette van (2010) *Een sjtetl in de tropen*, Amsterdam: KIT Publishers
- Fonk, Hans et. al. (1999) *Curaçao Architectuur & Stijl*. Curaçao: Stichting Curaçao Style,
- Fonk, Hans et. al. (2004) *Curaçao Dutch Caribbean Architecture & Style*. Curaçao: Curaçao Style Foundation.
- Gill, Ronald G. (2008) *Een eeuw architectuur op Curaçao*. Curaçao: Ronald G. Gill, (Original work published 1999)
- Klaus, Dennis (2009). BEN SMIT, a personal note, *The impact of Caribbean Modern Architecture, First regional DOCOMOMO seminar, hosted by the University of the Netherlands Antilles*, Curaçao, pp. 56-59
- Smit, Ben (2002). *Projecten Curaçao 1946 – 1969*. Curaçao: Ben Smit

Description_

The house is situated on the corner of Schout bij Nacht Doormanweg and Reigerweg, on a spacious site with many trees, which has a cooling effect on the living environment. The layout of the house is U-shaped, formed by several fairly loose building blocks, grouped around a terrace, enabling cross ventilation in all rooms. The different sections of the building are visually connected by the roofs.

The living and dining rooms are located on the west of the terrace, featuring ceiling-high windows and large glass sliding doors for daylighting. The living space integrates seamlessly with the front and rear terraces when the doors are open. Above the rear outdoor terrace, a spacious overhanging lightweight roof is supported by slender steel columns, emphasizing the Modern Movement principle of lightness. Beneath the kitchen, there is a cistern used for collecting rainwater, which is then used for cleaning and washing purposes.

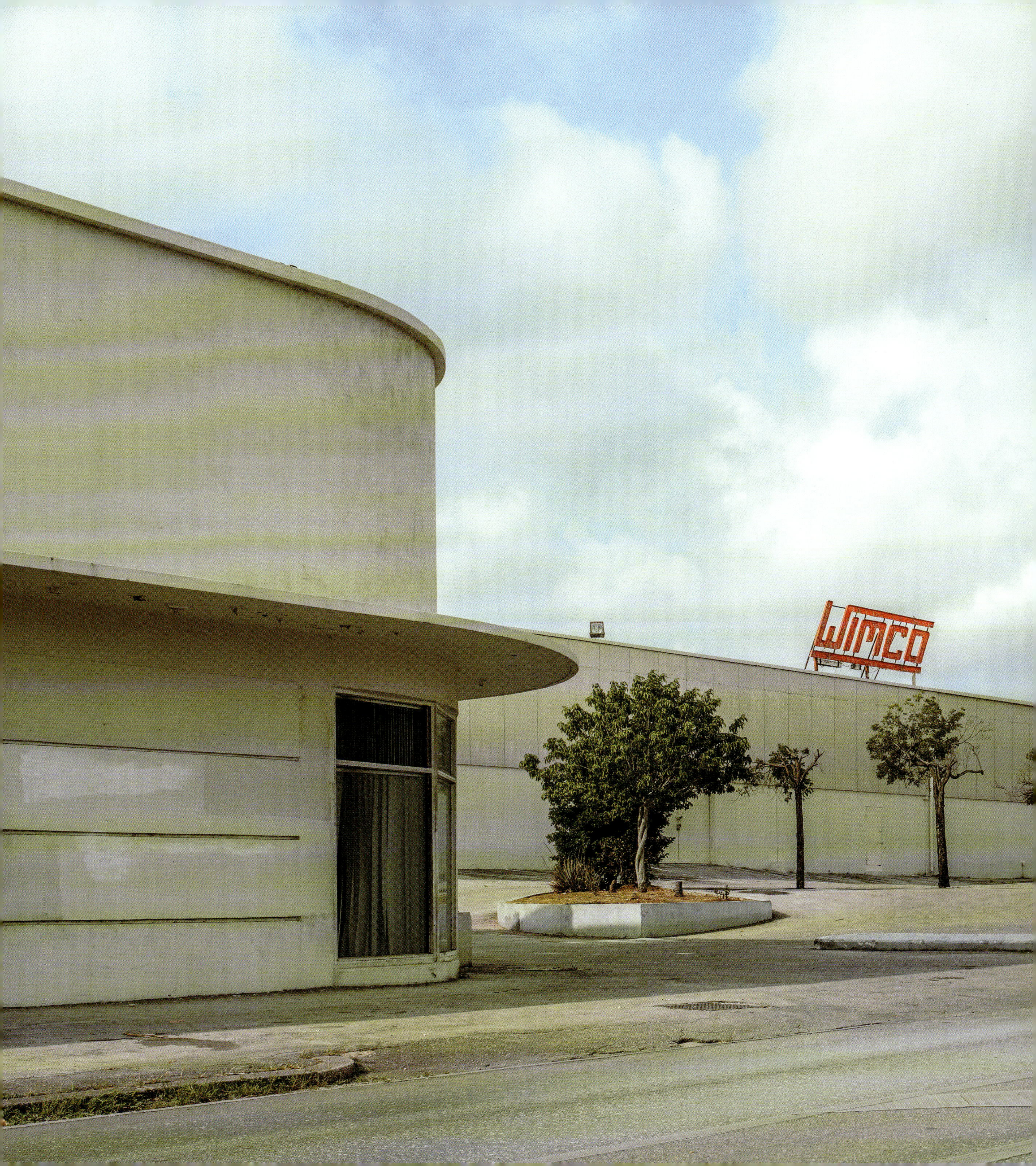
WIMCO

National grid reference: **12°06′21.4″N 68°54′44.2″W**

19.
PALAIS ROYAL
WIMCO_

SALIÑA

National Archive Curaçao / Coll. Fisher

Above the glass windows, broad concrete canopies were constructed to provide sun protection.

Historic Background_

In the 1950's, the economy of Curaçao was doing well due to the oil industry. Many businesses, including those originally located in the old center of Willemstad, relocated to the outskirts, particularly to the newly developed suburbs like the Saliña area. This neighborhood saw the establishment of several car showrooms selling American cars. One notable showroom was Palais Royal, the agent for Chrysler, Plymouth, and Fargo trucks. This enterprise was initiated by businessmen A. Moron and F. Brandao. The showroom, along with its garage and parking space, officially opened on May 16, 1953. (Amigoe, May 18, 1953).

Later, the building was sold to the West India Mercantile Company BV (WIMCO), which originally operated a store in the old center of Willemstad. In Saliña, WIMCO started a retail business in electrical household appliances, air-conditioning units, electronic devices, and commercial equipment. It grew into the largest appliance store in Curaçao. However, in 2019, WIMCO was declared bankrupt and closed its doors. The building was sold in 2021 and is currently awaiting redevelopment.

Architectural Design_

The modern 2000 m² showroom was designed by Pieter A. van Stuivenberg, a Dutch engineer who was a manager at the Technical Department of the "Landswatervoorzieningsdienst" (LWV), the Governmental Department for Water Supply. Besides designing for the LWV, he also worked for private clients. Many of Van Stuivenberg's designs were inspired by the so-called Miami Beach Art Deco movement in architecture, with the most notable example being the Cinelandia Cinema in the center of Willemstad. The showroom itself is simple in design, yet it clearly incorporates Art Deco elements. It was built by the then well-known contractor of Italian origin, Giovanni Pizziolo.

Description_

The building is situated at the corner of Saliña and Grebbelinieweg, with the location accentuated by a curved facade. This curved façade is flanked by vertical wall sections that project outward. Initially all of the façades of the showroom featured large shop windows, ensuring the cars inside were clearly visible. Above the glass windows, broad concrete canopies were constructed to provide sun protection. Unfortunately, part of the glass windows was later closed off.

References:

- Gill, Ronald G. (2008) *Een eeuw architectuur op Curaçao*. Curaçao: Ronald G. Gill, (Original work published 1999)
- Monsanto, Christel (2022) Pieter Antonie van Stuivenberg, architect. *De Archiefvriend, september 2022*

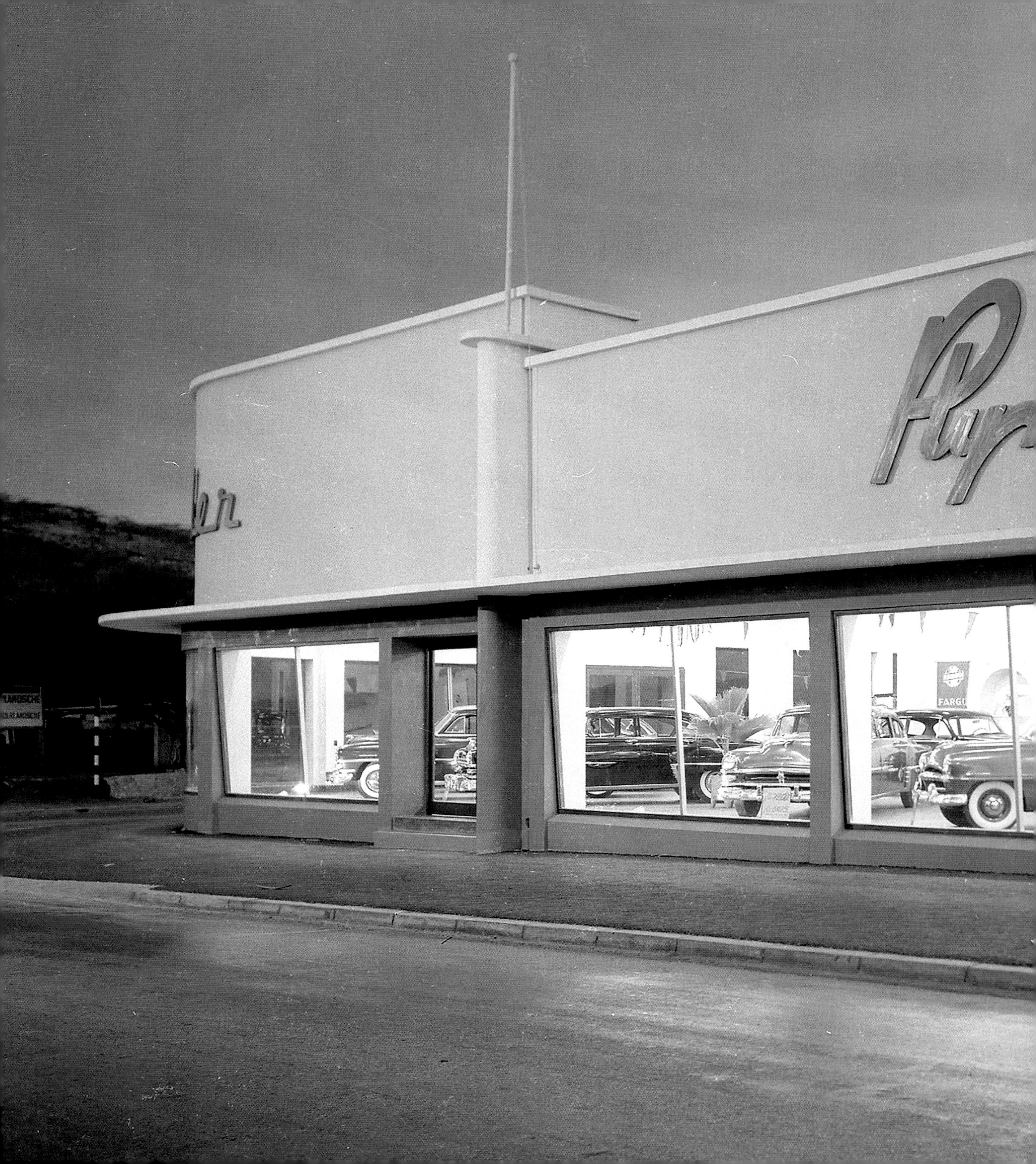
FARGO

National Archive Curaçao / Coll. Fisher

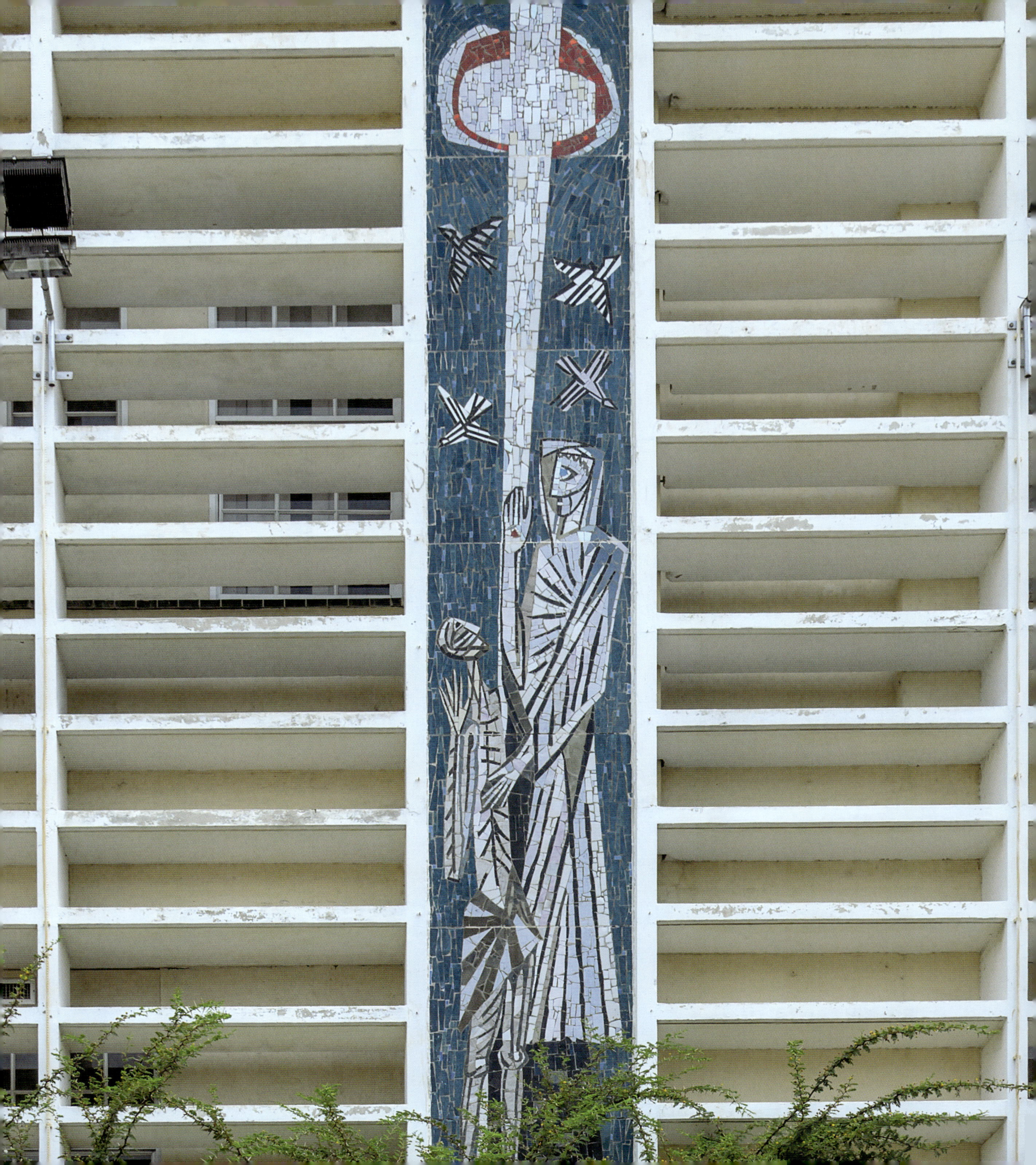

National grid reference: **12°06'30.9"N 68°56'24.2"W**

20.
ST. ELISABETH HOSPITAL - SOUTH-EAST WING_

PATER EUWENSWEG

The façades featured distinctive rotating blue aluminum vertical awnings that spanned the entire height of the floor.

National Archive Curaçao / Coll. Fisher

Historic Background_

The Catholic St. Elisabeth Hospital was the main hospital on Curaçao. Initiated by Monseigneur F.E.C. Kieckens, the first stone of the new guesthouse on the former Rifwater was laid by Governor van Lansberge in 1857. The hospital grew and modernized steadily over the ensuing century.

The original design underwent frequent and radical changes, resulting in the absence of any remaining 19th-century building parts.

From the middle of the 20th century, innovations in construction techniques and materials, along with the influence of international architectural styles, led to a transition from traditional architectural styles to modern styles such as "Nieuwe Bouwen" and Art Deco. Dutch architects, including A.J. Morel, ir. C.M. Bakker and Ben Smit, were involved in the renovations and expansions during this period.

In 1953, construction began on the last major expansion of the hospital on the east side of the complex, which opened in 1956. Initially, it had two floors. Later, in 1966-67, an additional floor was added, a provision that had been considered from the start. This section housed the children's, women's, and maternity wards.
However, with the opening of the newly built Curaçao Medical Center adjacent to it in November 2019, St. Elisabeth Hospital lost its function. Redevelopment of the complex is being studied.

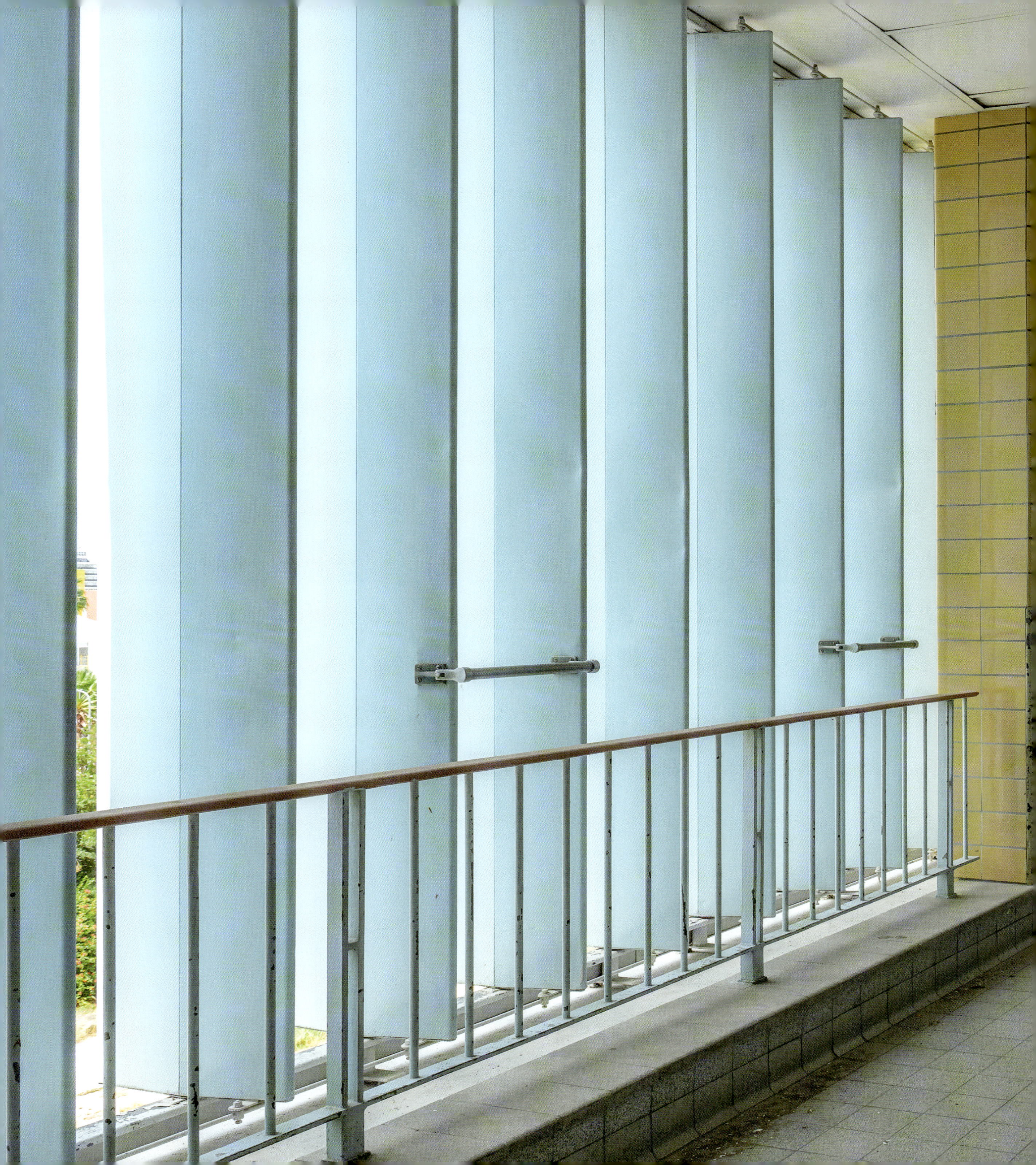

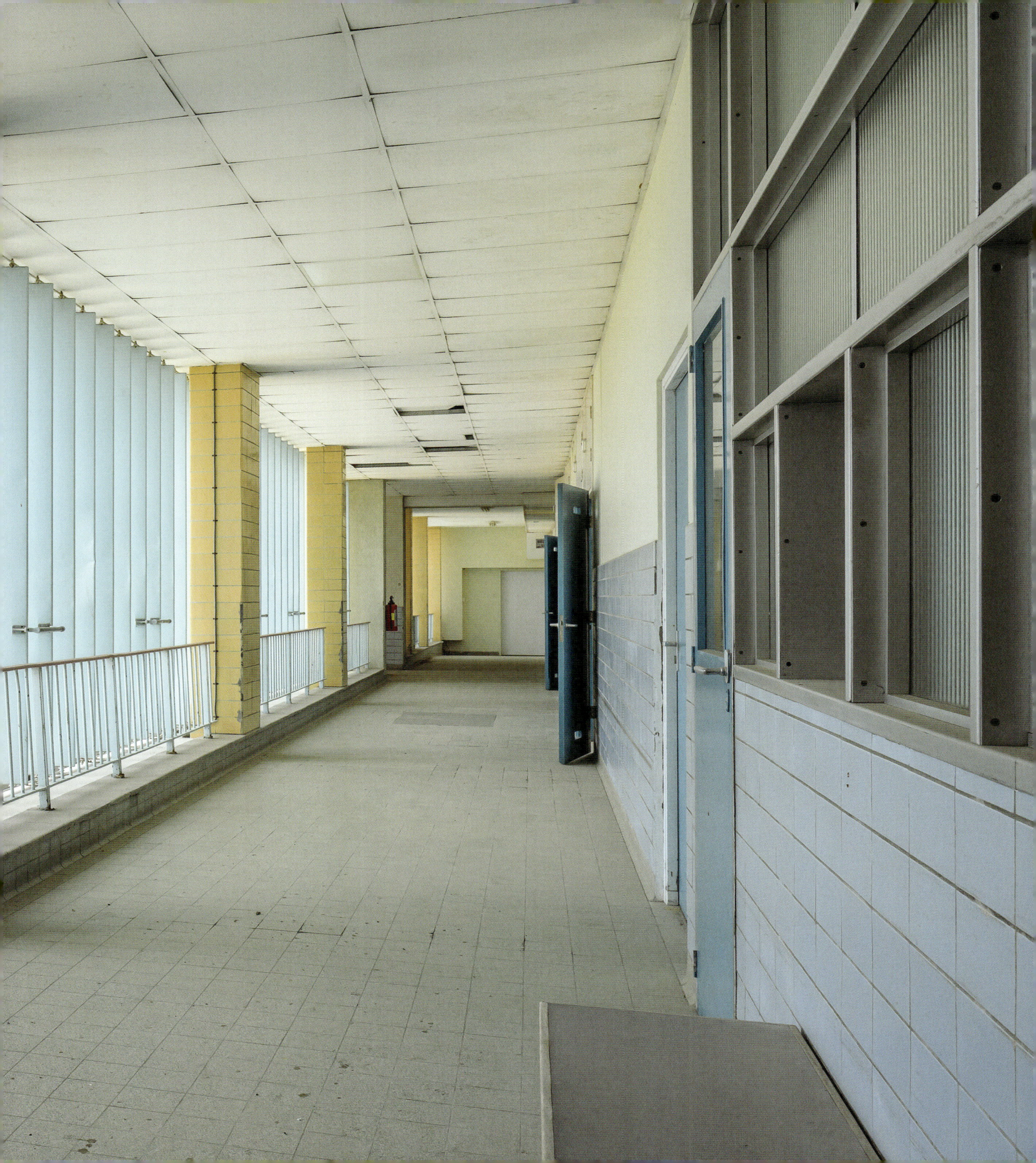

VERDIEPING

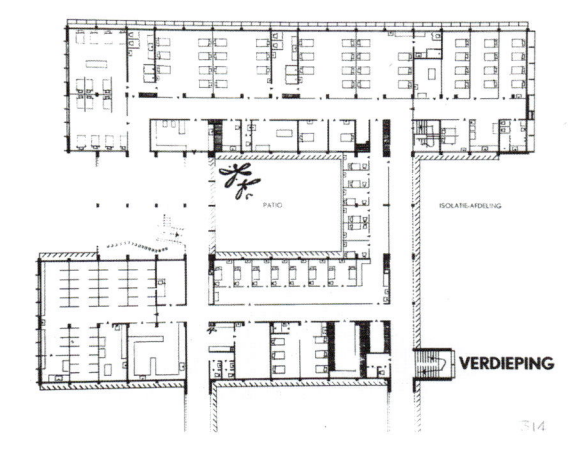

Architectural Design_

The east wing of the St. Elisabeth Hospital was designed by Ben Smit, who created several designs for the hospital during that period. Born in the Netherlands in 1922, Smit settled in Curaçao in 1943. After working for the Department of Public Works for three years, he established his own firm in 1946, becoming one of the first local architectural offices. He designed an impressive large number of buildings on the island, making him an influential architect from the 1940's until the 1960's.

Much attention has been paid to responsible tropical architecture in the design, with features such as cross ventilation and a shield against the low morning and afternoon sun. To minimize the influence of the sun, deep concrete grids were installed on the eastern façade and partly on the southern façade.

On the southern corridors facing the Pater Euwensweg, the façades featured distinctive rotating blue aluminum vertical awnings that spanned the entire height of the floor. These elements were frequently used by Ben Smit.

Vaginale spreider

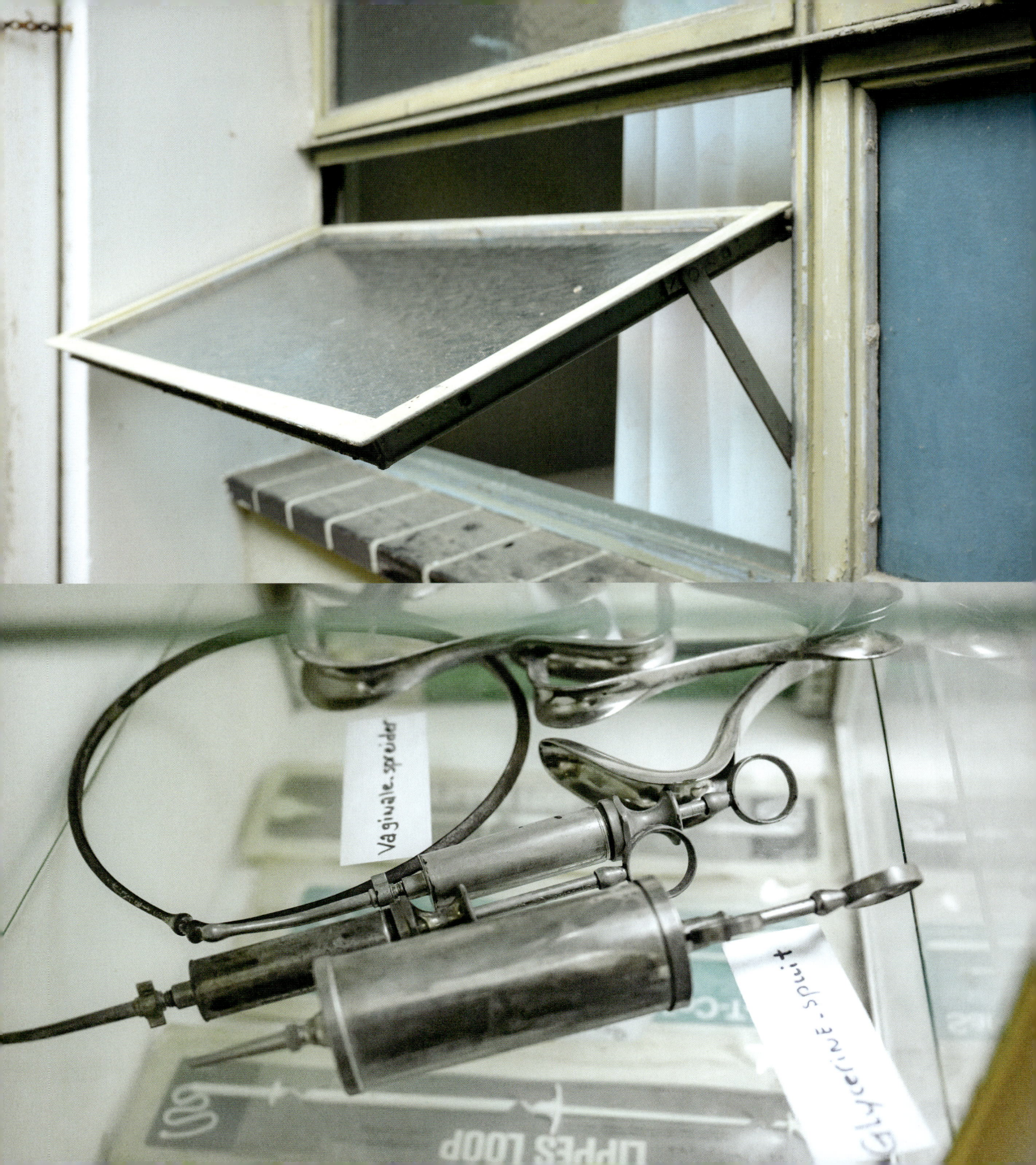

Glycerine-spuit

LIPPES LOOP

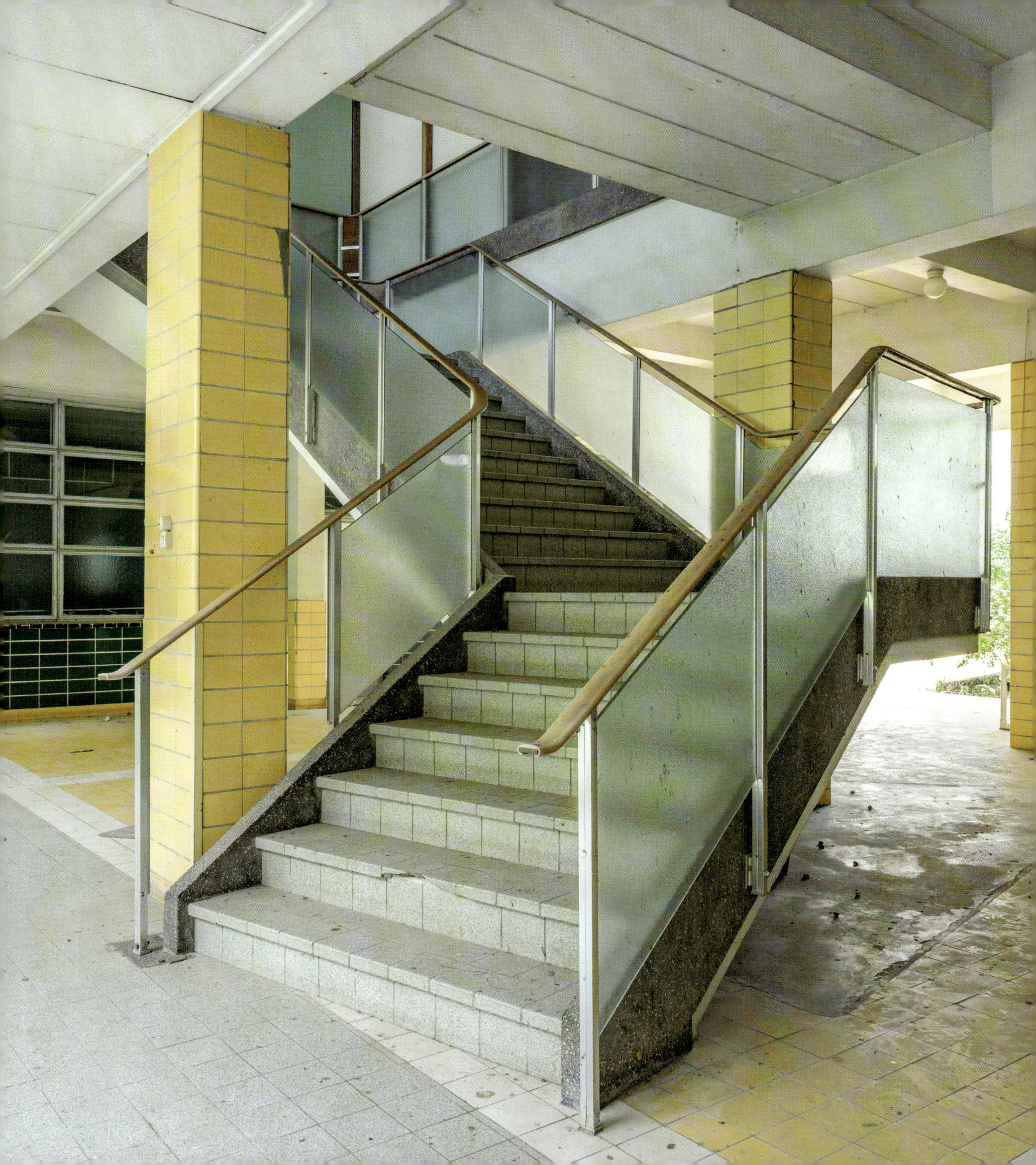

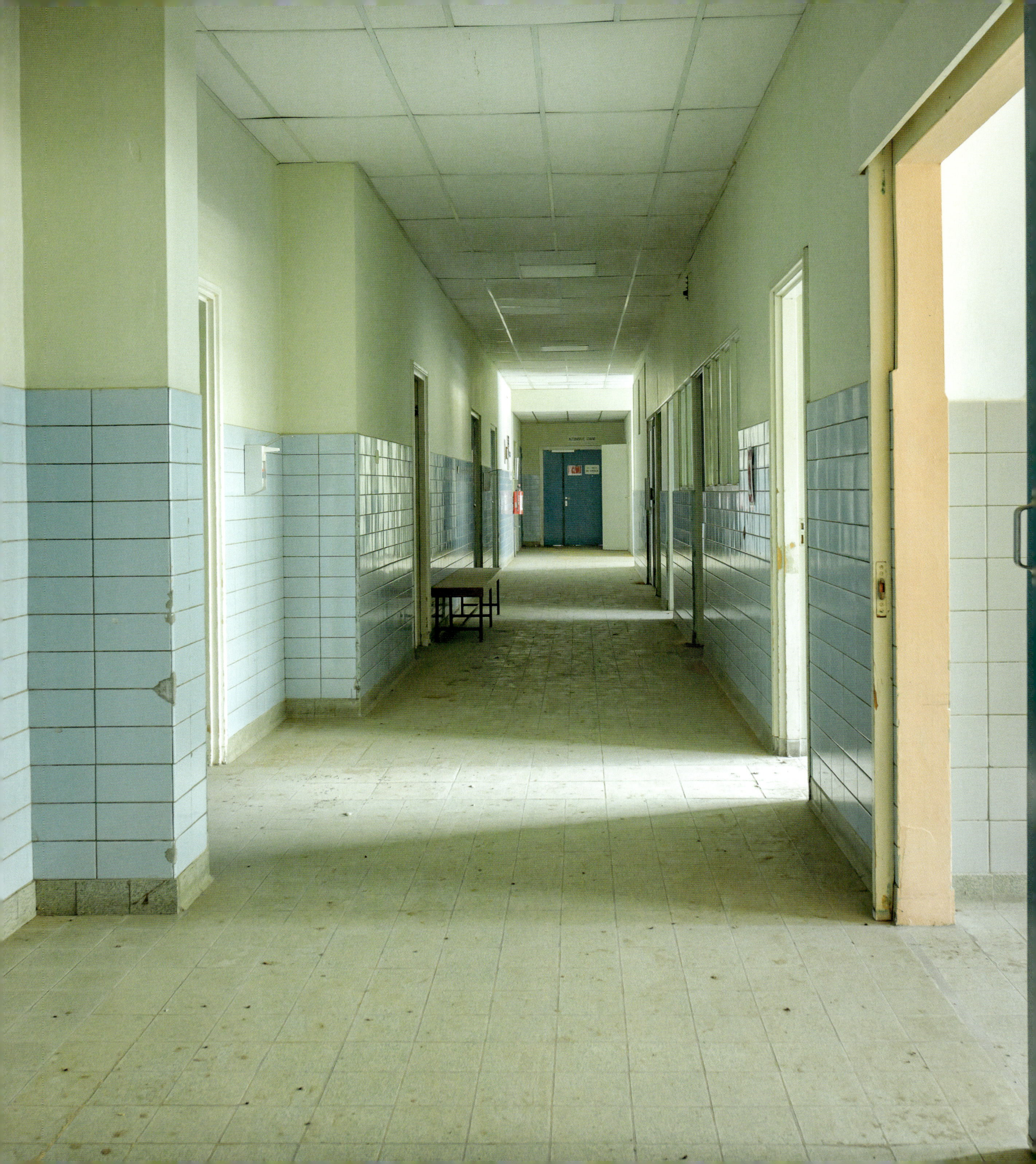

References:

- GEHLEN, Gerda (2022) *St. Elisabeth gasthuis.*
- Möhlmann o.p., M. (1955) *Stenen getuigen van honderd jaar sint elisabeth gasthuis . curaçao.* Curçao: St. Elisabeth Gasthuis
- Smit, Ben (2002). *Projecten Curaçao 1946 – 1969.* Curaçao: Ben Smit

Description_

To promote cross ventilation, patios were placed between the two wings, around which the rooms were arranged. The area surrounding the northern staircase is left completely open to the outside. Part of it was designed as a children's playground enclosed by low security glass panels. Originally, the windows and room partitions were made of steel with panels of clear or frosted glass. The windows were designed with an ingenious tilt system.

Against the main southern façade, between the concrete grids, a narrow vertical tile tableau was added with an image of Saint Francis of Assisi. Recognizable by the stigmata (wounds) in his hands and feet, Saint Francis is the patron saint of the Sisters of Breda. The birds and the leper at his feet are also characteristic attributes of Saint Francis. The tableau was created by the Rotterdam artist Valdemar (Wally) Hansen Elenbaas (1912-2008).

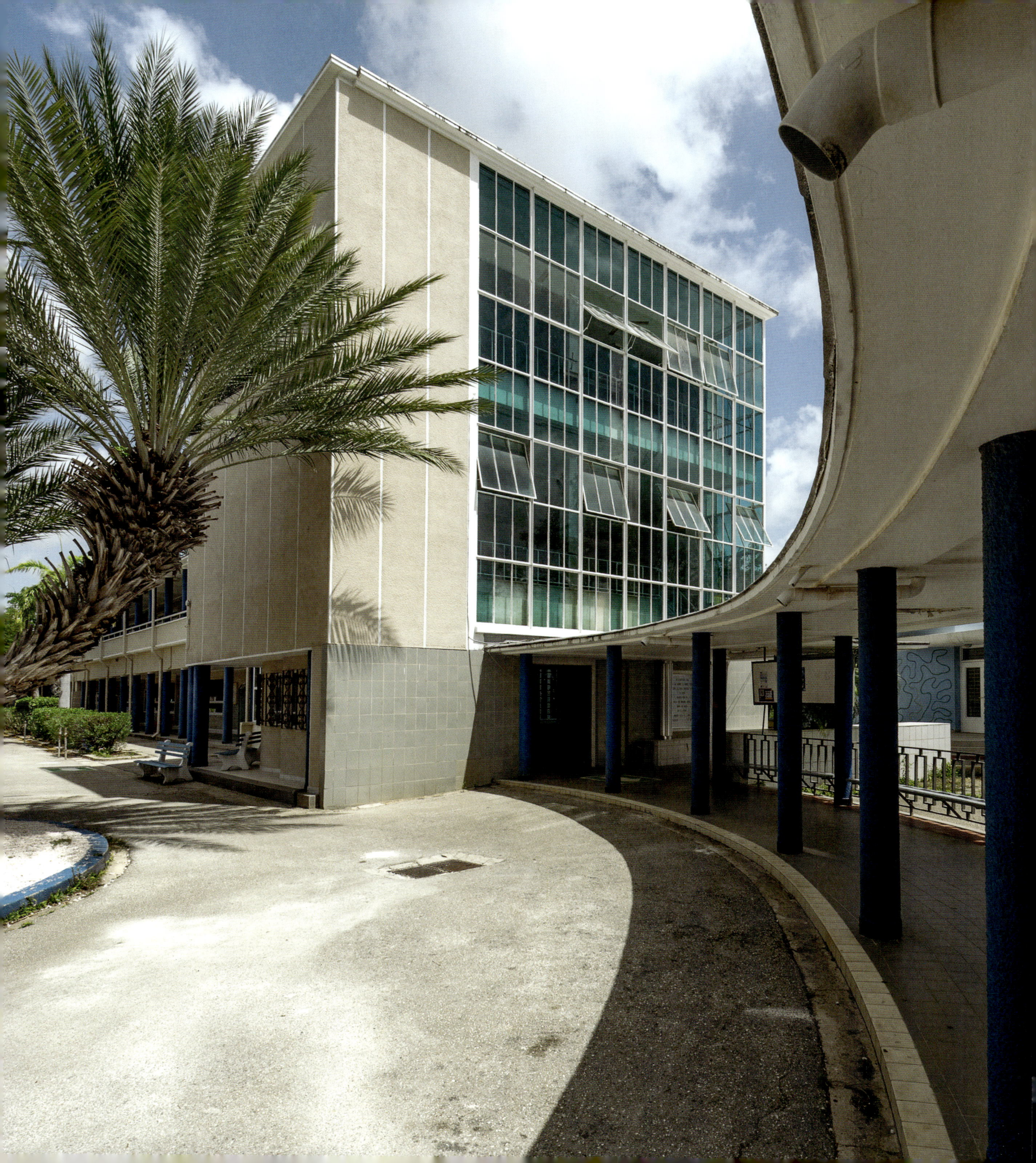

National grid reference: **12°08'19.8"N 68°54'23.4"W**

21. PETER STUYVESANT COLLEGE
KOLEGIO ALEJANDRO PAULA_

SCHOTTEGATWEG NOORD 105

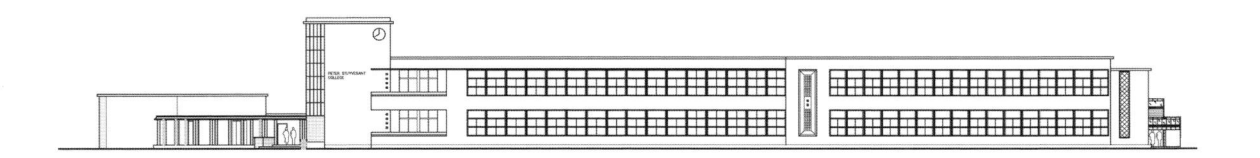

Kolegio Alejandro Paula. Drawing: IMD Design / Rosberg Engineering, 2016

National Archive Curaçao / Coll. Fisher

Characteristic elements of the school include the semi-circular, fully open gallery with benches that connect the high- and low-rise buildings.

Historic Background_

The population of Curaçao quadrupled in the first half of the 20th century due to industrialization. In the decades after the Second World War, large projects such as a new harbor, public housing, and infrastructure were realized. A school building program was established to construct the necessary new school facilities, resulting in the construction of both Catholic and public secondary schools.

One of these schools was Peter Stuyvesant College, which was renamed Kolegio Alejandro Paula in 2011. It is a public secondary school. In January 1952, it was decided to locate the school on the (then) northern outskirts of Willemstad. The school opened on September 6, 1954.

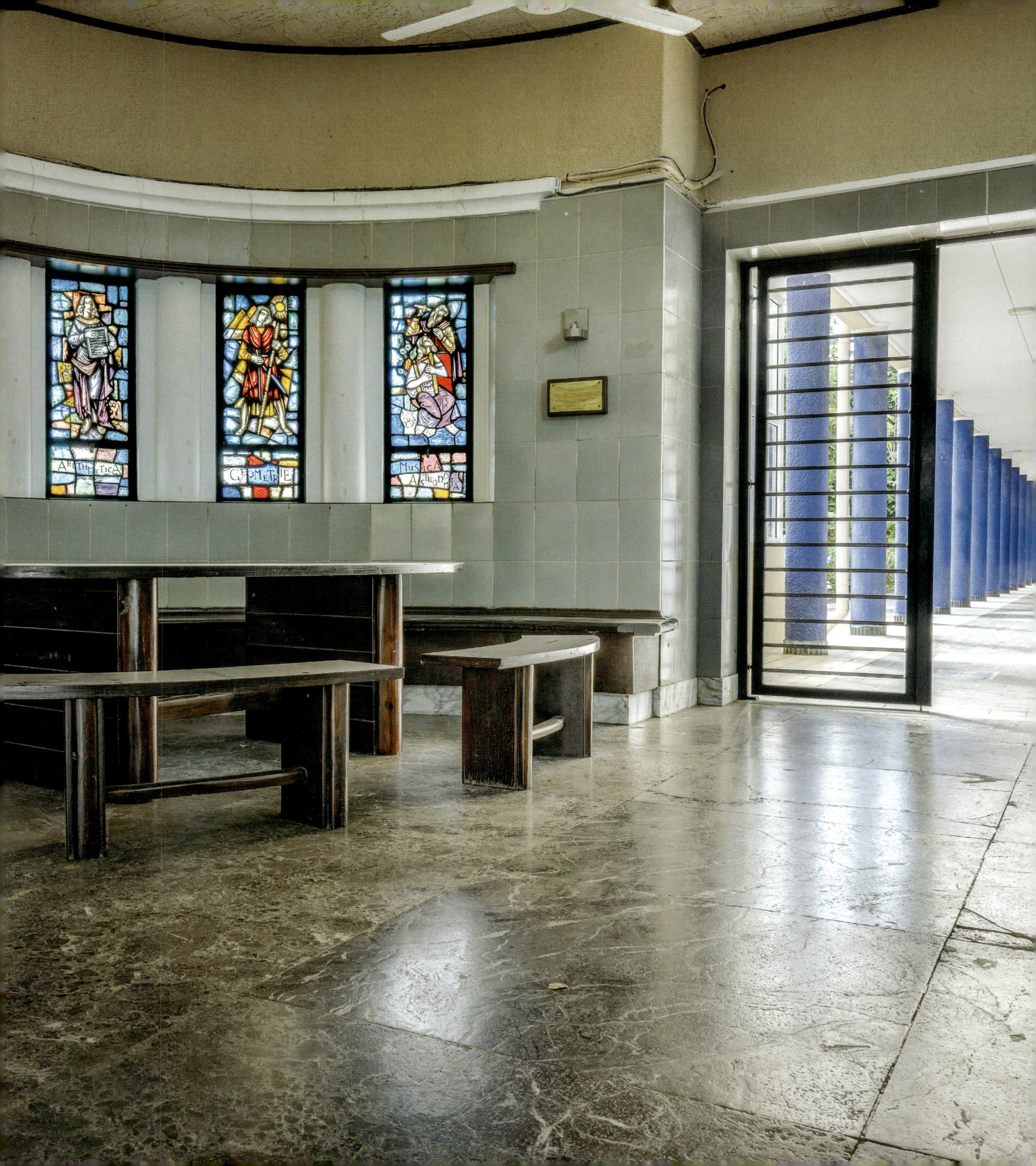
ARITHMETICA
GEOMETRIE
MUSICA
ASTRONOMIA

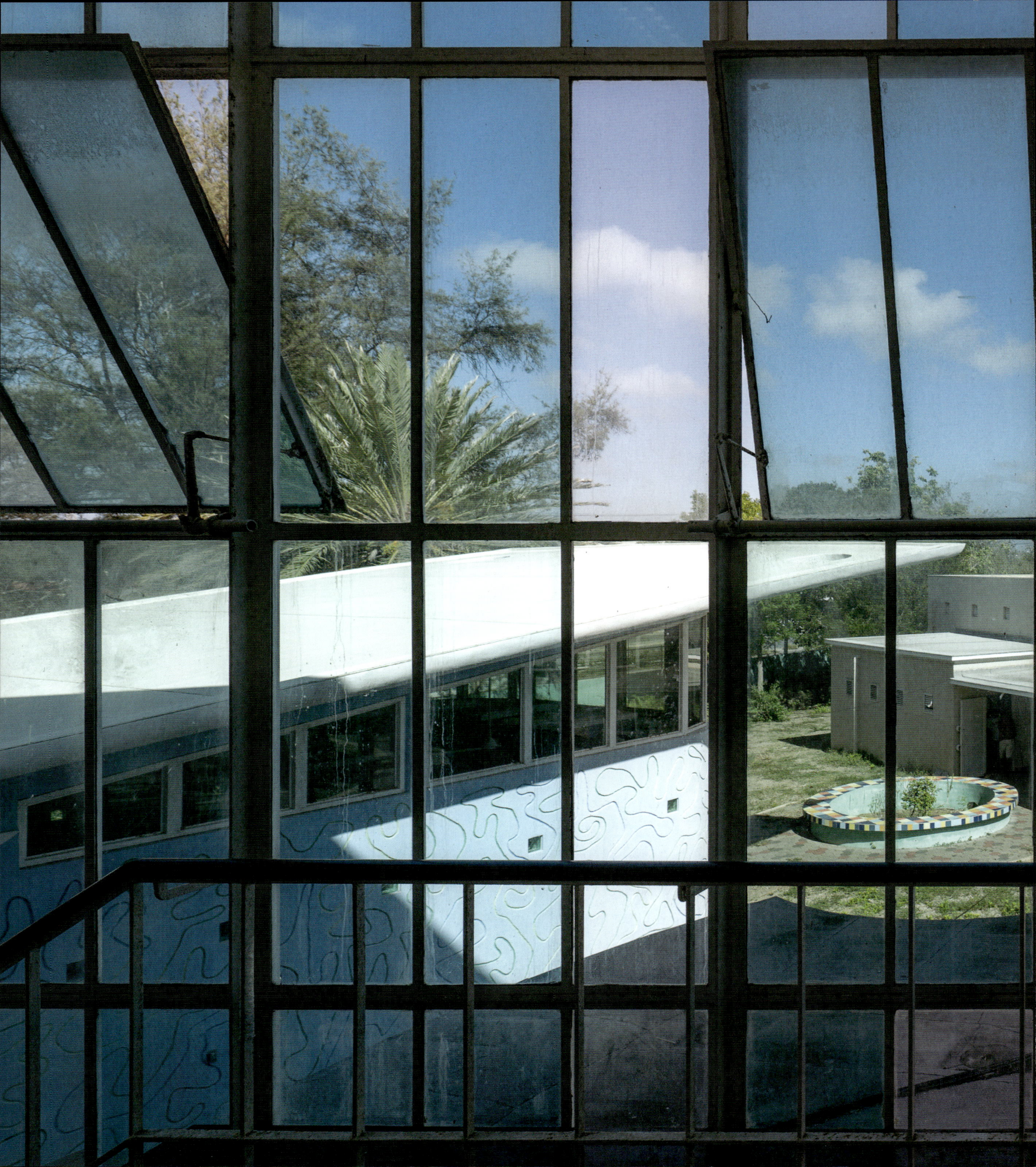

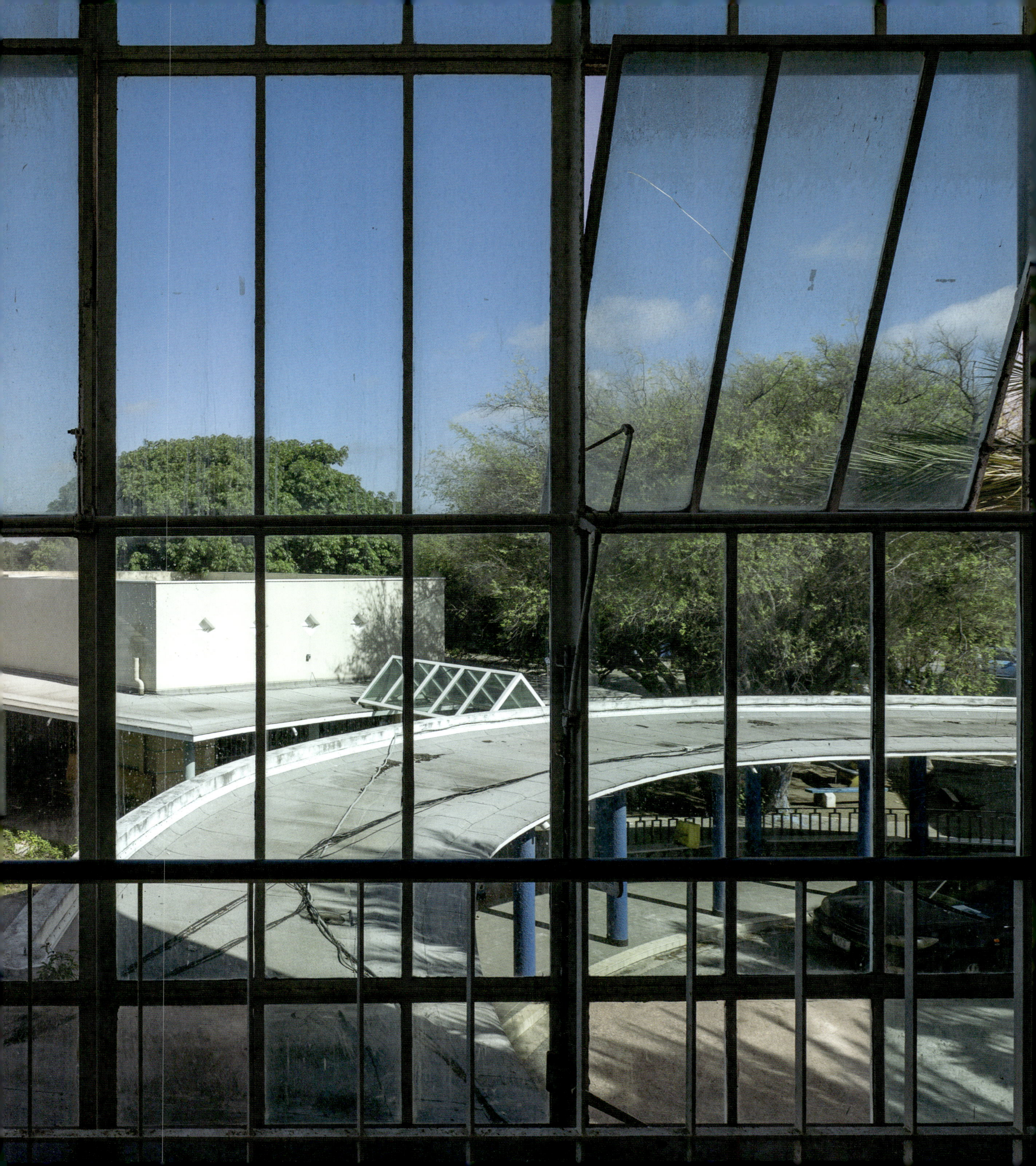

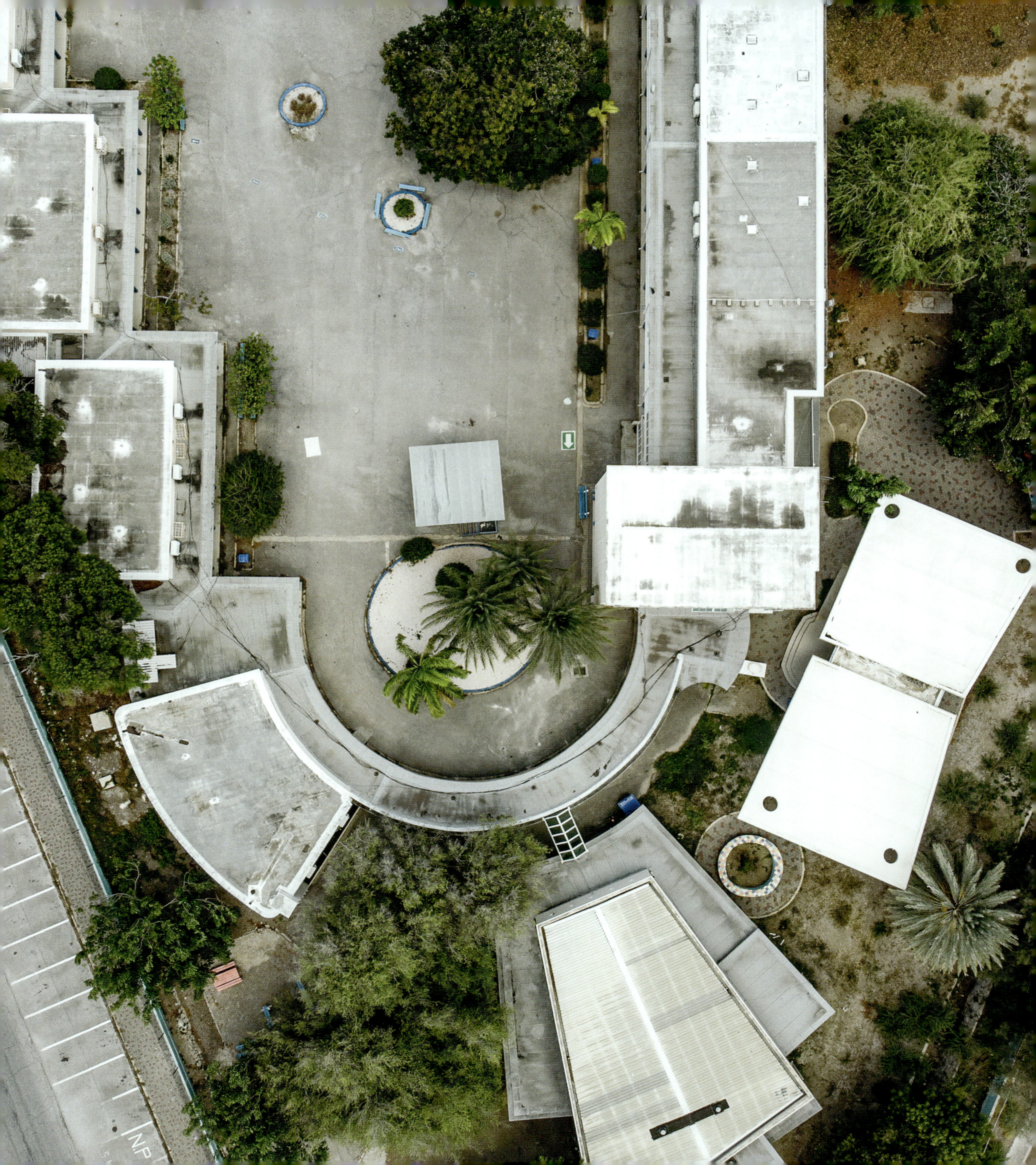

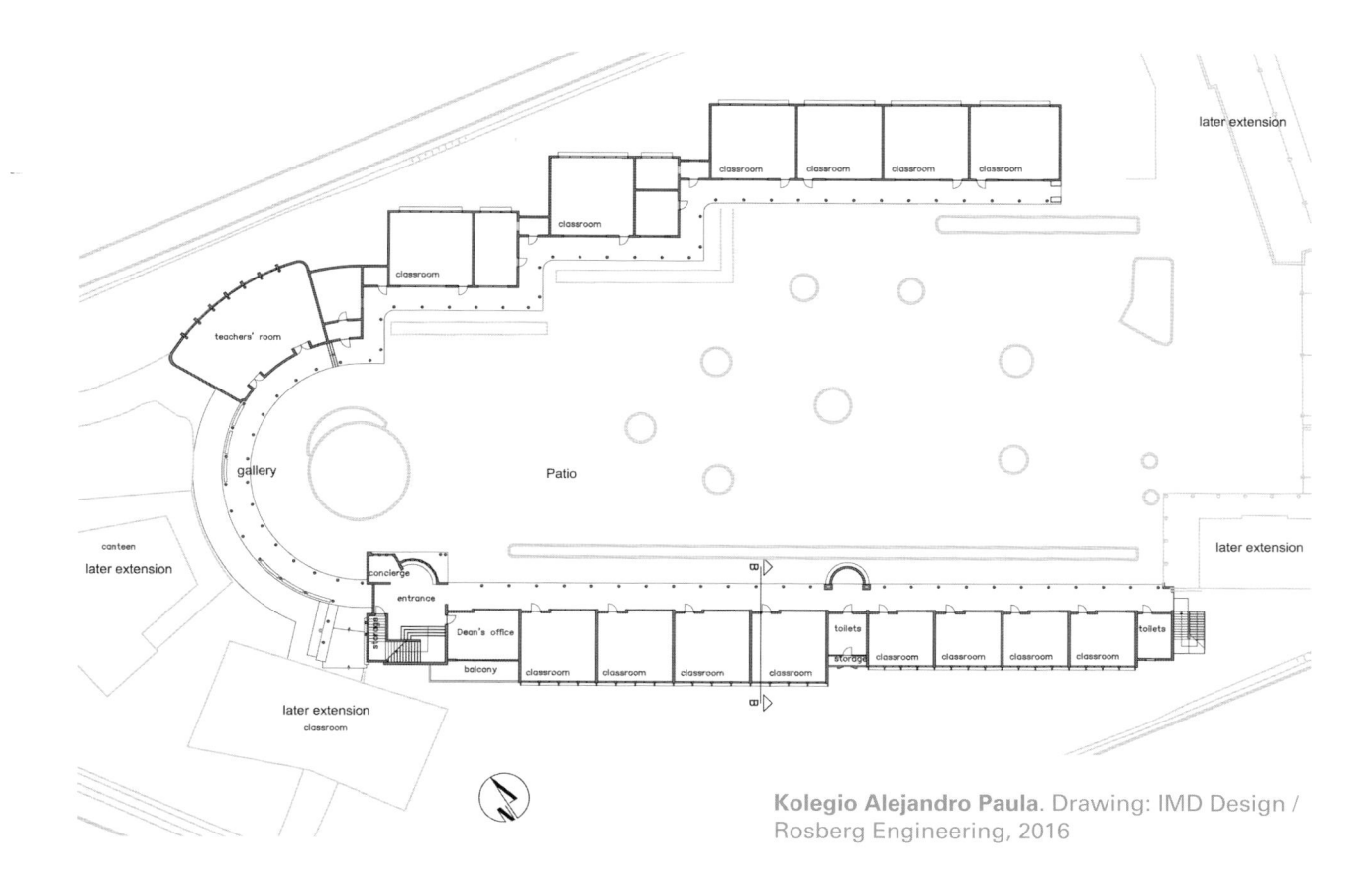

Kolegio Alejandro Paula. Drawing: IMD Design / Rosberg Engineering, 2016

Architectural Design_

The school was designed by Ir. Anton de Vries, an architect at the Public Works Department. During his career there, he designed several schools on the island, including Radulphus College, another secondary school that opened a year earlier. Notably, the Radulphus College, a Catholic institution, features more traditional architecture, while Peter Stuyvesant College, a public school, showcases a modern architectural style. Despite this contrast, there are various similarities in detail between these two schools.

The original assignment was to design a school with 16 classrooms and 6 classrooms for practical instructions, along with additional supporting rooms for the school principal, teachers, toilets, etc. The school is an example of the Dutch Modern Movement architectural style known as "Nieuwe Bouwen", adapted to the tropics.

The designer took into account the prevailing eastern wind direction when situating the various blocks. To achieve this, the building blocks were slightly rotated in relation to the elongated construction site. All classrooms were interconnected by wide galleries, which also provided ample shaded areas.

Along the long southwestern façade of the two-story building, in front of the 16 classrooms, a concrete grid, known as "brise-soleil" as the Swiss-French architect Le Corbusier called them, was added to provide shade.

Behind this grid, large pivoting glass windows were positioned to maximize ventilation within the classrooms.

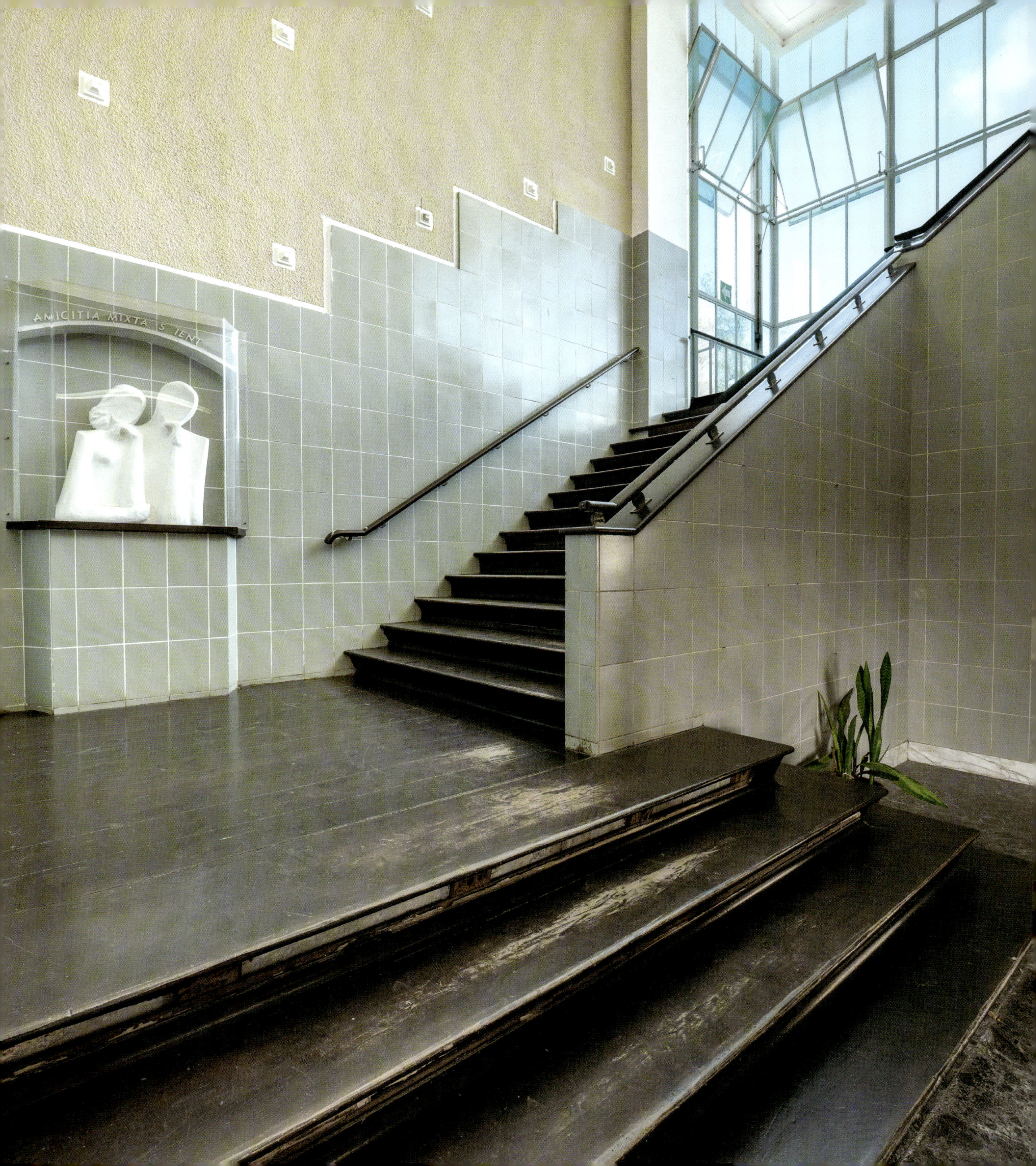
AMICITIA MIXTA S IENT

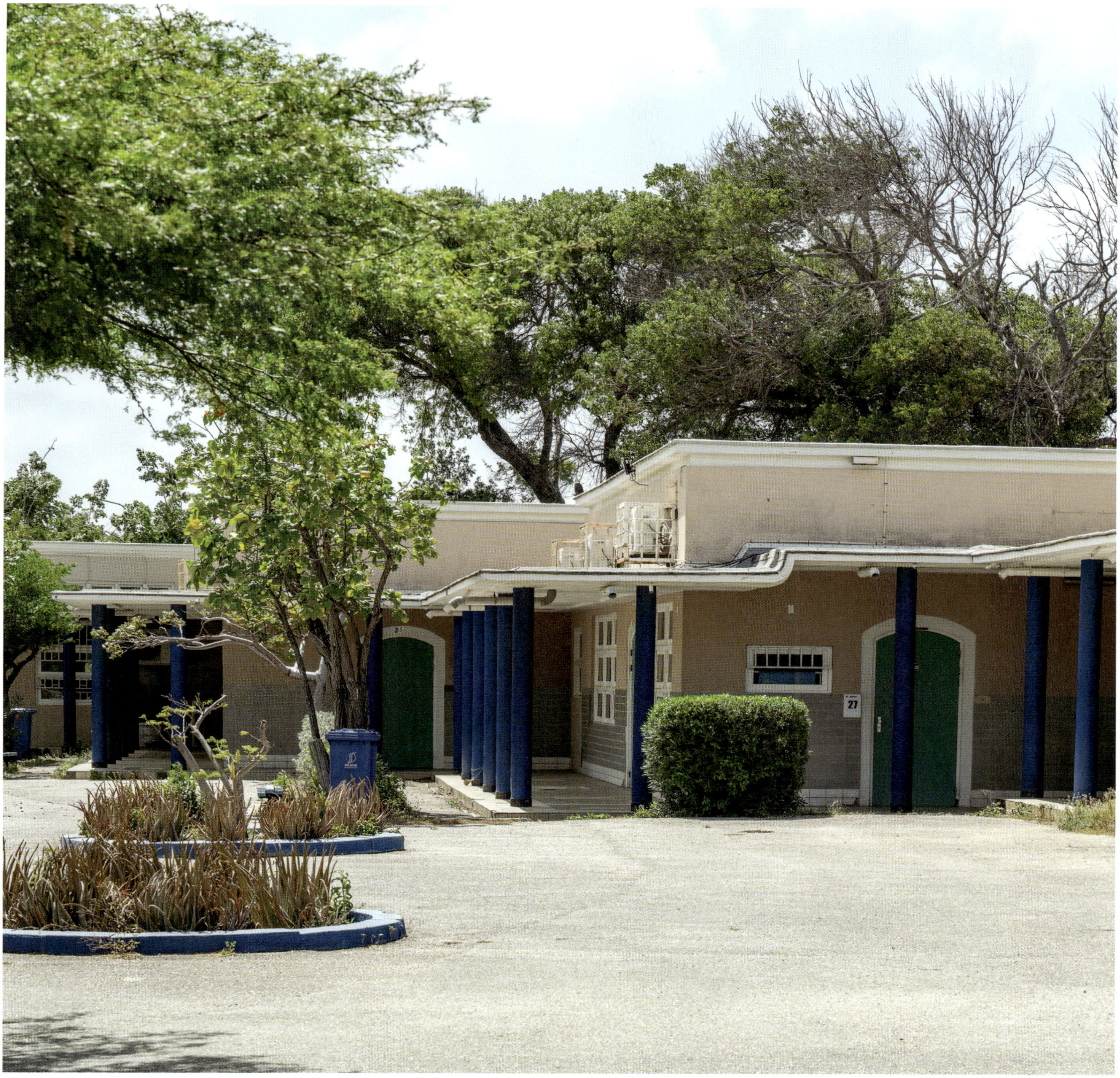
27

do_co_mo_mo_curaçao

Description_

The original design featured a large central square. On the northern side of the square were low-rise buildings housing large classrooms for chemistry, physics, mathematics, biology, and art. On the southern side of the square, there was an elongated two-story block with 16 classrooms, culminating in a three-story tower.

Characteristic elements of the school include the semi-circular, fully open gallery with benches that connect the high- and low-rise buildings, as well as the three-story western tower.
The concrete columns that accentuate the galleries are prominent features throughout the building. In the low-rise section, these columns support staggered concrete roofs, adapting to changes in terrain height.

The western facade of the three-story tower is almost entirely made of glass, which is unusual considering the otherwise well-designed climatic considerations of the building, particularly for the tropics.

Despite being equipped with green-tinted "anti-sun" glass and windows, which can be opened completely, the interior spaces, consisting of the stairwell and the large art classroom, become uncomfortably hot in the afternoon.

A few decades ago, several two-story classroom blocks were added to the eastern side of the original complex. In 1995, a new canteen opened, built as an independent structure west of the semi-circular gallery. Designed by Ir. Anko van der Woude (IMD Design) it shares the fundamental design elements of the original building: flat concrete roofs and galleries supported by round concrete columns. Around 2015, two study rooms/computer labs were built southwest of the tower. Designed by Ir. Willy Juliana (S.O.S. - Stichting Onderhoud Scholen), they feature characteristic sloping concrete roofs with large overhangs.

References:

- Bade, J.J. and H.J. Boukema (1966) *Skein - Documentaire van het Peter Stuyvesant College 1941-1966*, Curaçao: Peter Stuyvesant College,
- Gill, Ronald G. (2008) *Een eeuw architectuur op Curaçao*. Curaçao: Ronald G. Gill, (Original work published 1999)
- Woude, Anko van der (1991) Naar een tropische architectuur in de moderne tijd: analyse van een schoolgebouw; in: *Onderwijs in de steigers*, Curaçao: Peter Stuyvesant College,
- Woude, Anko van der (2009) Modernistic Tropical Peter Stuyvesant College (PSC); *The impact of Caribbean Modern Architecture, First regional DOCOMOMO seminar, hosted by the University of the Netherlands Antilles*, Curaçao, pp. 63-65

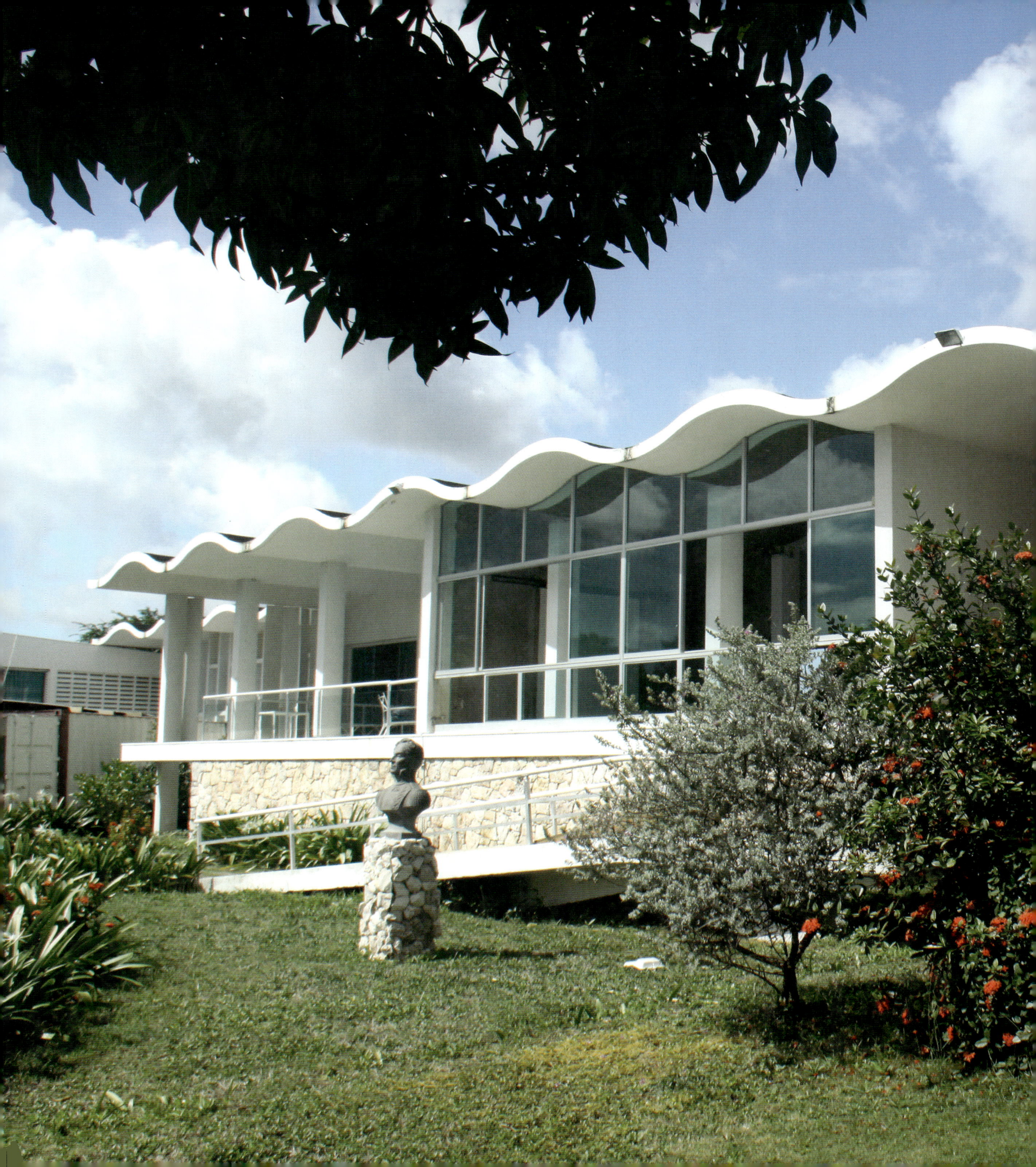

National grid reference: **12°06'33.7"N 68°55'34.3"W**

22.
CASA SIMON BOLIVAR_

PRESIDENT ROMULO BETANCOURT BOULEVARD - SERU ARRARAT

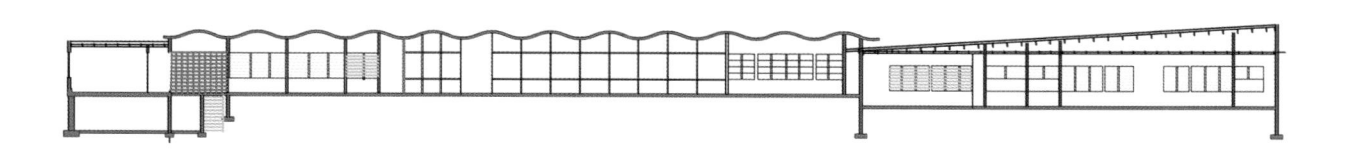

Casa Simon Bolivar. Drawing: Ben Smit, c. 1956 / Rosberg Engineering, 2016

The most salient feature is the undulated shape of the roof over the central part of the building.

Historic Background_

Casa Simon Bolivar is the residence of the Consul General of Venezuela in Curaçao. The building was a gift from the government of the Netherlands Antilles to the Venezuelan government as a token of friendship between the two countries and to honor the freedom fighter Simon Bolivar.

Just a few years earlier, on March 15, 1950, practically across from the Casa Simon Bolivar on the hill of Arrarat, the Roosevelt House was opened as the residence of the Consul General of the United States. This was the local government's gift of land and building to the United States as an expression of gratitude for U.S. protection during World War II. The design was by A.A. van Ammers, an architect at the Curaçao Public Works Department.

For the design of the Casa Simon Bolivar, the government chose a different route. Several local architects were selected to submit a design for the building. There were five entries, and in March 1956, the design by Ben Smit was chosen, and he was given the assignment. The official conveyance of the building and land to the Venezuelan government, and opening of the residence, took place on December 2, 1957.

Coll. Mongui Maduro Library

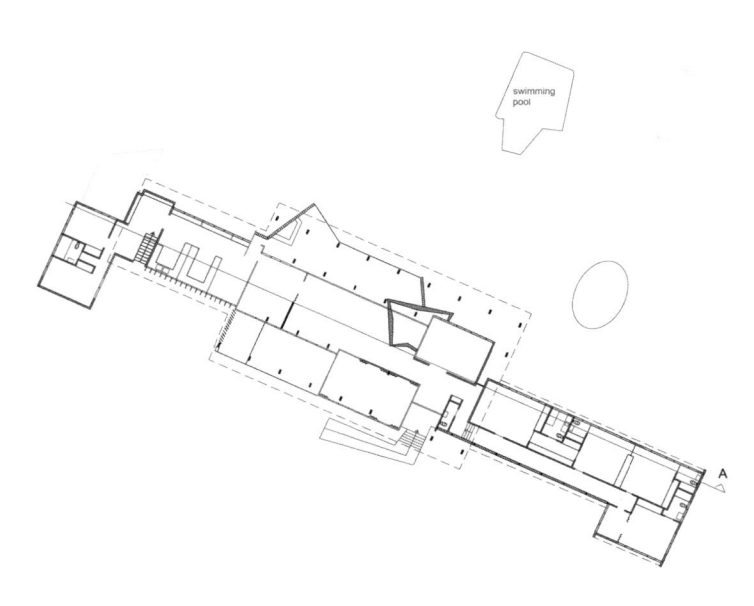

Casa Simon Bolivar. Drawing: Ben Smit, c. 1956 / Rosberg Engineering, 2016

Architectural Design_

The architect Ben Smit was born in the Netherlands in 1922 and established himself in Curaçao in 1943. After working for the Department of Public Works for three years, he founded his own firm in 1946, one of the first local architectural offices. From the mid-1940s until the end of the 1960s he was one of the most influential architects in Curaçao

The house stands on top of the Arrarat hill and offers a panoramic view of historic Willemstad to the South and the large harbour and oil refinery to the North. The residence is elongated in an East-West direction. Ben Smit's architecture took into account the climatic conditions, avoiding the strong tropical sun and optimizing the use of the east wind orientation. The most salient feature is the undulated shape of the roof over the central part of the building, which according to the architect, was influenced by Brazilian modern architecture.

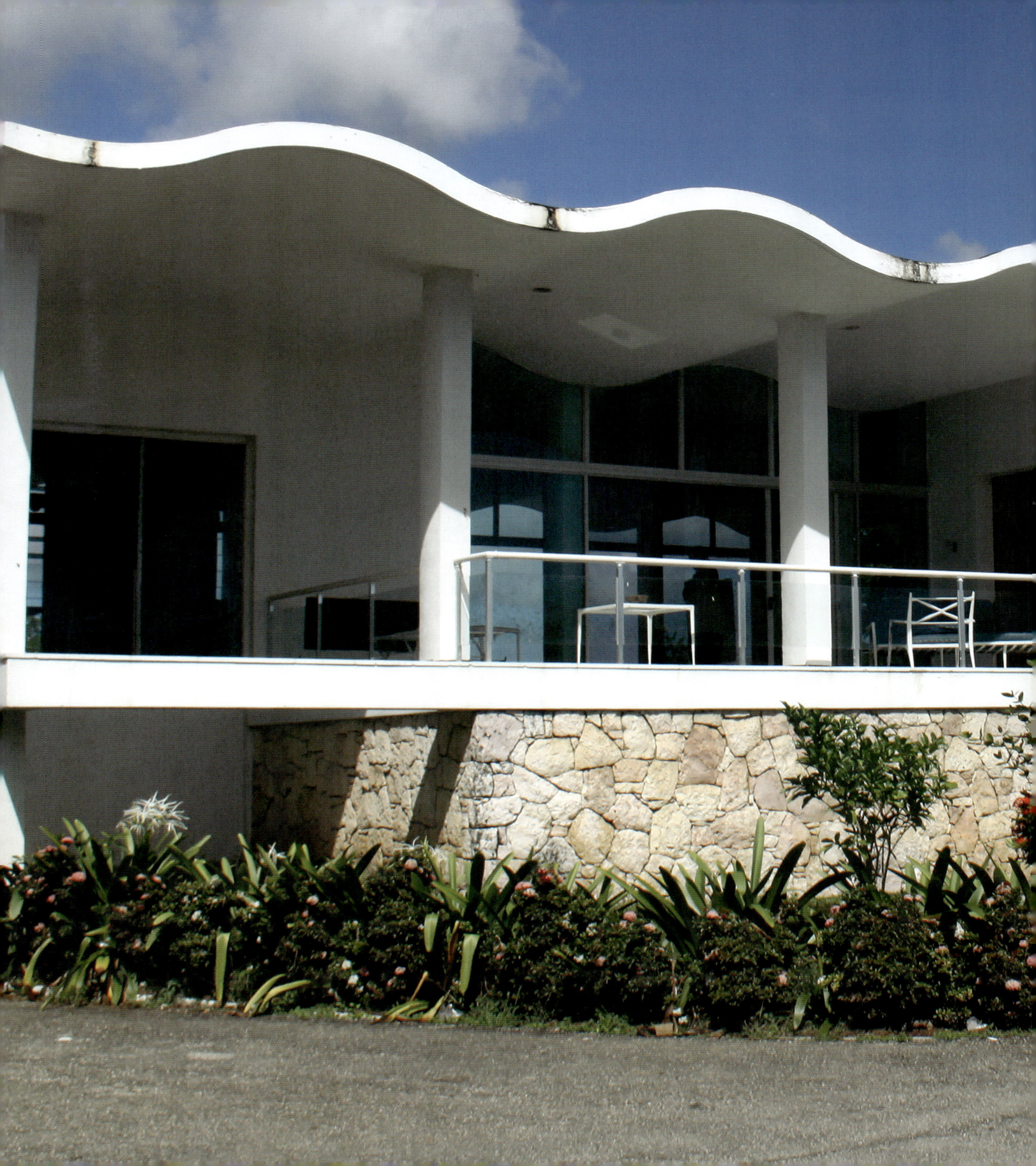

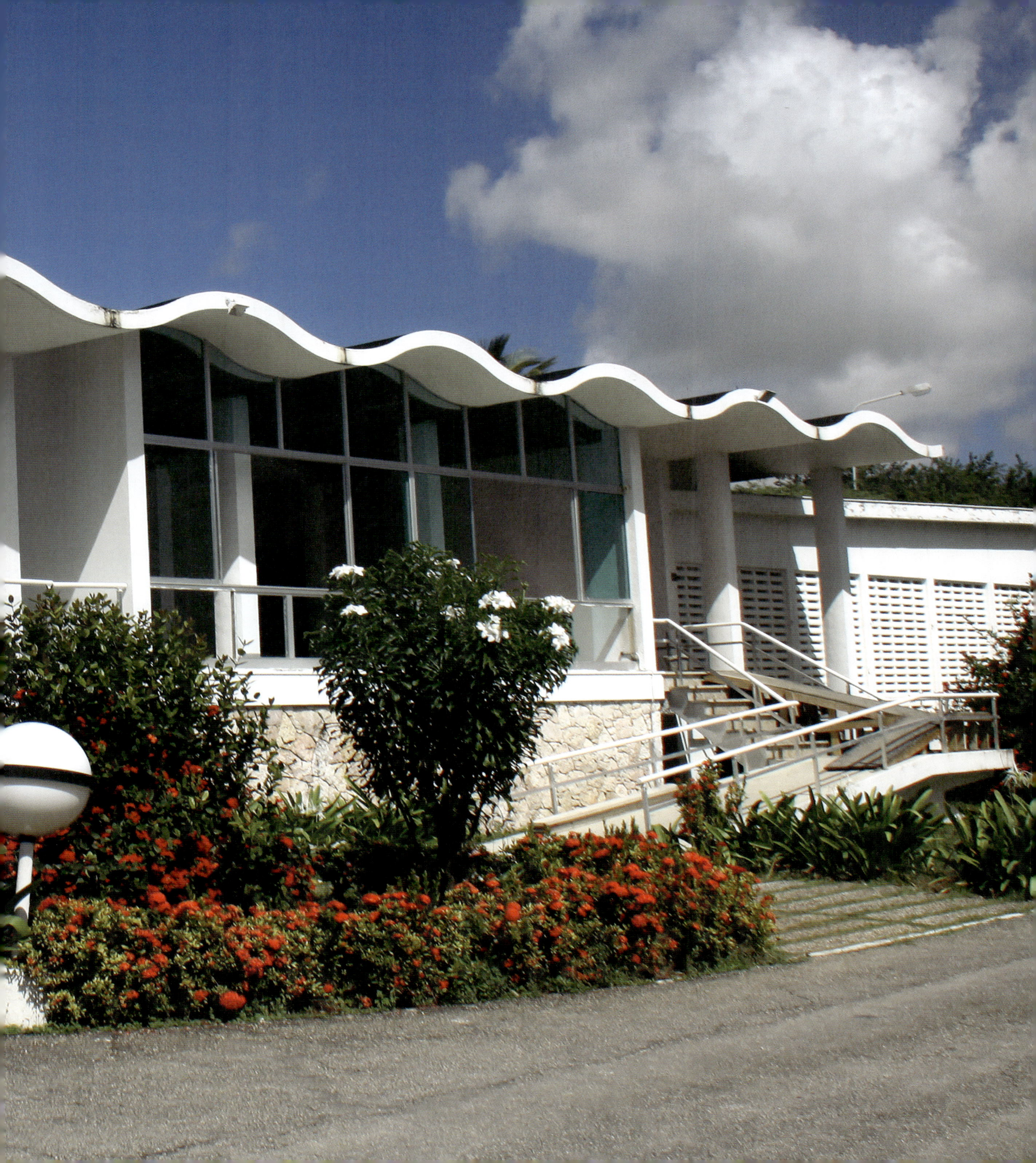

References:

- AMIGOE DI CURAÇAO, 21.03.1956; 02.12.1957; 03.121957
- Fonk, Hans. et al. (2004) *Curaçao Dutch Caribbean Architecture & Style*. Curaçao; Curaçao Style Foundation, pp 107-109
- Gill, Ronald G. (2008) *Een eeuw architectuur op Curaçao*. Curaçao: Ronald G. Gill, (Original work published 1999)
- Klaus, Dennis (2009) BEN SMIT, a personal note, *The impact of Caribbean Modern Architecture, First regional DOCOMOMO seminar, hosted by the University of the Netherlands Antilles*, Curaçao, pp. 56-59
- Smit, Ben (2002). *Projecten Curaçao 1946 – 1969*. Curaçao: Ben Smit

Unfortunately, Docomomo did not receive permission from the Venezuelan government to take recent photos of Casa Simon Bolivar.

Description_

The residence is spacious, open to the garden, and offers excellent facilities for receptions. The reception area is centrally located and provides ample natural ventilation. It is accessible via a ramp in front of the residence. Further into this central area, partly flowing into each other, are the living room, the dining room, and library. Terraces are located on the north and south sides. To the west of the central area are the kitchen, pantry and servant's quarters, while to the east are the dormitories with bathrooms.

The undulated roof of the central part of the building is made of reinforced concrete supported by concrete columns. The walls are constructed of plastered concrete blocks. Smit utilized local materials wherever possible, but the floor in the central area is made of cement-colored Italian marble. There are various aluminum sliding doors with sun-resistant glass to the north and south terraces. The servants' area and dormitories feature almost flat roofs. Noteworthy is the west wing with the service bedrooms, which are elevated on triangular concrete columns, a necessary design feature due to the sloping terrain.

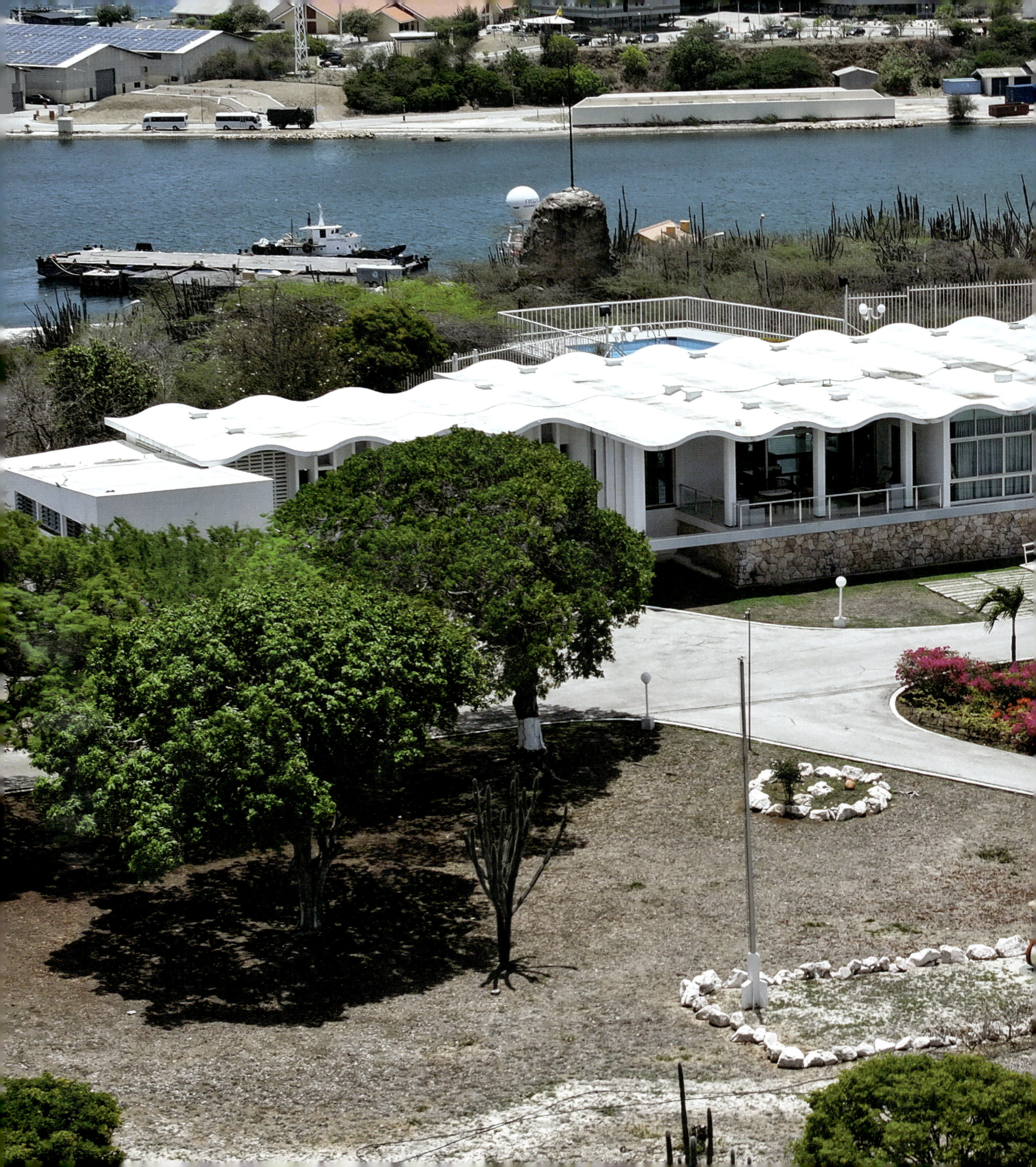

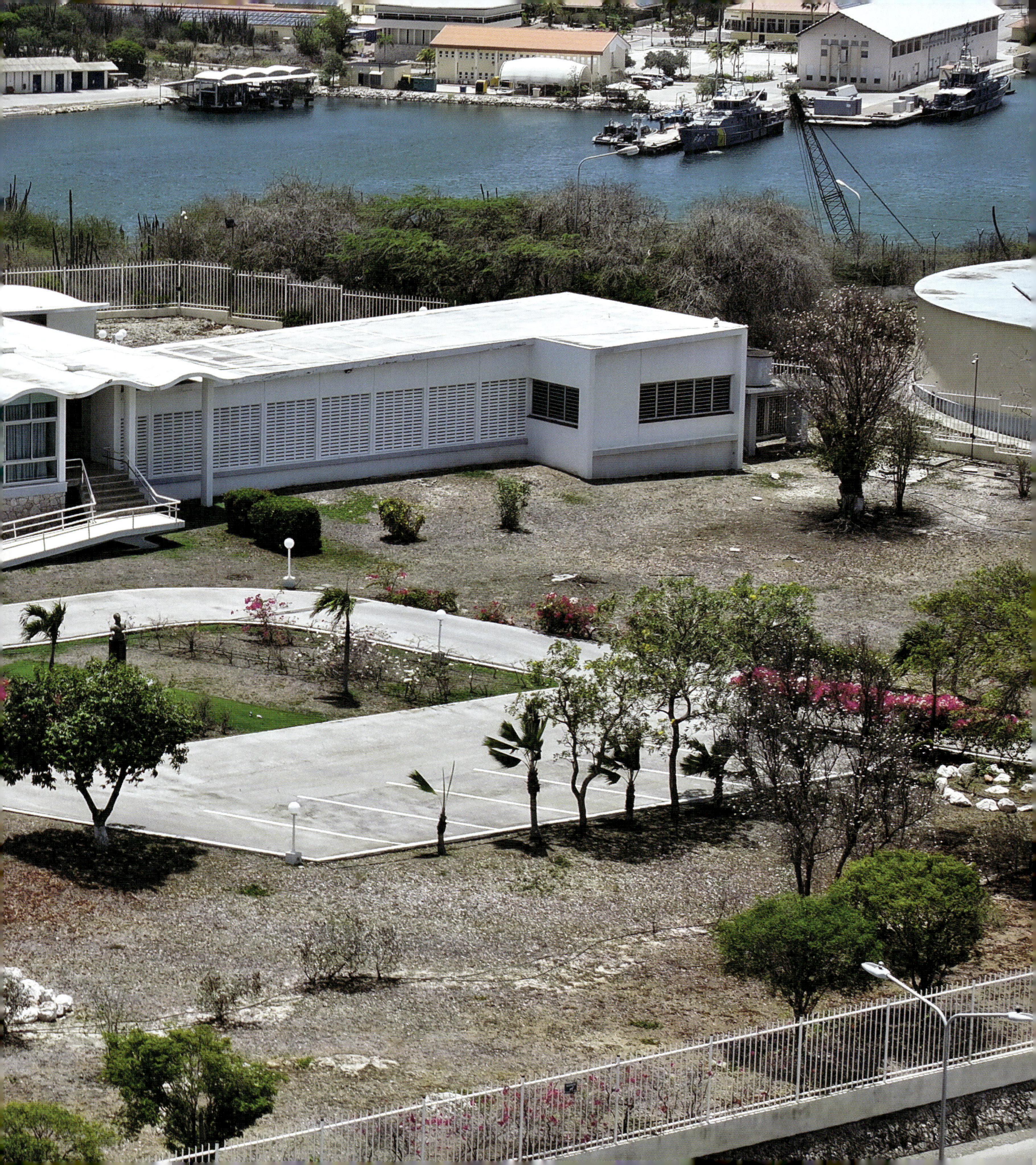

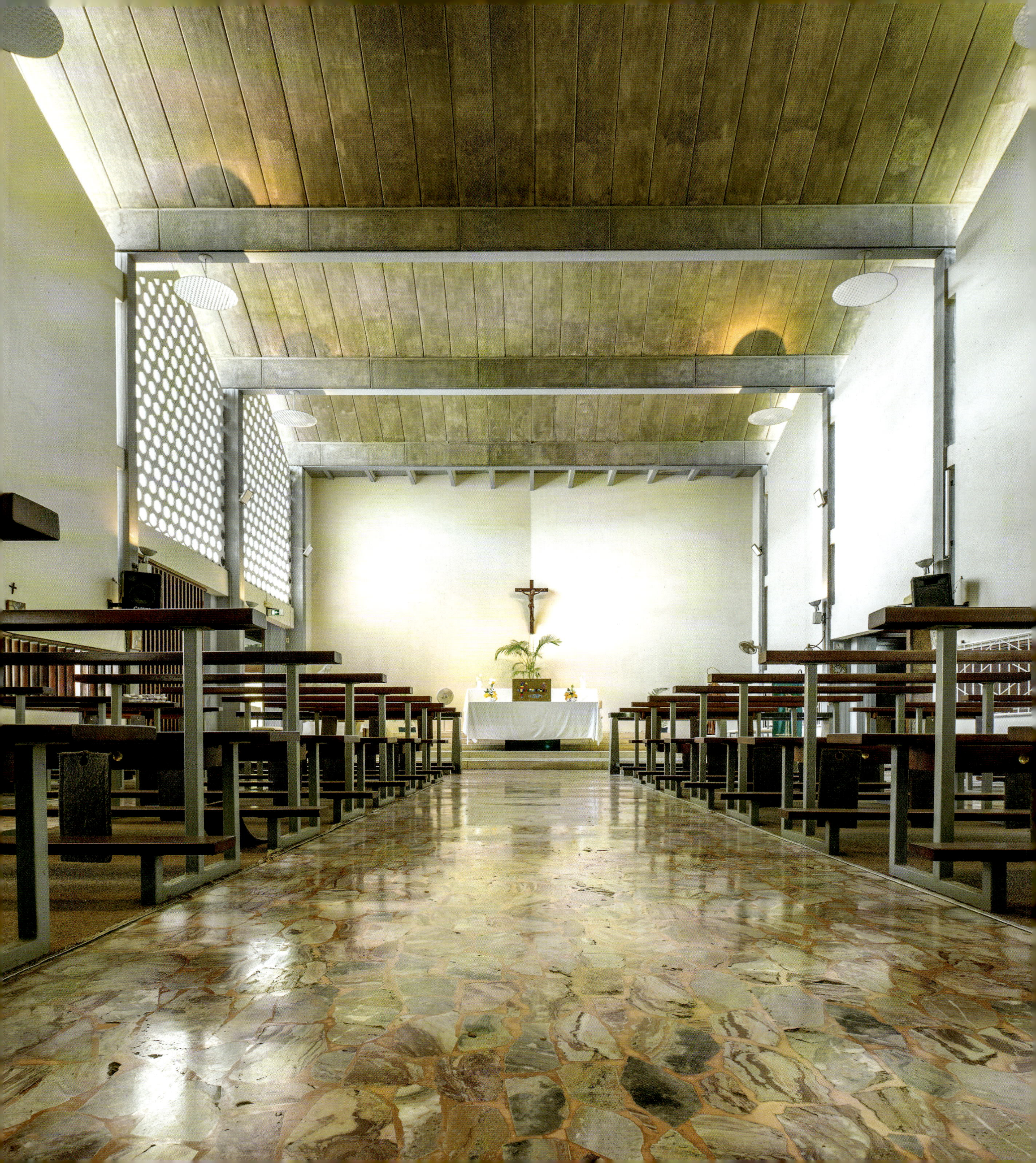

National grid reference: **12°07'01.9"N 68°56'52.4"W**

23.
ALVERNA CHAPEL & MONASTERY_

GOUVERNEUR VAN LANSBERGEWEG

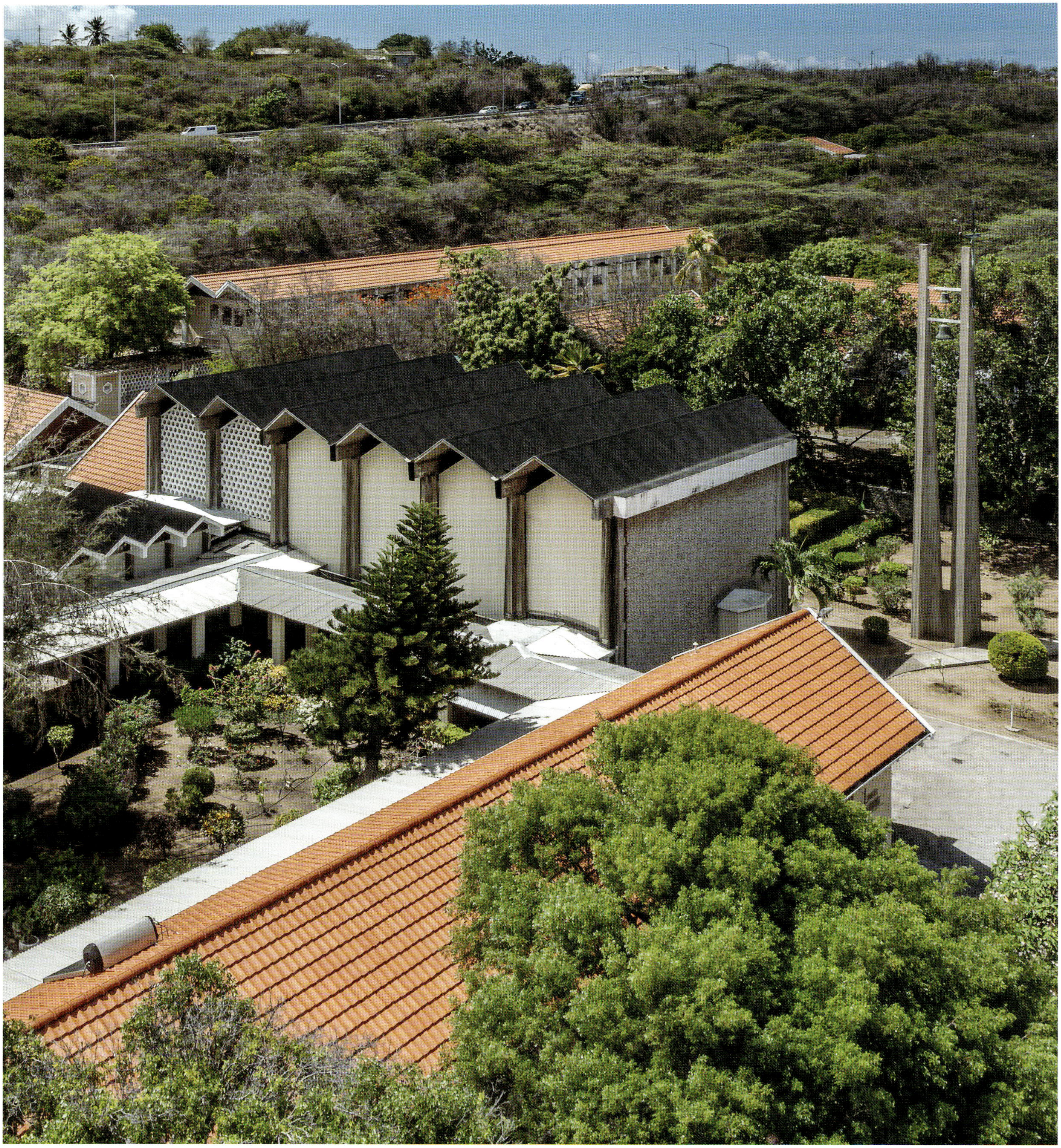

Coll. Mongui Maduro Library

The centrally located chapel, with its zigzag-shaped roof, is a masterpiece.

Historic Background_

In 1842, the first religious sisters from the Netherlands arrived in Curaçao. Their mission was threefold: to provide an education for children (both boys and girls) of all classes, to found a boarding school for girls from the upper classes, and to set up mission posts in the outer districts of the island. In the 19th and 20th century, the nuns erected schools and other buildings to fulfill these purposes.

The last complex established by the Congregation of Franciscan Sisters of Mariadal from Roosendaal (Netherlands) in 1957/1958 was the convent and girls' boarding school Alverna. The nuns of the congregation lived in the new convent. Most of the pupils at the boarding school came from the other Dutch Caribbean islands to Curaçao for their secondary school education at the nearby Maria Immaculata Lyceum or Maria College.

In the 1970s, when secondary education became possible on the other islands, the boarding school closed. The boarding school building became a retirement home called Nos Lanterno. Due to a reduction in the number of nuns over the years, the two-story dormitory for the nuns was demolished in the beginning of this century. Since then, they have lived in a separate northern part of the monastery. The last three nuns living there left the island and moved to the Netherlands in July 2024. The complex is now managed by Birgen di Rosario, a foundation for elderly care. The former monastery rooms are at this moment, available for rental to seniors and non-religious individuals.

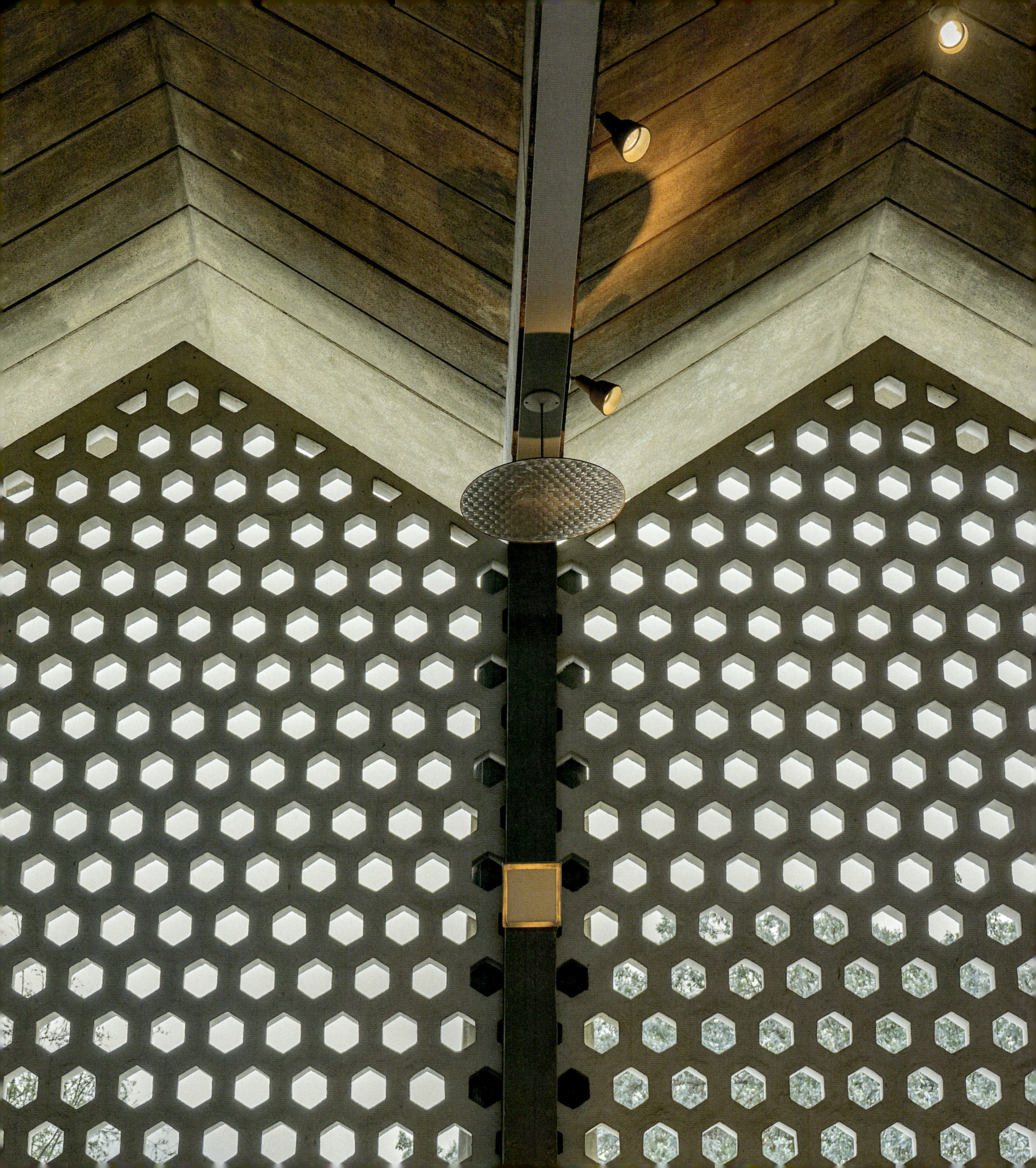

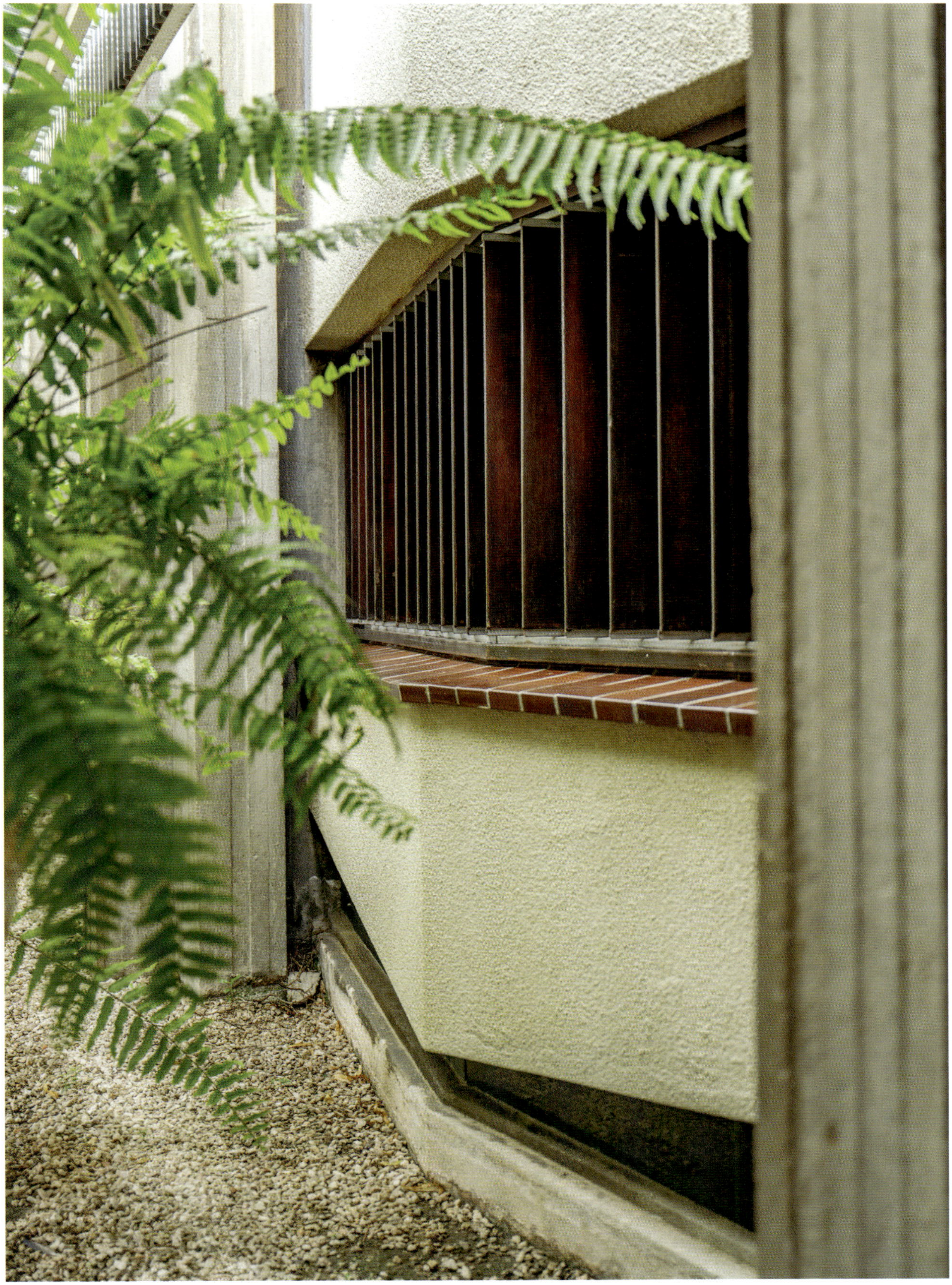

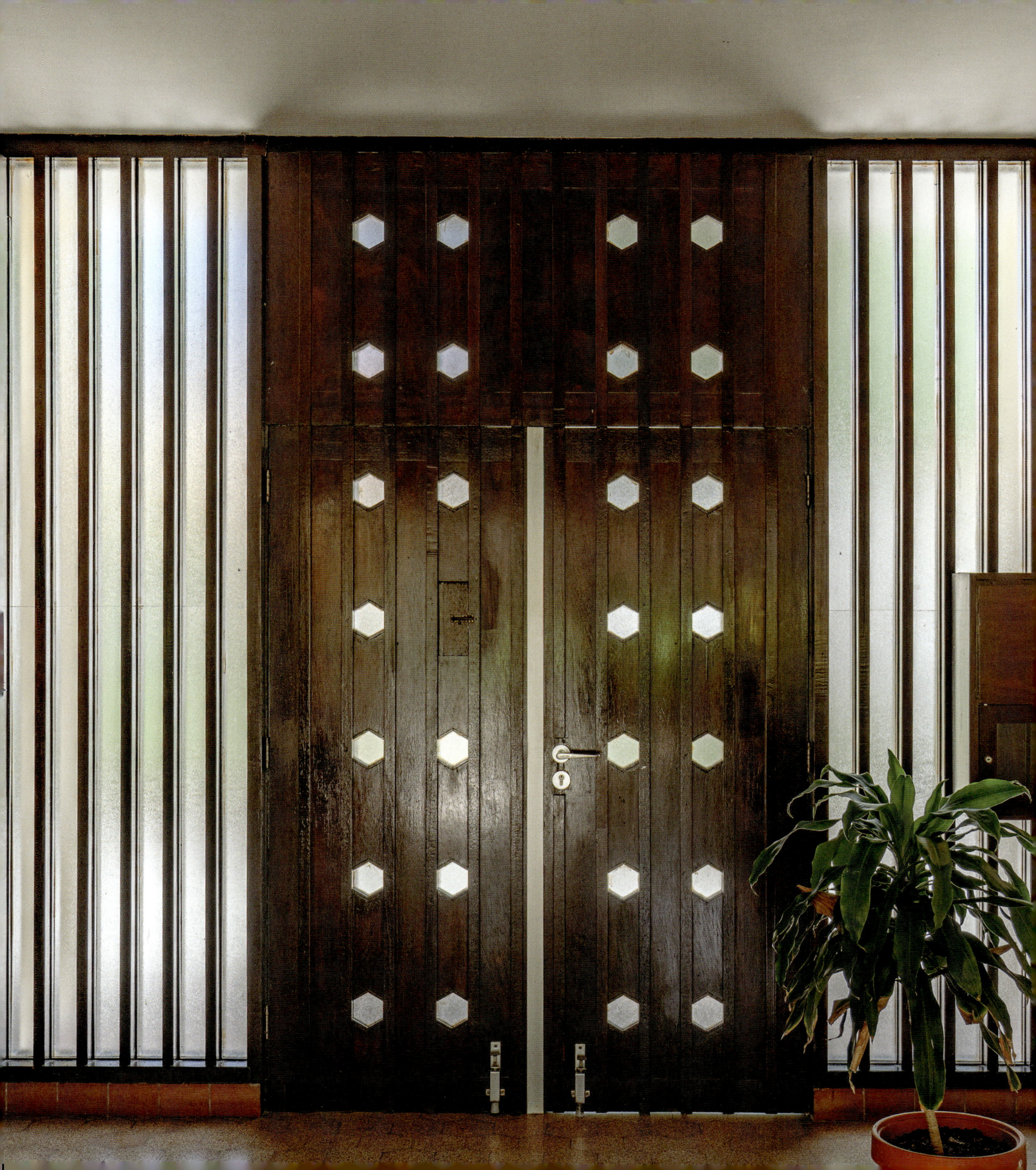

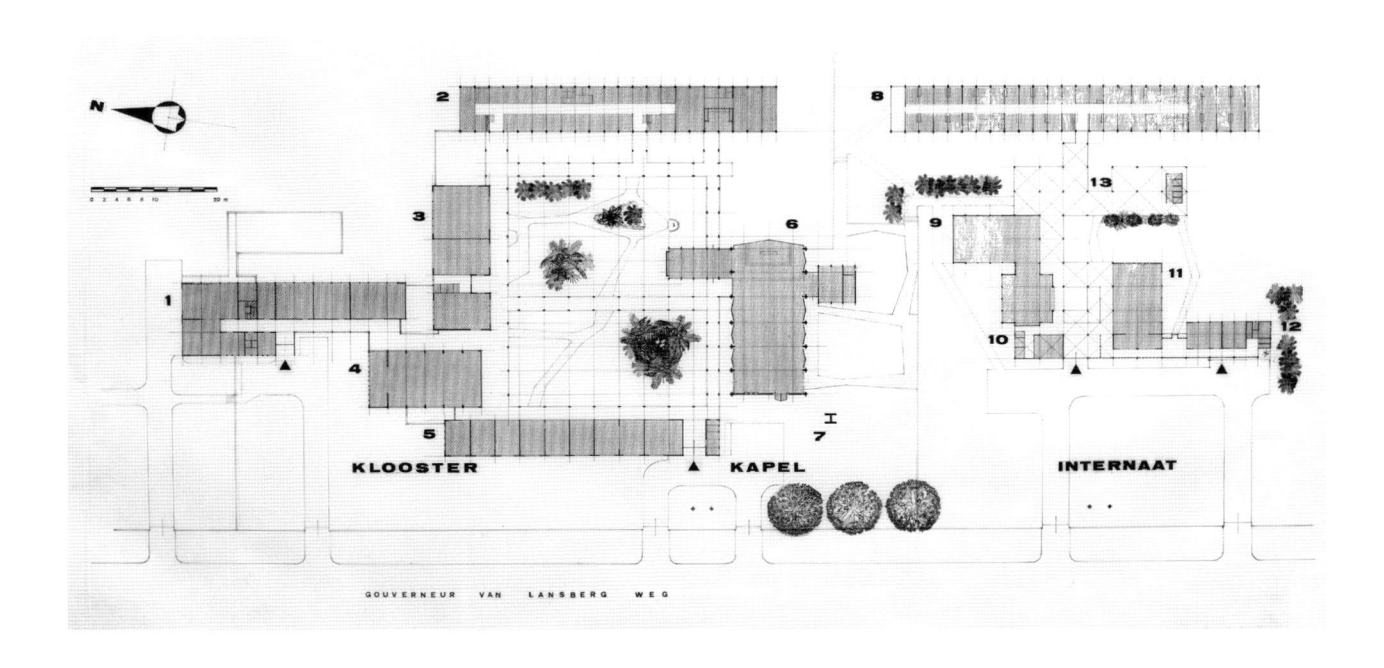

Alverna Chapel. Drawing: Ben Smit, c. 1956

Architectural Design_

The Dutch architect Ben Smit designed the chapel, the monastery and the boarding school. He settled in Curaçao in 1943 and founded his own firm, one of the first local architectural offices on the island, in 1946. His style was inspired by the Brazilian movement in modern architecture, and he became known for his natural, tropical designs. Until his return to the Netherlands in 1969, he was very influential as a proponent of the Modern Movement in architecture.

In consultation with his clients, the Franciscan sisters, it was decided to use mainly natural materials. The centrally located chapel, with its zigzag-shaped roof, is a masterpiece. The aim was to provide good natural ventilation and daylight without compromising privacy. Walls visually separated from the roof, concrete columns, and even the floor, along with strips of tinted glass, determine the atmosphere and spatial effect. Hexagonal forms appear in various ways throughout the complex, from open windows in walls to complete concrete wall elements with hexagonal openings. Even the floor tiles have a hexagonal shape. The meters-high walls, entirely covered with local coral stone, are also striking and characteristic of the chapel of Alverna.

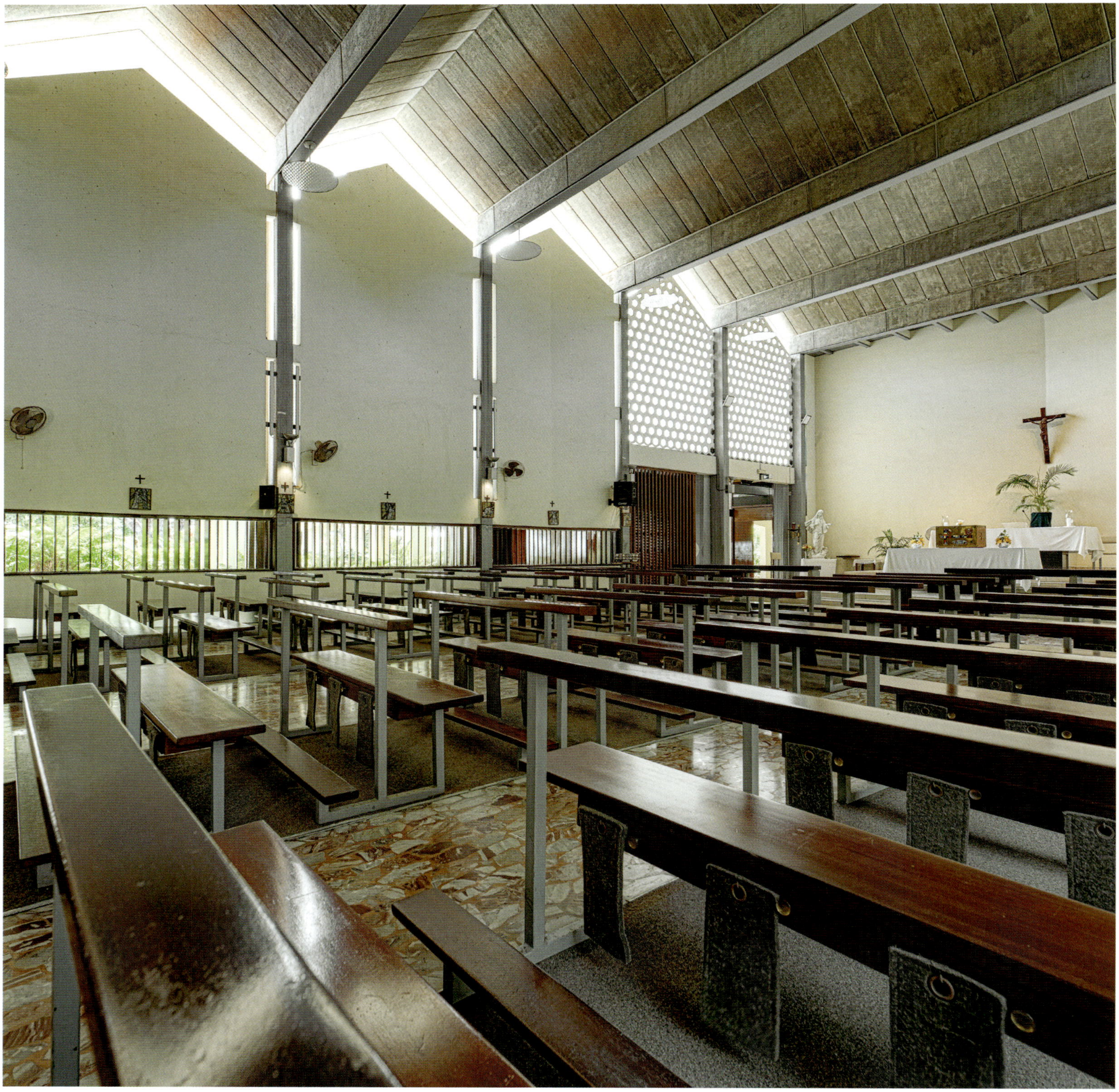

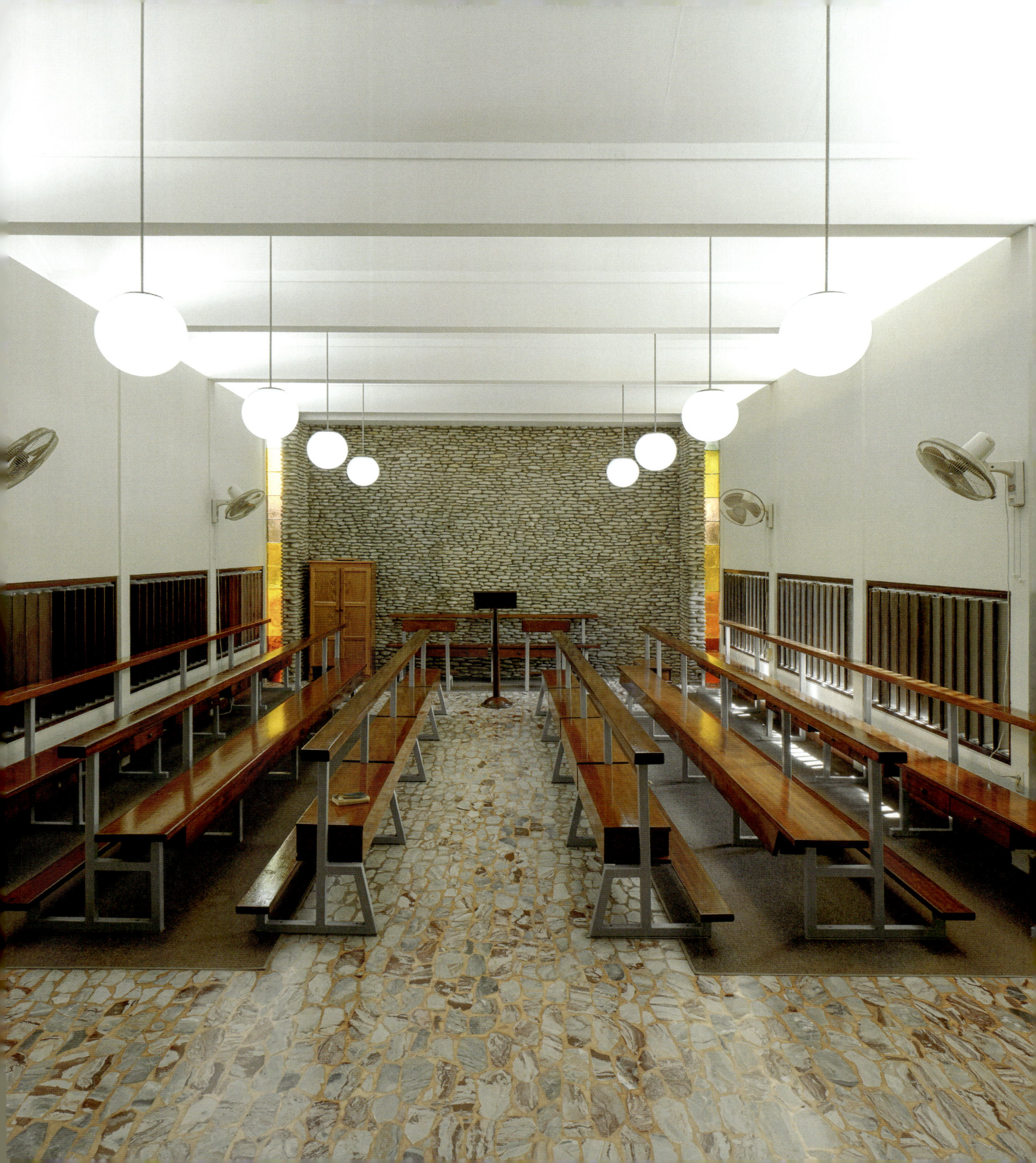

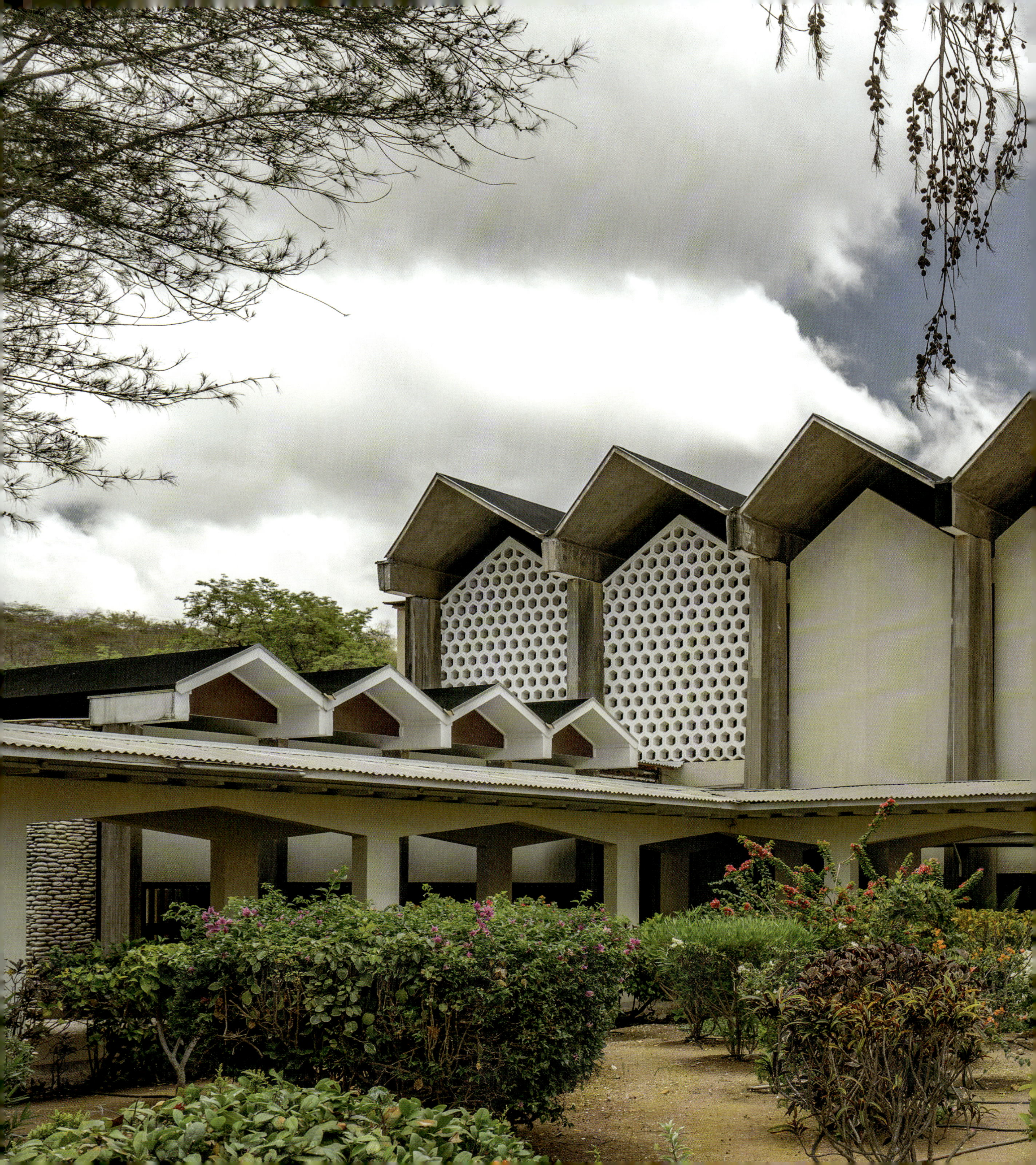

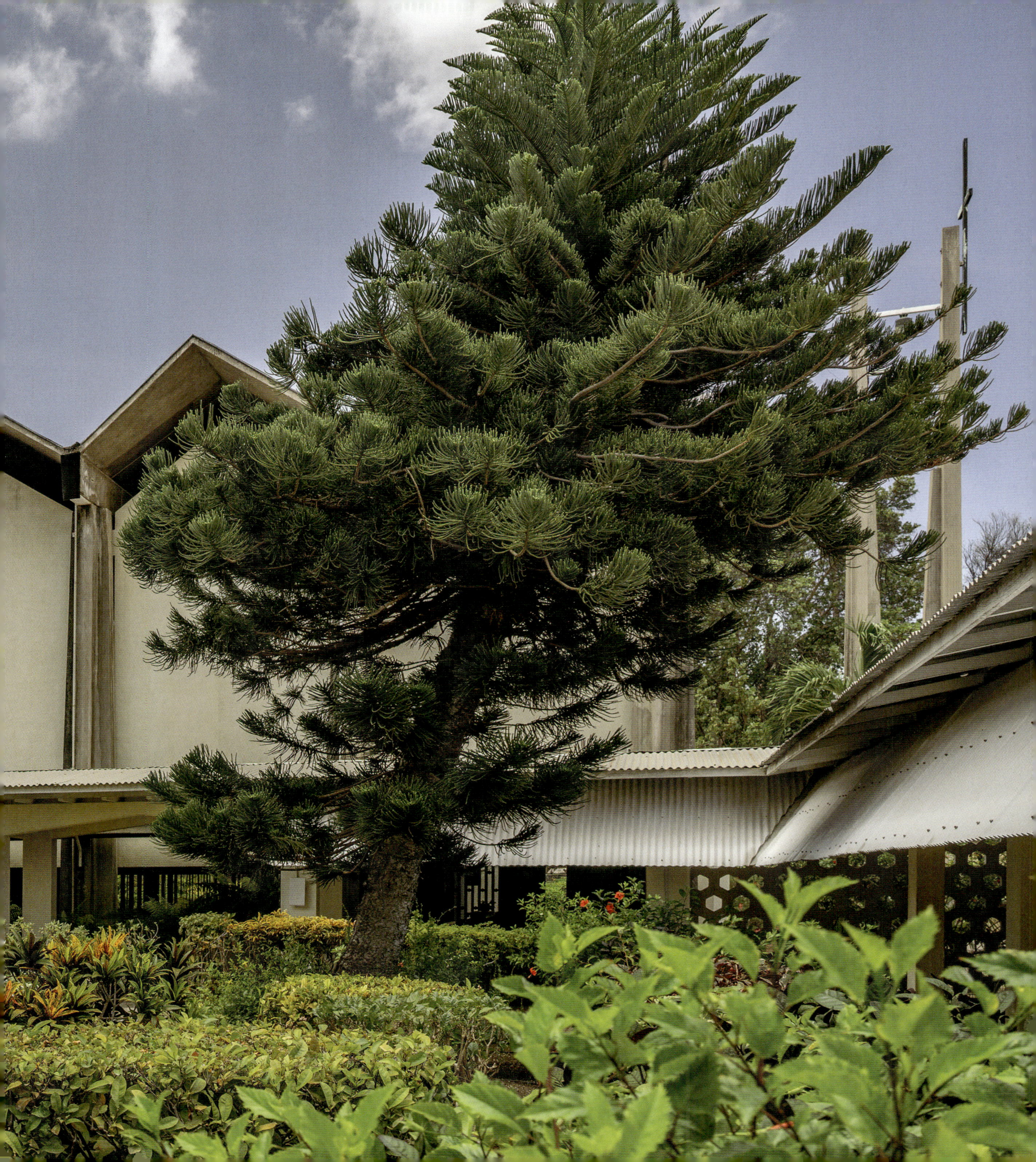

Coll. Mongui Maduro Library

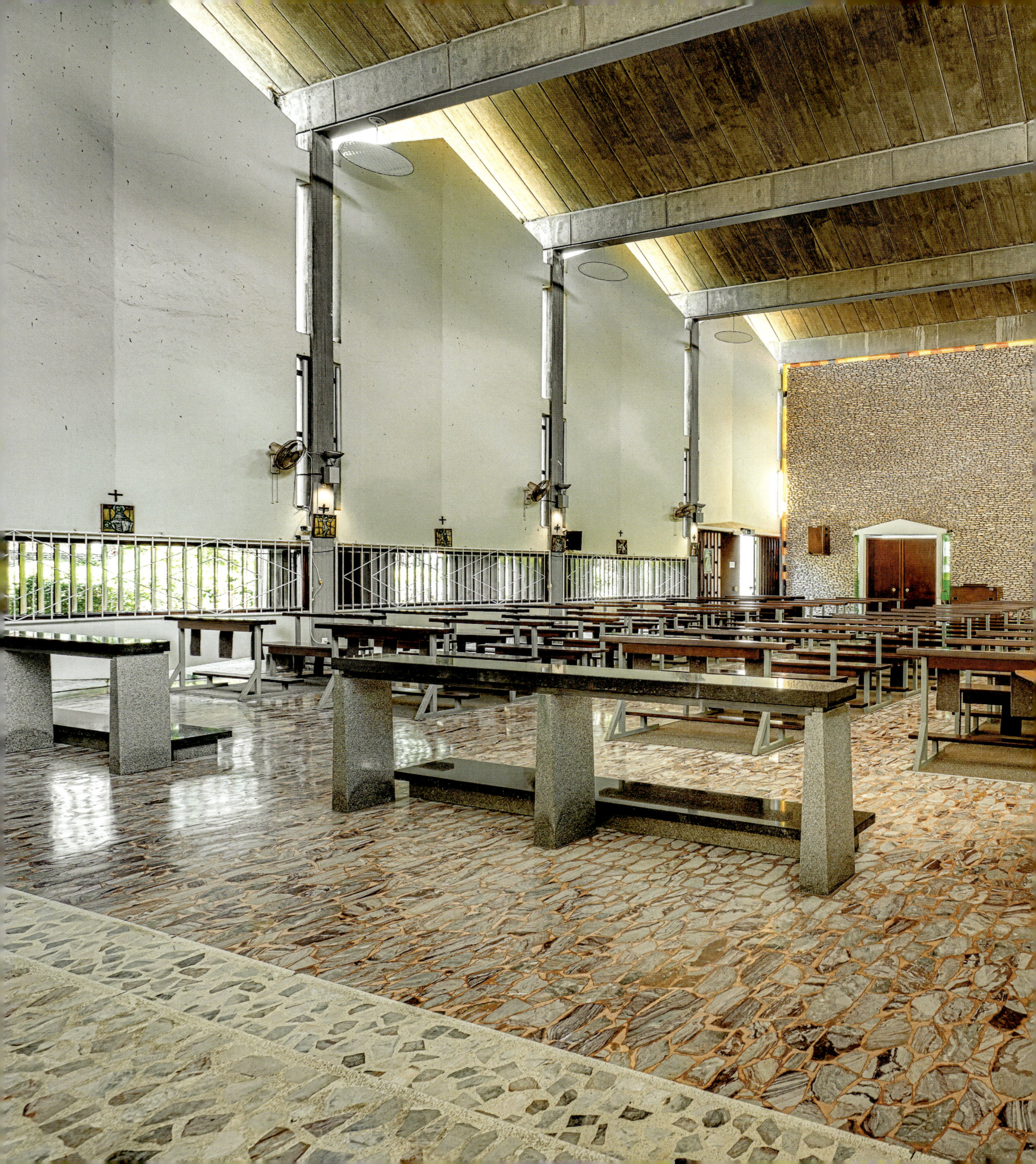

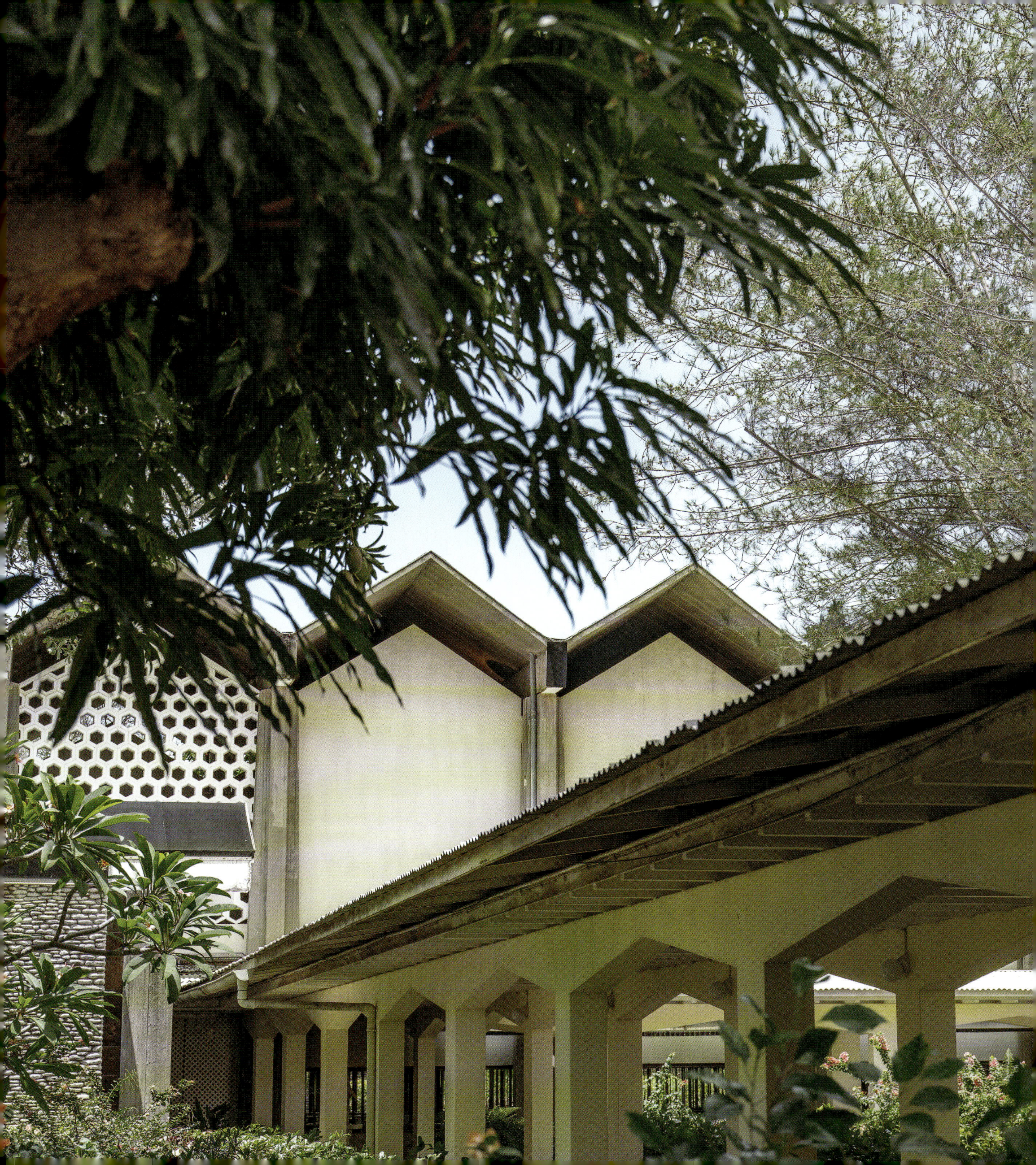

References:

- Smit, Ben. (2002). *Projecten Curaçao 1946 – 1969*. Curaçao: Ben Smit
- www.mariadal.nl

Description_

The extensive building complex consists of three parts: the monastery to the North, the girls' boarding school to the South, and the chapel in the middle. The buildings of the complex are generally simple, rectangular-shaped structures with gable roofs. However, it is the chapel that clearly stands out in terms of design language. Despite their individuality, the buildings are connected by covered, broad, open galleries with spacious gardens in between.

The monastery part faces inward, while the boarding school is partially open to the exterior. The monastery area includes the chapel, the administration, the refectory, the workspaces, the dormitories on two floors and the service areas.

The boarding school located on the southern side of the complex had dormitories on two floors, study rooms, a dining room, a recreation room and service areas. At present, they are all part of the retirement home.

ROZENDAELS

National grid reference: **12°06'05.6"N 68°55'22.8"W**

24.
ROZENDAELS_

PENSTRAAT 35 – 35A

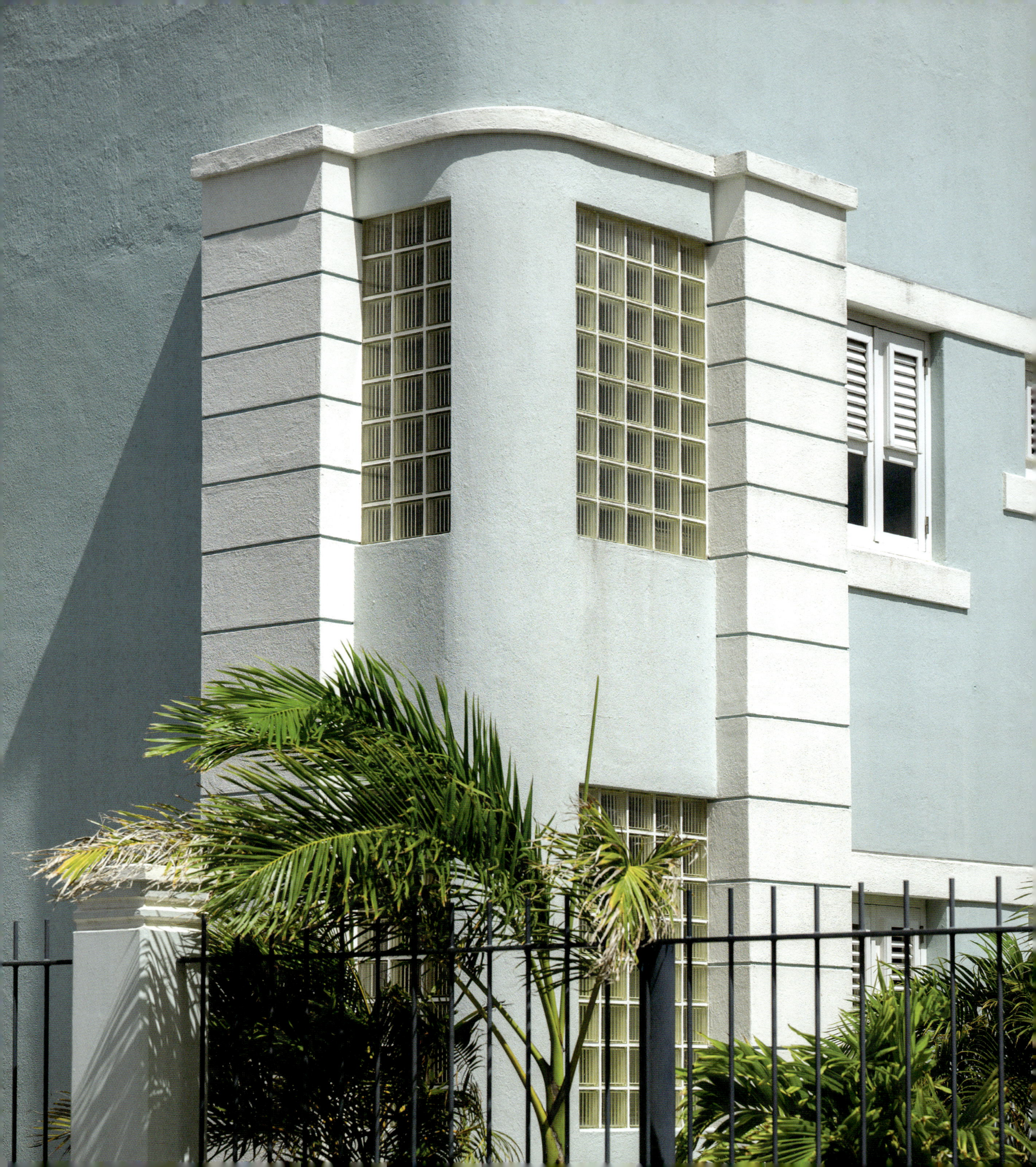

the Art Deco elements include the chequered plastered vertical lines with glass construction blocks.

Historic Background_

The Penstraat is the road that runs along the coast from Willemstad to the eastern part of the island. As early as the 18th century, spacious mansions were built on both sides of the road for the well-to-do of the island.

The residential house on the Penstraat 35-35a was built in 1957 by Stanley Levy Maduro, a member of the Sephardic elite, who held various high positions on the island. In 2000, the building was sold. The new owner restored the building to its original state to the greatest extent possible. Later additions were removed, and the layout and furnishings of the interior were restored. The building subsequently served as an office for a number of years. At present it houses a restaurant on the ground floor and an office on the first floor. The building was officially listed as a protected monument in 2018.

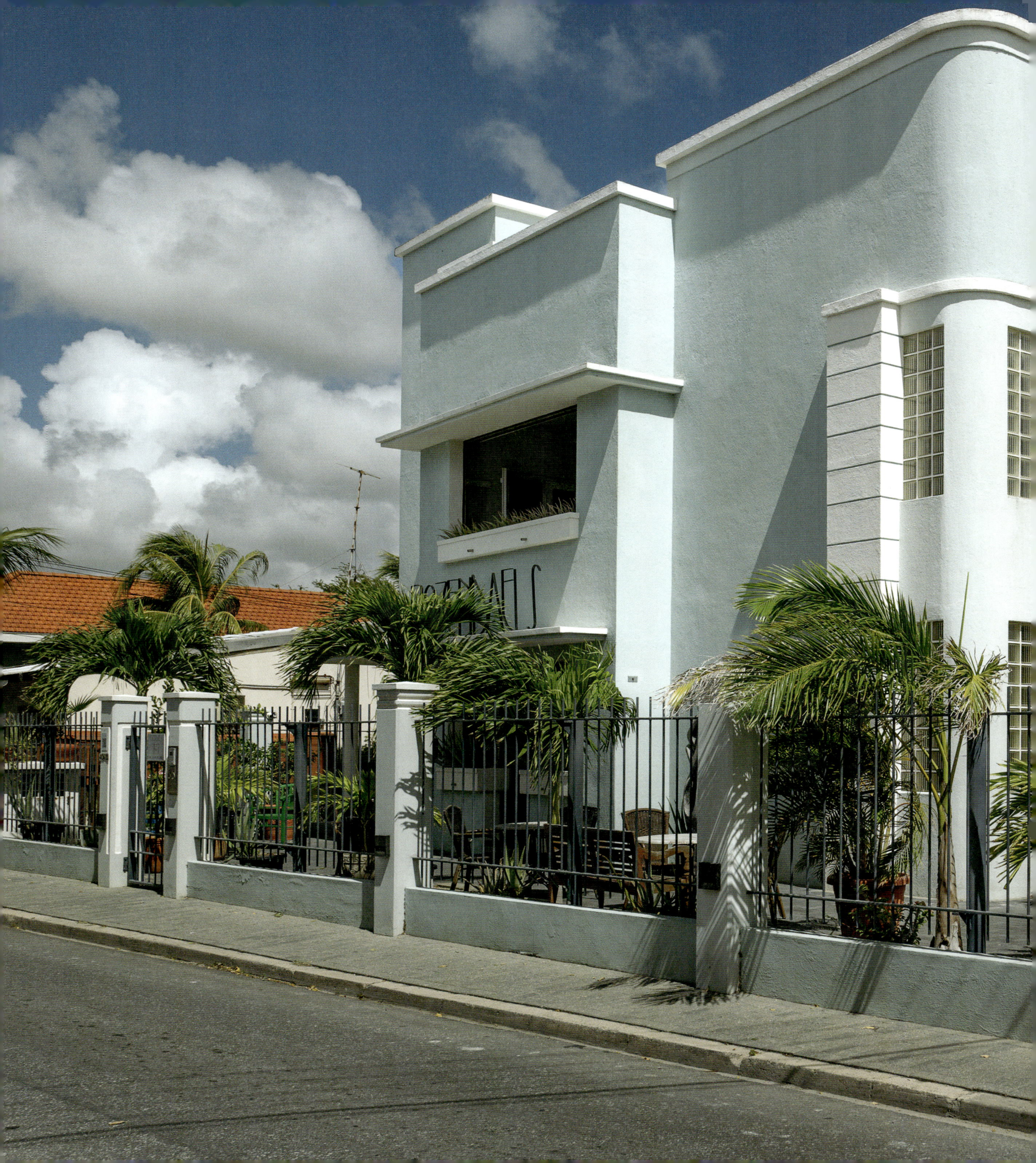

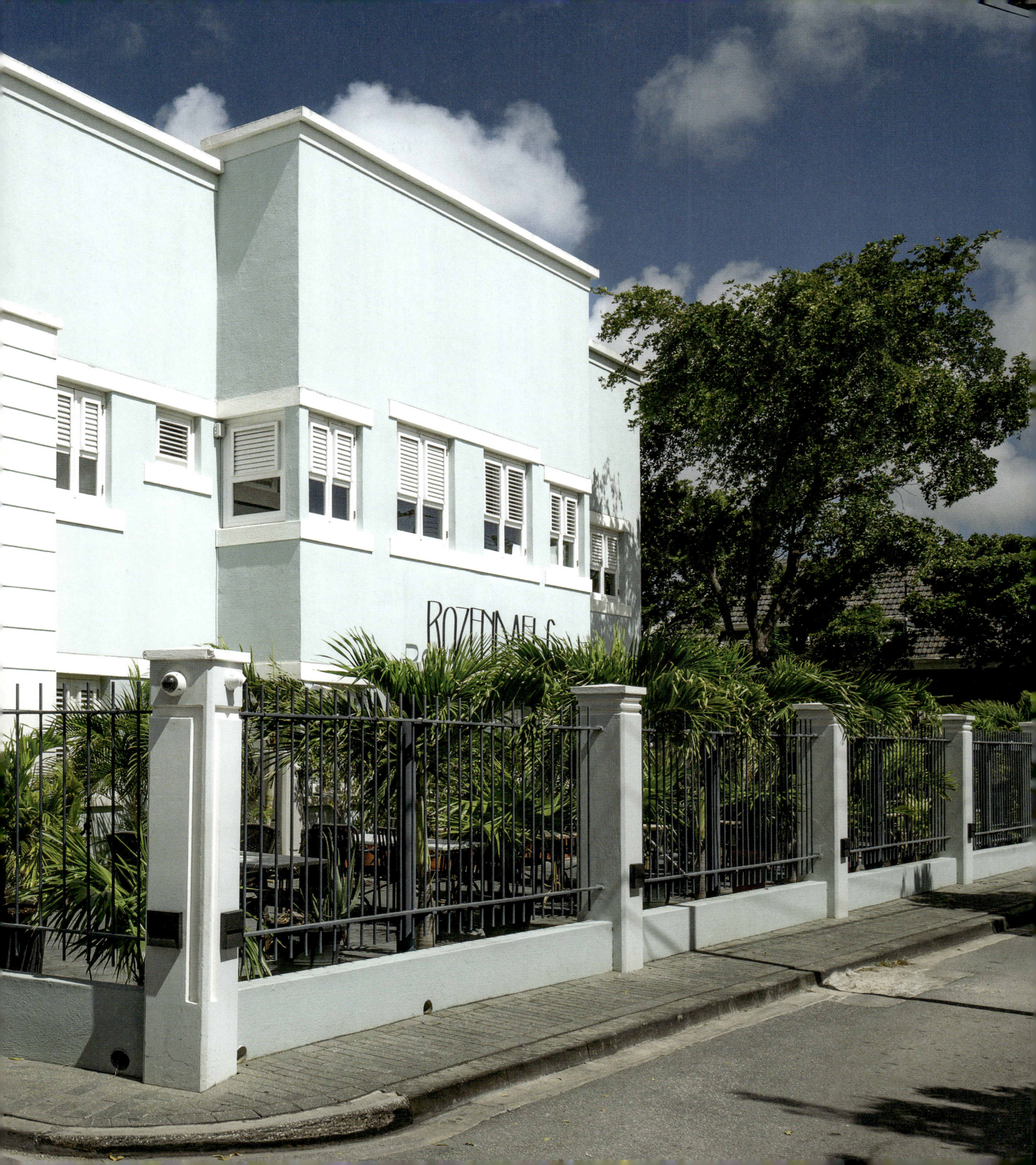

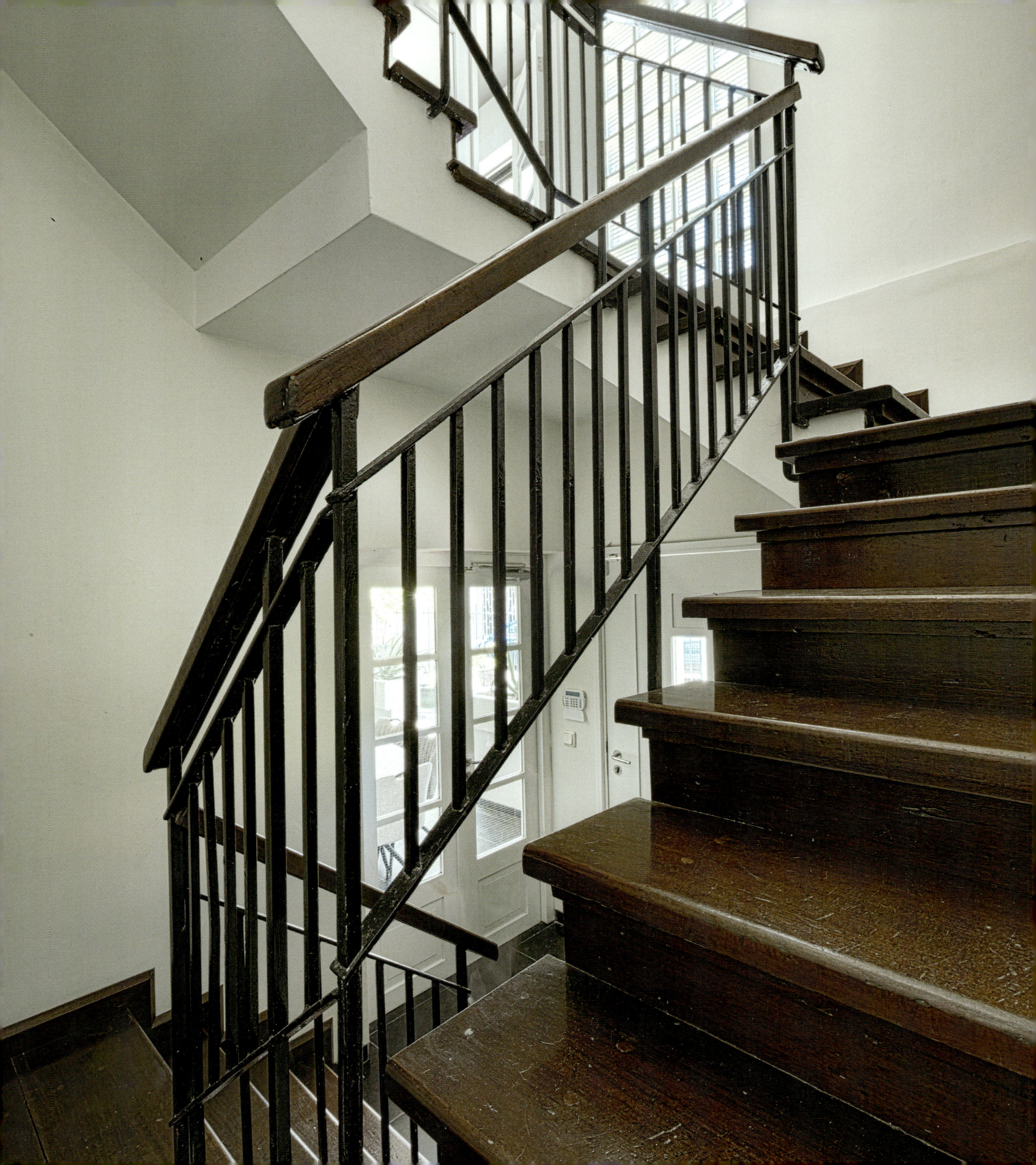

Architectural Design_

The house is built in the Art Deco style. The name of the designer is not known, although it is said to have been designed by a Miami-based architect with a Russian background. That makes this building an example of U.S.-influenced architecture on mid-20th century Curaçao architecture. The contractor was the then well-known contractor of Italian origin, Giovanni Pizziolo.

Some of the Art Deco elements include the chequered plastered vertical lines with glass construction blocks on the soft curved east-south front and at the western stairwell.

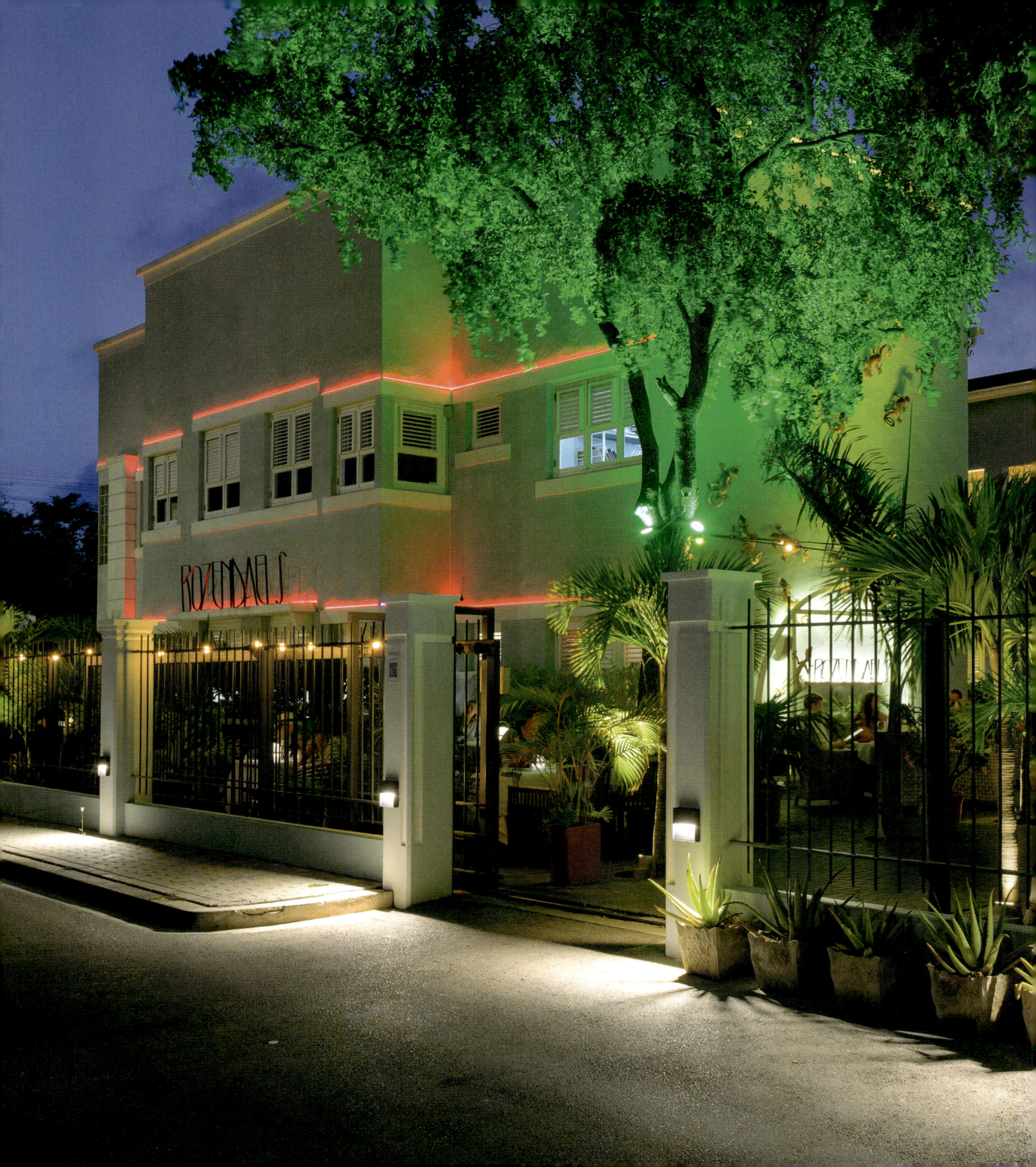
ROZENDAEL'S

Description_

The two-floor building is situated on a corner lot and has a U-shaped floorplan with a patio in the middle, which is open to the back. It consists of different building volumes that connect to each other. As is often the case in the tropics with an eastern trade wind, the bedrooms are located on the eastern side, while the kitchen and service areas on the western side. The front large central section has a terrace on top. Typical features are also the recessed balconies at the façade on the ground and first floor of the central section.

References:

- www.curacaomonuments.org/sites/penstraat-35/

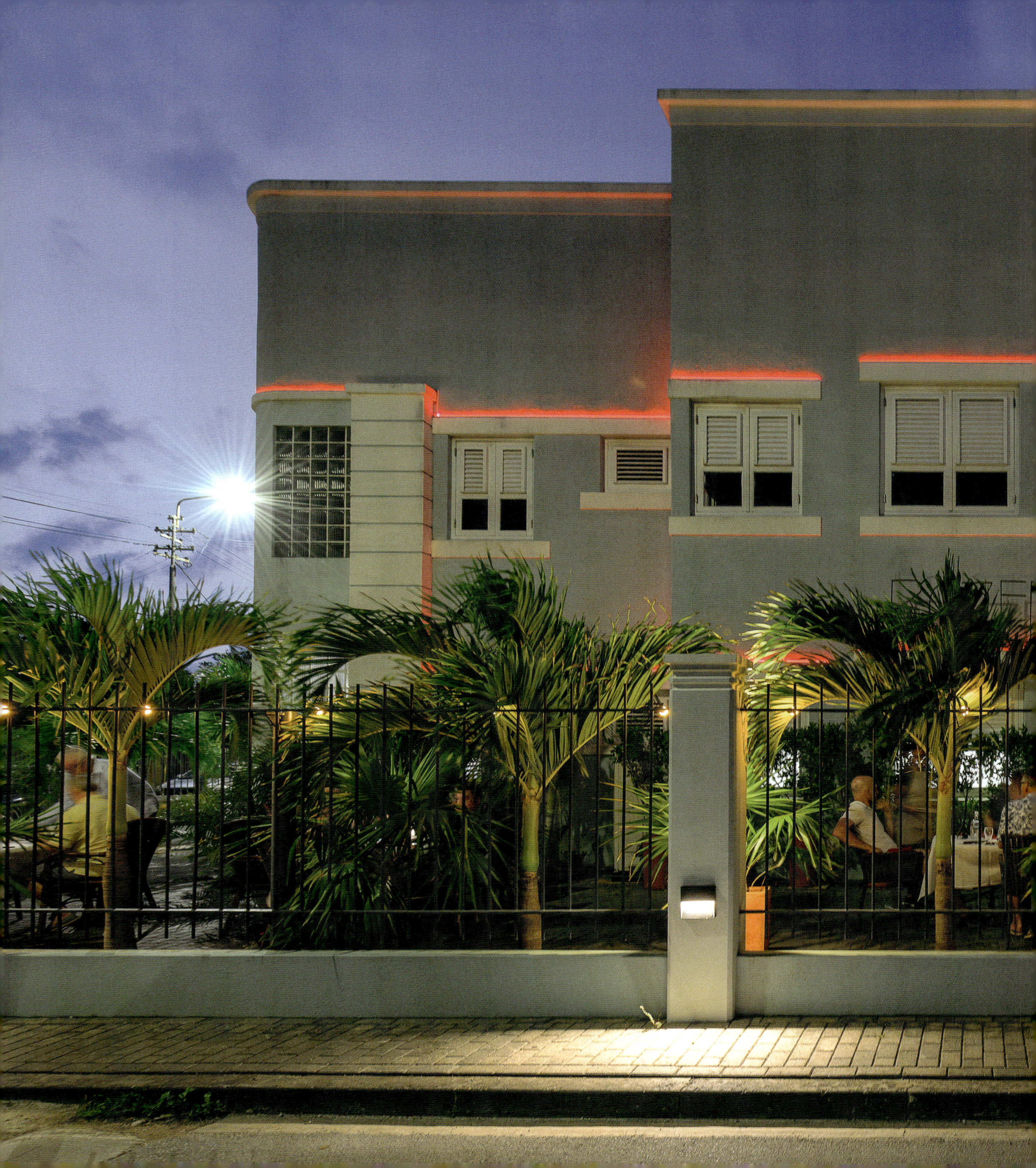

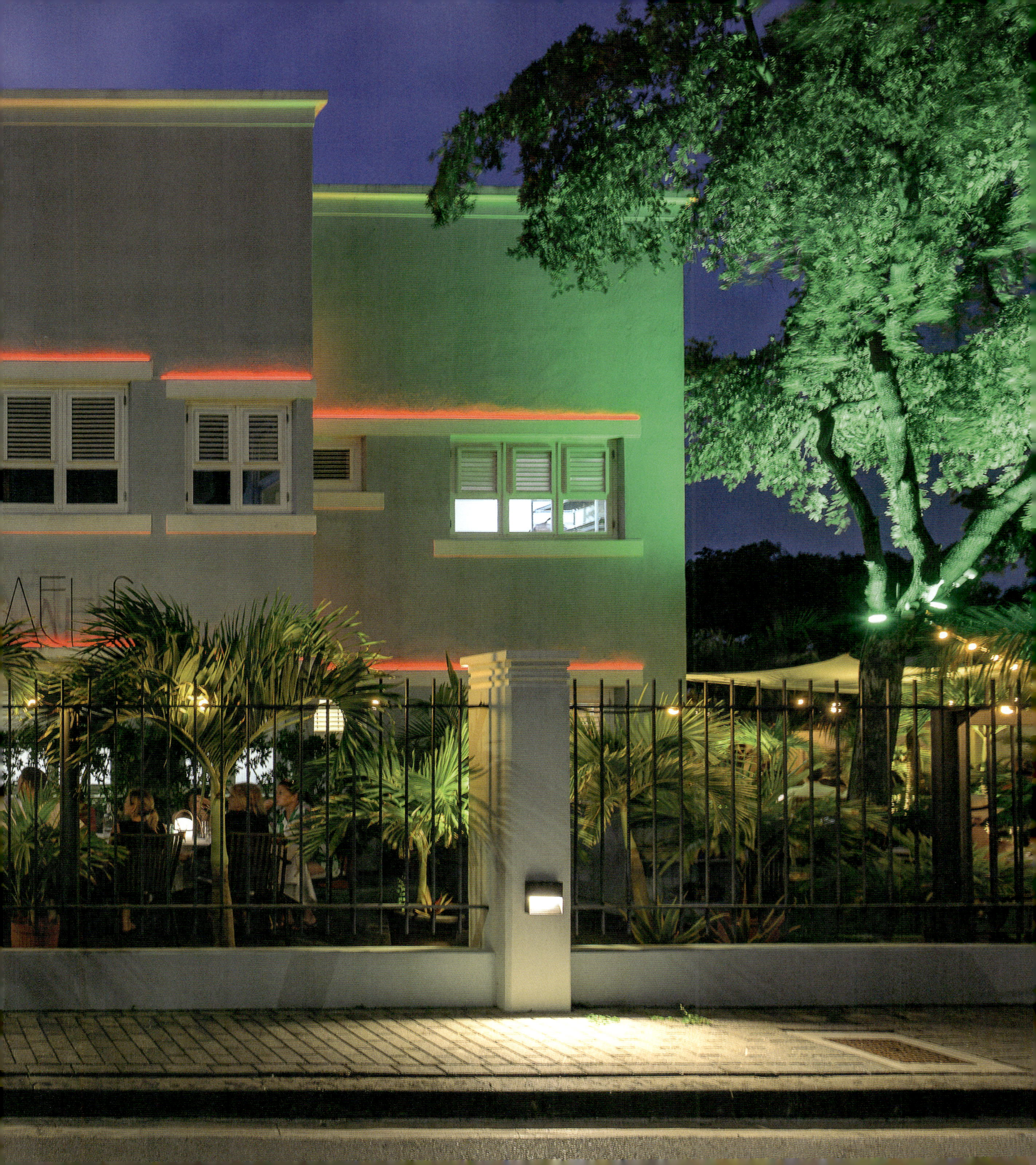

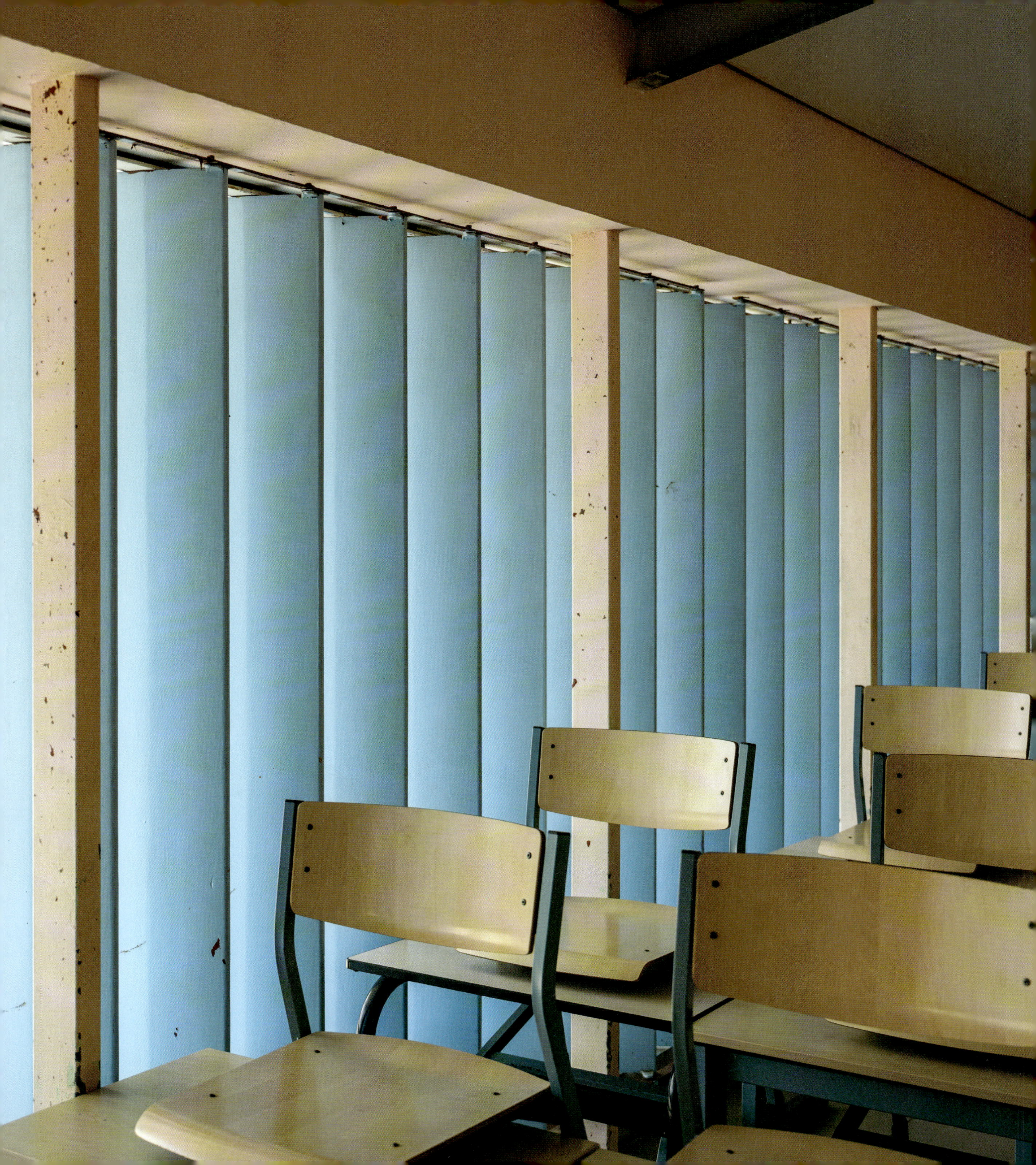

National grid reference: **12°07'47.6"N 68°54'03.7"W**

25. PROTESTANT LOWER TECHNICAL SCHOOL _

CAS CORAWEG

National Archive Curaçao / Coll. Fisher

This main block is the most distinctive and eye-catching part of the school, characterized by its elongated façade with uneven rectangular openings.

Historic Background_

The "Protestants Lagere Technische School" PLTS (Protestant Lower Technical School) was built by the foundation "Stichting Protestants Nijverheidsonderwijs" and financed with Dutch multi-year development funds. The cornerstone was laid on August 29, 1967, by Dutch Deputy Prime Minister Drs. J.A. Bakker, who was also responsible for providing financial aid and support to Suriname and the Netherlands Antilles.

The school opened in November 1968. Later, the foundation's name was changed to "Vereniging voor Protestants Christelijk Onderwijs" (VPCO), and the school became known as VSBO Marnix College Cas Cora.
The project was designed by the architect Henk J. Nolte. Born in the Netherlands in 1915, Nolte spent his youth in Curaçao, where his father worked at the refinery. After finishing his studies at the "Academie van Bouwkunst" in Amsterdam, he returned to Curaçao in 1946 and worked for the Department of Public Works. In 1962, he established himself as an independent architect.

do.co.mo.mo_curaçao

225

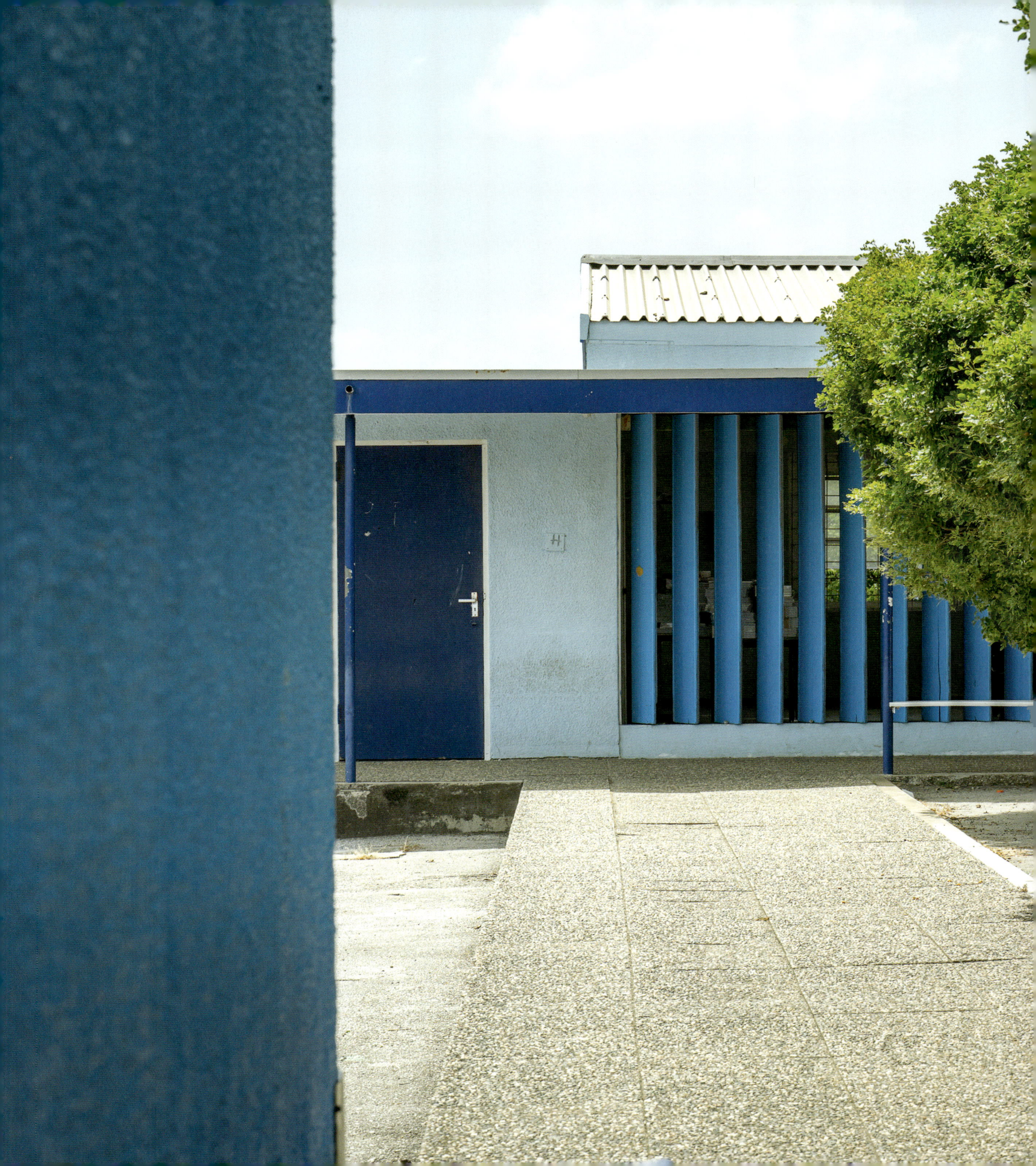

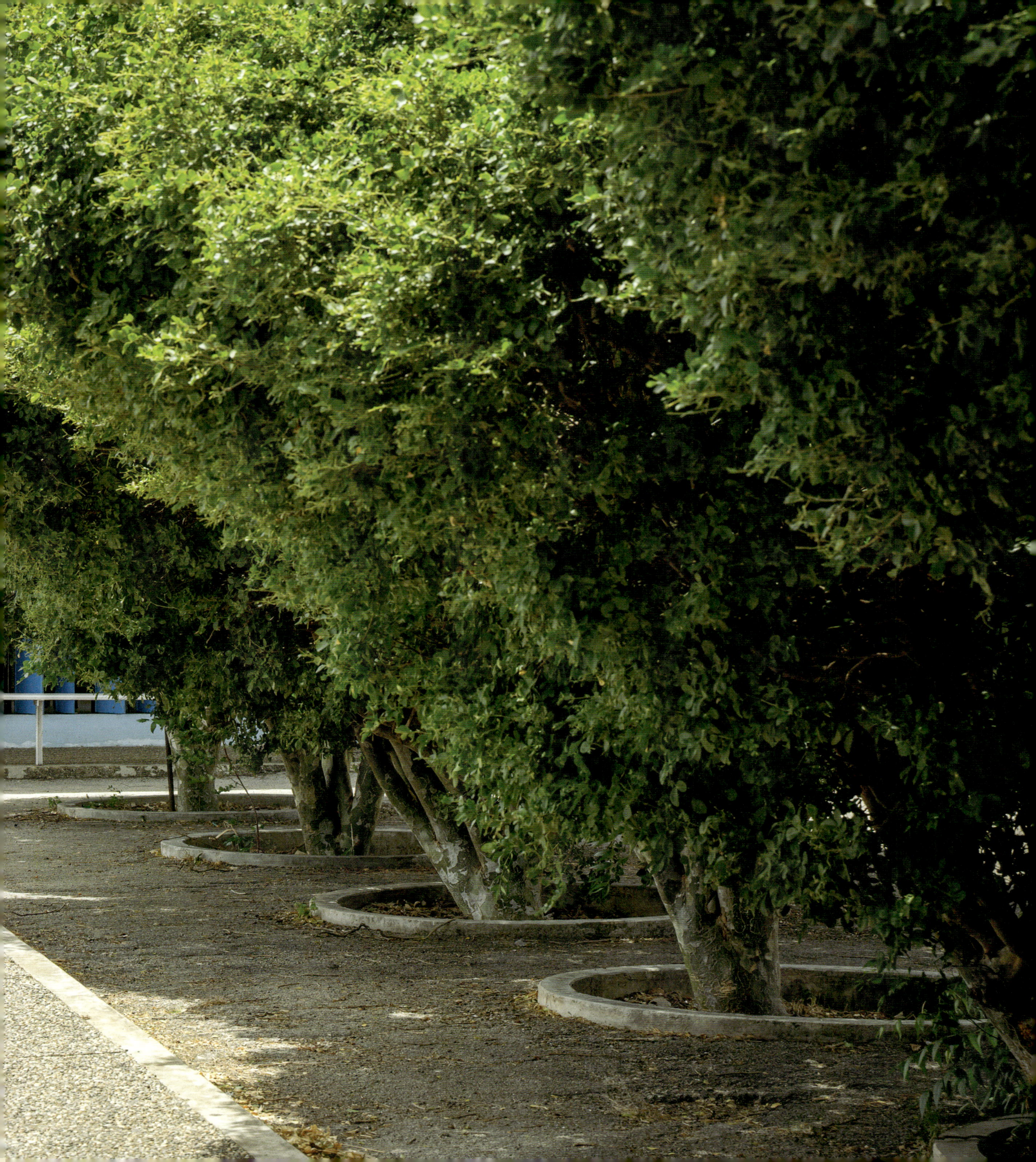

do.co.mo.mo_curaçao

Architectural Design_

The spacious complex is located on a hill, consisting of three levels that rise towards the rear, separated by slopes.

The central part of the school features a courtyard and sports field enclosed by buildings, with the main building on the street side.

This main block is the most distinctive and eye-catching part of the school, characterized by its elongated façade with uneven rectangular openings. This unique detached façade also functions as sun protection for the rooms behind it.

Aquilis Civilis (SHONKI) Hal

Marnix College 1986 - 2016

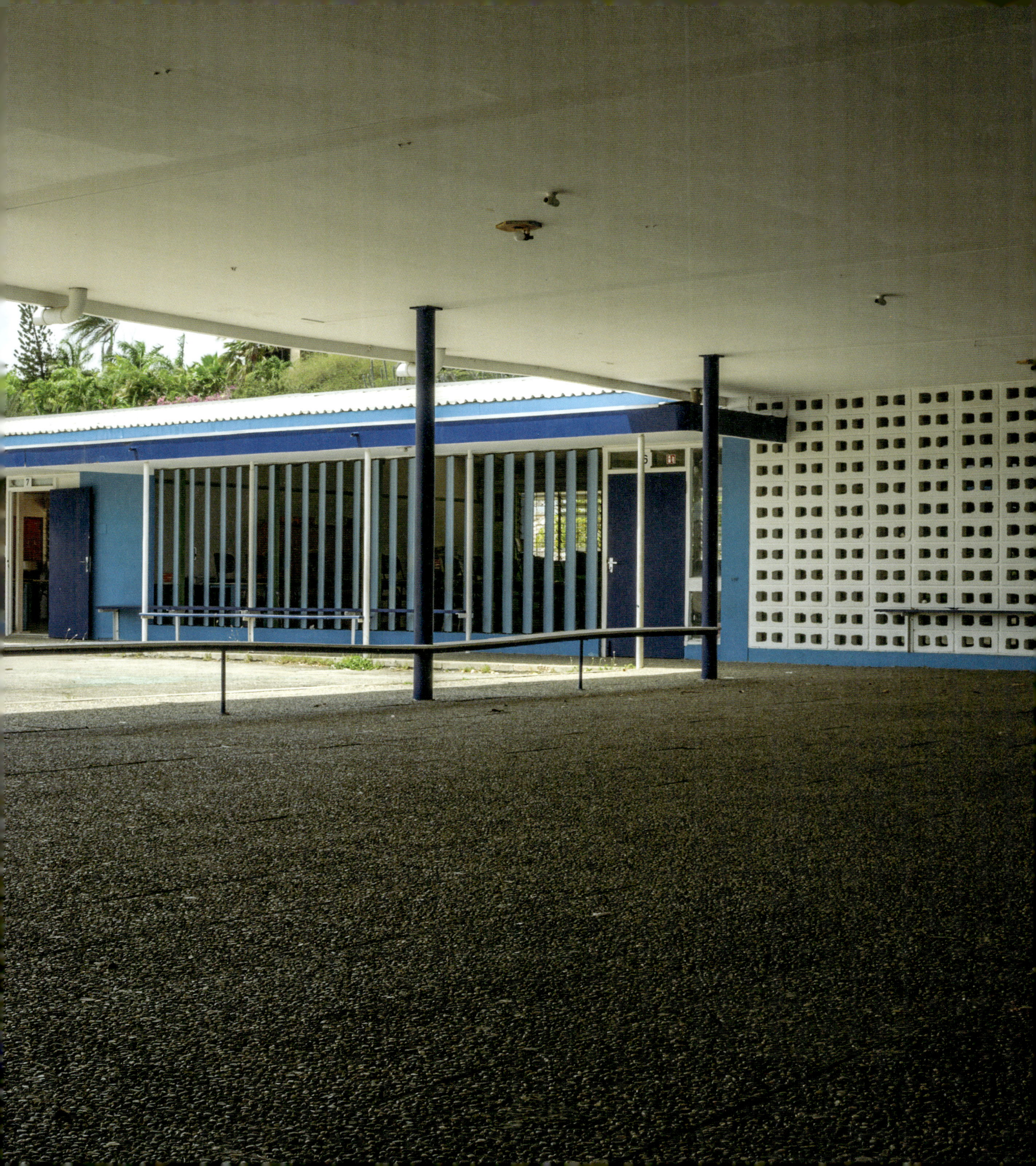

References:

- Gill, Ronald G. (2008) *Een eeuw architectuur op Curaçao*. Curaçao: Ronald G. Gill, (Original work published 1999)
- Julian Labraña, Fernando, (z.j.) *Het werk van H.J. NOLTE architect bna*, Curaçao

Description_

The complex was designed with simple classrooms for both theoretical and practical training, and is well-spaced for adequate ventilation. The complex was built with a slim steel construction.

Unique, and very tropical are the façades of the classrooms around the courtyard, consisting entirely of rotating slats that span almost the entire height of the front. These slats function as sun protection and provide perfect cross ventilation.

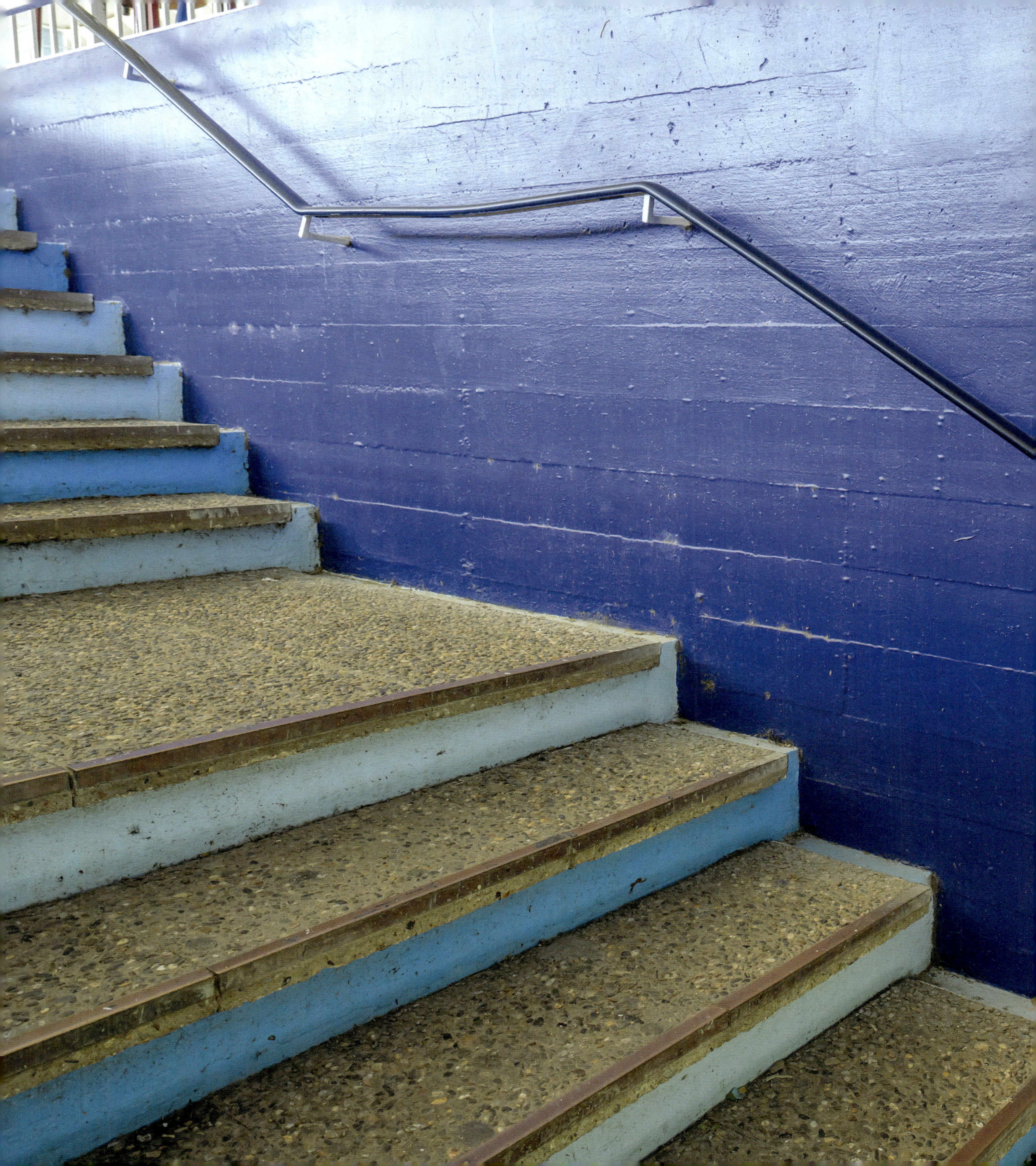

MAP OF CURAÇAO _

do.co.mo.mo_curaçao

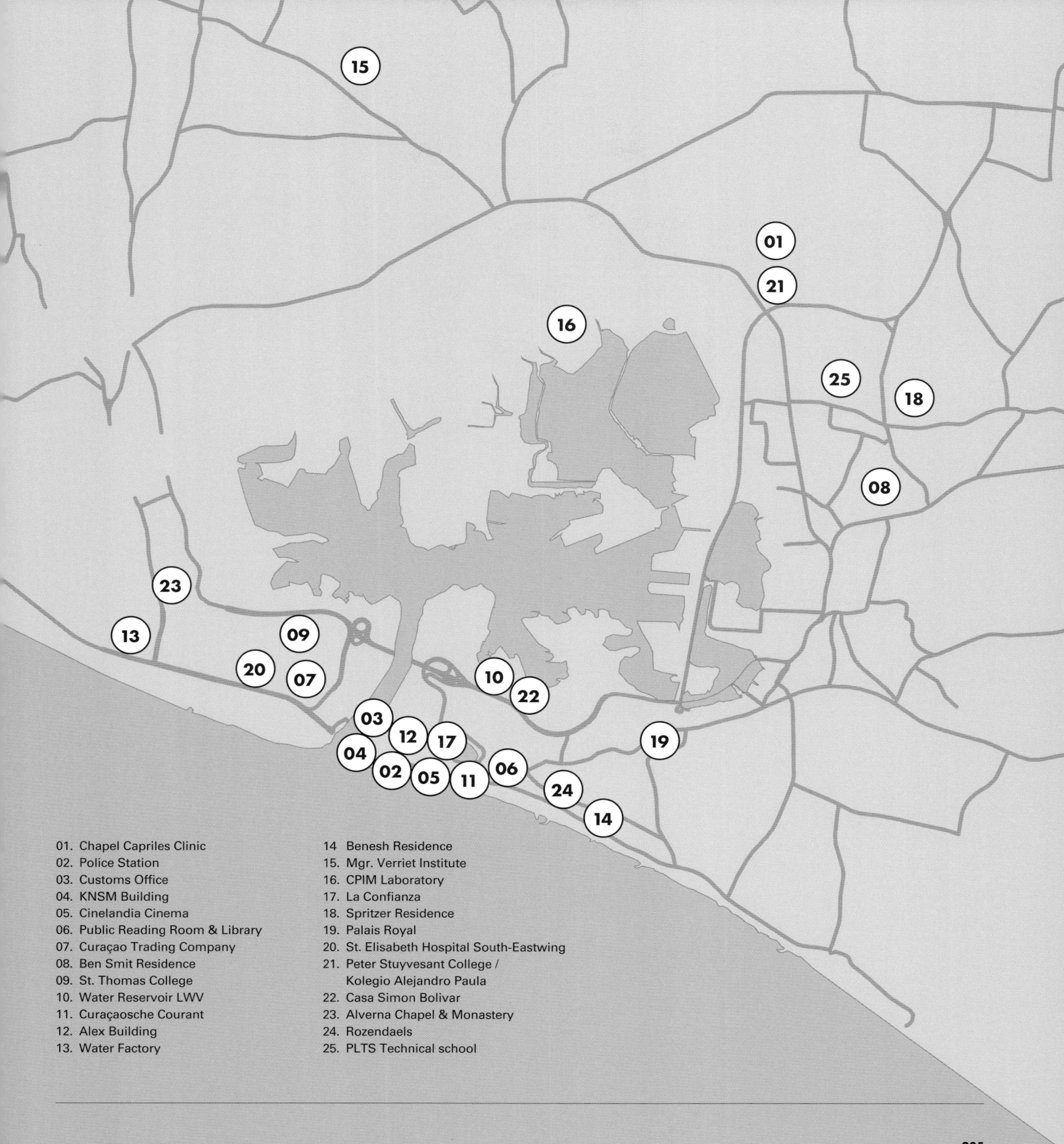

01. Chapel Capriles Clinic
02. Police Station
03. Customs Office
04. KNSM Building
05. Cinelandia Cinema
06. Public Reading Room & Library
07. Curaçao Trading Company
08. Ben Smit Residence
09. St. Thomas College
10. Water Reservoir LWV
11. Curaçaosche Courant
12. Alex Building
13. Water Factory
14. Benesh Residence
15. Mgr. Verriet Institute
16. CPIM Laboratory
17. La Confianza
18. Spritzer Residence
19. Palais Royal
20. St. Elisabeth Hospital South-Eastwing
21. Peter Stuyvesant College / Kolegio Alejandro Paula
22. Casa Simon Bolivar
23. Alverna Chapel & Monastery
24. Rozendaels
25. PLTS Technical school

BIBLIOG-
RAPHY_

- Bade, J.J. and H.J. Boukema (1966) Skein - Documentaire van het Peter Stuyvesant College 1941-1966, Curaçao: Peter Stuyvesant College.
- Bosch-Kruimel, Fosca (2007) Johan van Walbeeckplein 6/13; Monumento Habri '07 – Pietermaai Smal, Curaçao: Fundashon Pro Monumento.
- Bosh-Kruimel, Fosca (2009) Johan van Walbeeckplein 6 / 13; The impact of Caribbean Modern Architecture, First regional DOCOMOMO seminar, hosted by the University of the Netherlands Antilles, Curaçao.
- Ditzhuijzen, Jeannette van (1995) Monumento Habro '95 - Otrobanda, Fundashon Pro Monumento.
- Ditzhuijzen Jeannette van (2010) Een sjtetl in de tropen, Amsterdam: KIT Publishers.
- Fonk, Hans et. al. (1999) Curaçao Architectuur & Stijl. Curaçao: Stichting Curaçao Style.
- Fonk, Hans et. al. (2004) Curaçao Dutch Caribbean Architecture & Style. Curaçao: Curaçao Style Foundation.
- Gehlen, Gerda (2009) The KNSM Building, unplastered brick, strikingly modern; The impact of Caribbean Modern Architecture, First regional DOCOMOMO seminar, hosted by the University of the Netherlands Antilles, Curaçao.
- Gehlen, Gerda (2017) Het gebouw van de K.N.S.M.; Monumento Habri '17 – Punda, Curacao, Fundashon Pro Monumento.
- Gehlen, Gerda & Ditzhuijzen, Jeannette van, (2017) Warda di Polis – Police Station; MONUMENTO HABRI '17 – Punda, Curaçao: Fundashon Pro Monumento.
- Gehlen, Gerda (2022) St. Elisabeth gasthuis.
- Gill, Ronald (1990) The architecture of Rietveld on Curaçao. Building up the future from the past. Zutphen: De Walburg Pers.
- Gill, Ronald G. (2008) Een eeuw architectuur op Curaçao. Curaçao: Ronald G. Gill, (Original work published 1999).
- Gill, Ronald (2009) Gerrit Rietveld's Verriet Institute for diasabled children; The impact of Caribbean Modern Architecture, First regional DOCOMOMO seminar, hosted by the University of the Netherlands Antilles, Curaçao.
- Gomez Casseres, Charles (2004) PUNDA PUNDA. Curaçao: Charles Gomes Casseres.
- Hartog, Dr. Joh. (1961) CURAÇAO – Van Kolonie tot Autonomie, deel II. Aruba: De Wit.
- Heer, Jan de (2011) Rietveld en Curaçao, Rotterdam: Uitgeverij 010.
- Julian Labraña, Fernando, (z.j.) Het werk van H.J. NOLTE architect bna, Curaçao.
- Klaus, Dennis (2009). BEN SMIT, a personal note, The impact of Caribbean Modern Architecture, First regional DOCOMOMO seminar, hosted by the University of the Netherlands Antilles, Curaçao.
- Knap, Ger. H., (1956) Gekroonde Koopvaart, Reisresultaat van honderd jaar zeevaart door de Koninklijke Nederlandsche Stoomboot-maatschappij N.V. 1856 – 1956. Amsterdam: J.H. de Bussy.
- Landswatervoorzieningsdienst (1953) Gedenkboek Landswatervoorziening in de Nederlandse Antillen: 1 januari 1928 – 1 januari 1953, Curaçao.

- Lobo, Ronny (2009) Refining oil, Redefining architecture - The former Shell office and laboratories; The impact of Caribbean Modern Architecture, First regional DOCOMOMO seminar, hosted by the University of the Netherlands Antilles, Curaçao.
- Maduro-Molhuijsen, Helma (2013) Johan Heinrich Werner, de 'doodgezwegen' architect; De Archiefvriend, maart 2013.
- Möhlmann o.p., M. (1955) Stenen getuigen van honderd jaar sint elisabeth gasthuis . curaçao. Curçao: St. Elisabeth Gasthuis.
- Monsanto, Christel (2022) Pieter Antonie van Stuivenberg, architect. De Archiefvriend, september 2022.
- Monsanto, Christel (2022) Ir. Cornelis Marinus (Kees) Bakker, architect (1903 Hilversum – 1989 Toronto). De Archiefvriend, december 2022.
- Newton, Michael A. (1990) Fo'i porta, The Wilhelminapark and its surroundings. Building up the future from the past. Zutphen: De Walburg Pers.
- Newton, Michael (2009) OGEM & Customs office – The first modern movement in Curaçao; The impact of Caribbean Modern Architecture, First regional DOCOMOMO seminar, hosted by the University of the Netherlands Antilles, Curaçao.
- Oirschot, Anton van, et al. (1986) De Fraters van Zwijsen - 100 jaar fraters op de Nederlandse Antillen; Zutphen: De Walburg Pers.
- ONS ZEEWEZEN (1961) Orgaan van de Koninklijke Nederlandse Vereniging 'Onze Vloot', januari 1961, Antillennummer.
- Paul, P. (1959) Gedenkboek Tien jaar Korps Politie Nederlandse Antillen: 1949 – 1 oktober – 1959. Curaçao.
- Reichardt, Joke en Veendendaal, Peter (2024) Inspired by Dudok . Dudok.org / Dudok Architectuur centrum.
- Saavedra Bruno, Sofia (2009) The Cultural importance of saving Cinelandia; The impact of Caribbean Modern Architecture, First regional DOCOMOMO seminar, hosted by the University of the Netherlands Antilles, Curaçao.
- Smit, Ben. (2002). Projecten Curaçao 1946 – 1969. Curaçao: Ben Smit
- Verschoor, J.A.J. (1962) Gedenkboek ter gelegenheid van het 150-jarig bestaan van drukkerij " DE CURAÇAOSCHE COURANT" N.V. ; Curaçao: Curaçaosche Courant.
- Woude, Anko van der (1991) Naar een tropische architectuur in de moderne tijd: analyse van een schoolgebouw; in: Onderwijs in de steigers, Curaçao: Peter Stuyvesant College,
- Woude, Anko van der (2009) Modernistic Tropical Peter Stuyvesant College (PSC);
- The impact of Caribbean Modern Architecture, First regional DOCOMOMO seminar, hosted by the University of the Netherlands Antilles, Curaçao.

INDEX_

- Abspoel, C.A. (Kees) - 134
- Alex building – 9, 98
- Alverna Chapel & Monastery - 9
- Angloweg 9 – 69, 71
- Annabay – 28, 36, 39
- APNA - 54
- Aqualectra – 85, 86, 102
- Archaeological Antropological Institute Netherlands Antilles (AAINA) - 54
- Ashkenazi - 140
- Bakker, Cornelis Martinus (Kees) Bakker – 8, 9, 57, 67, 83, 94, 95
- Bakker, drs. J.A. - 224
- Bauhaus - 7
- Beaujon, R. - 103
- Beiderwellen, Jacobus - 24
- Benesch, dr. Julius - 113
- Berger, Melanie - 113
- Bernadine - 113
- Botica Nueva - 98
- Brandao, F. - 156
- Breedestraat – Punda - 24, 35
- Breuer, Marcel - 7
- Brionplein - 8
- Brise-soleil – 7, 70, 73, 144, 149, 179
- Brothers of Tilburg - 82
- Capriles, dr. David Ricardo - 14
- Cas Coraweg – 223, 224
- Casa Simon Bolivar – 9, 185, 186, 187, 235
- Chapel Capriles Clinic – 8, 13, 14, 17, 20, 235
- Cinelandia Cinema – 9, 47, 48, 49, 51, 157, 235
- Congregation of Franciscan Sisters of Mariadal (Roosendaal) - 197
- Construction Bureau KNSM - 39
- CPIM Laboratory – 129, 131, 235
- Curaçao Trading Company (CTC) – 65, 66, 235
- Curaçaosche Courant – 9, 93, 94, 95, 235
- Customs Office – 8, 27, 28, 31, 32, 235
- Damacor - 144
- Damplein – 54, 57
- De Ruyterkade – 94, 139, 140, 141
- Department of Public Works – 17, 24, 28, 31, 32, 57, 67, 70, 83, 95, 99, 118, 140, 144, 167, 179, 186, 187, 224
- Dudok, W.M. - 8, 39
- Emmastad - 129
- Engels, dr. – 118, 121
- Fensohn - 82
- Gill, Ronald – 3, 118
- Girobank - 141
- Gouverneur van Lansbergeweg - 195
- Groot Kwartier -14
- Gropius, Walter - 7

- Handelskade – 8, 31, 32, 66
- Hansen Elenbaas, Valdemar - 171
- Hendrikplein - 47
- Irausquin, Alex - 98
- Irausquin, Ruben - 98
- Juliana, Willy - 183
- Kieckens, Monseigneur F. - 163
- Klaus, Dennis - 54
- KNSM – 8, 35, 36, 39, 42, 235
- Kolegio Alejandro Paula – 173, 174, 179, 235
- Korpodeko - 36
- L.B. Smithplein – 81, 82
- La Confianza -139, 140, 141, 235
- Landswatervoorzieningsdienst LWV – 9, 49, 85, 86, 88, 101, 102, 103, 106, 157, 235
- Lansberge - 163
- Le Corbusier – 7, 70, 149, 179
- Lendering - 82
- Lienden, dr van – 14, 17
- Maduro, Stanley Levy - 213
- Mahaai – 70, 144
- Mgr. Verriet Institute – 9, 117, 118, 121, 125, 235
- Mies van der Rohe, Ludwig - 7
- Morel, A.J. - 163
- Moron, A. – 48, 156
- Mundo Nobo – 9, 101, 102
- National Archaeological Antropological Memory Management - 54
- Nederhost - 17
- Niemeyer, Oscar – 7, 70
- Nolte, Henk – 7, 8, 9, 118, 125, 224
- Palais Royal – 155, 156, 235
- Pater Euwensweg – 161, 167
- Pellicer Hernandez, Alfredo - 48
- Penstraat – 86, 102, 111, 113, 115, 211, 213
- Peter Stuyvesant College – 9, 173, 174, 179, 235
- Pizziolo, Giovanni – 24, 157, 217
- Plasa Jojo Correa – 97, 99
- PLTS – 7, 9, 223, 224, 235
- Police Station – 8, 23, 24, 235
- President Romulo Betancourt Boulevard – 85, 185
- Project Planners and Designers - 125
- Public Reading Room & Library – 9, 53, 54, 67, 235
- Radulphus College - 179
- RdK -131
- Rietveld, Gerrit Thomas – 9, 118, 121, 125
- Riffort - 102
- Roodeweg – 65, 66, 82
- Roosevelt House - 186
- Rozendaels – 211, 235
- Saavedra Bruno, Sofia - 3
- Saint Fransis of Assisi - 171
- Salina – 155, 156, 157
- Salon Habana - 48
- Salsbachweg - 117
- Schottegat – 28, 131
- Schottegatweg Noord - 173
- Schout bij Nacht Doormanweg – 143, 153
- Sephardic - 213
- Seru Ararat – 86, 185, 186, 187
- SGR group - 125
- Sha and Lio Caprileskade - 27
- SHELL – 8, 28, 67, 95, 99, 131, 134
- Sisters of Breda - 171
- Slobbe, van - 24
- Smit, Ben – 7, 8, 9, 69, 70, 71, 73, 115, 144, 149, 163, 185, 186, 187, 191, 201, 235
- Spritzer, Erno – 7, 9, 143, 144, 149, 235
- St. Elisabeth Hospital – 7, 9, 82, 161, 163, 235
- St. Thomas College – 9, 81, 82, 235
- St.Martinus Mavo - 82
- Stuivenberg, Pieter van – 9, 39, 49, 51, 88, 106, 157
- Technical University Delft – 67, 95, 99
- Theaterstraat – 93, 94, 95
- UNESCO – 7, 121
- Vries, Anton de – 8, 140, 179
- Walbeeckplein, Johan van – 53, 54
- Water Factory – 9, 101, 235
- Water Reservoir – 9, 85, 86, 91, 235
- Werner, Johan Heinrich / Hans / Henk – 8, 17, 31
- West-End – 9, 49
- White and Trafers - 134
- Wilhelminaplein – 23, 24
- Wimco – 155, 156
- Wit Gele Kruis - 118
- Wiznitzer - 140
- Woei a Sioe, Jacqueline - 54
- Woude, Anko van der - 183

COLOPHON_

Modern Architecture of Curaçao 1930–1960 is published by DoCoMoMo Curaçao in collaboration with Stichting LM Publishers.

Text	**Michael A. Newton** architect / architectural historian
Photography	**Ton Verkuijlen** professional photographer
President DoCoMo - Curaçao	**Ronny Lobo**
Research	**Mongui Maduro Library**
Historical photos	**National Archives of Curaçao**
Text correction	**Esty da Costa**
Graphic Design	**Salt (Carl Ariza)**
Production	**Hightrade B.V.**

© 2024 DoCoMoMo Curaçao / Michael A. Newton / LM Publishers Edam

ISBN: 9789460229800

This book was supported by:

Stimuleringsfonds Creatieve Industrie
Administratiekantoor Newton N.V.
Landmark Real Estate N.V.
Maduro & Curiel's Bank N.V.
Refineria di Korsou (RDK) N.V.
S.A.L. (Mongui) Maduro Foundation
Stadsherstel Willemstad N.V.
Stichting Curaçao Style
Stichting Monumentenfonds Curaçao
Stichting Monumentenzorg Curaçao

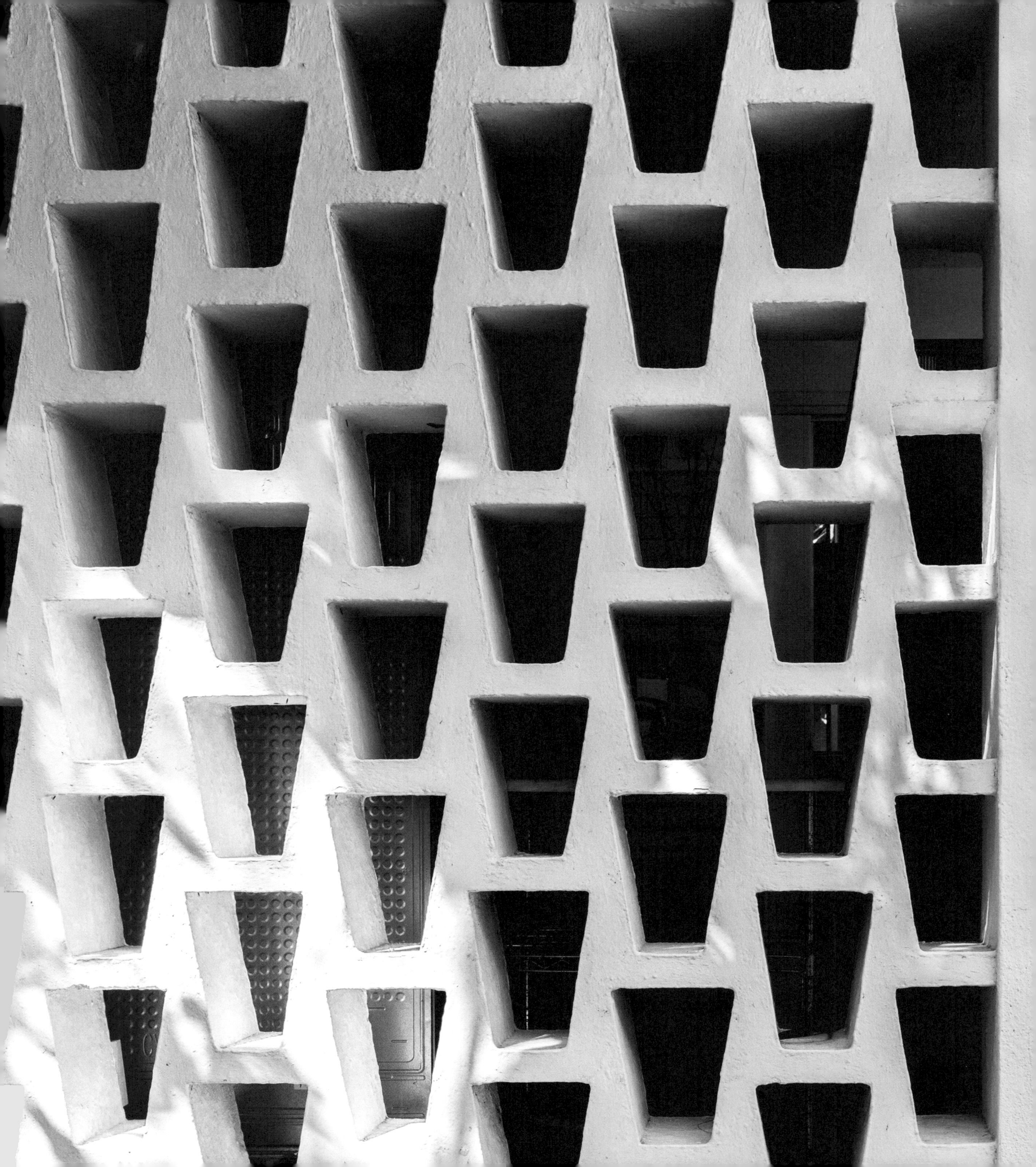